Identities in Crisis in Iran

Identities in Crisis in Iran

Politics, Culture, and Religion

Edited by Ronen A. Cohen

LEXINGTON BOOKS
Lanham • Boulder • New York • London

Published by Lexington Books
An imprint of The Rowman & Littlefield Publishing Group, Inc.
4501 Forbes Boulevard, Suite 200, Lanham, Maryland 20706
www.rowman.com

Unit A, Whitacre Mews, 26-34 Stannary Street, London SE11 4AB

British Library Cataloguing in Publication Information Available

Library of Congress Cataloging-in-Publication Data

Library of Congress Cataloging-in-Publication Data Available

ISBN 978-1-4985-0641-0 (hardback: alk. paper)
ISBN 978-1-4985-0643-4 (pbk: alk. paper)
ISBN 978-1-4985-0642-7 (ebook)

∞ ™ The paper used in this publication meets the minimum requirements of American
National Standard for Information Sciences Permanence of Paper for Printed Library
Materials, ANSI/NISO Z39.48-1992.

Printed in the United States of America

Contents

Acknowledgments

The difference between writing monographs and the editing of a collection of essays seems to be that the former is harder and more exhausting—and it is. The advantage of doing the latter, however, is that one gets the opportunity to meet and communicate with many scholars, some of whom are veteran and some new to the field. Accepting this mission to collect chapters from scholars from different countries and universities, from Israel and abroad, and to group them under the umbrella of one theme (with probably too many facets and interpretations) has, I believe, ultimately proven to be fruitful and satisfactory.

This mission could not have become a reality without the valuable, even priceless, contribution made by the wonderfully professional, "blind" peer-reviewers; so to all those "behind the scenes" people thank you very much for your kind and valued assistance. I would also like to thank several mentors and professional colleagues without whose excellent advice I could not have navigated this mission: Dr. Soli Shahvar from the Department of Middle Eastern History and The Ezri Center for Iran and Gulf Studies at the University of Haifa; Prof. Ali Ansari, Director of the Institute for Iranian Studies, member of the School Research Committee, chair in the Middle East studies department at the University of St. Andrews, UK; Dr. Ron Fuchs, from the Department of Art History at the University of Haifa and from the School of Architecture at Ariel University; Dr. Liora Hendelman-Baavur, from the Department of Middle Eastern and African History at the Tel Aviv University; my editors at Lexington Books—Ms. Sabah Ghulamali, who embraced this project, Mr. Brian Hill for his patience and professional advice and, of course, my new editor, Ms. Nicolette Amstutz, who proved to be wonderful and diligent and who brought this project to its final stages. Of course, I also want to thank my devoted, legendary professional editor Sammy, Mr. Samuel Beris, who makes my books more readable.

Special thanks are also given to all my colleagues who helped me by stimulating me with good ideas and advice and helping me with technical matters: to Prof. Alexander Bligh, acting dean of the Faculty of Social Sciences and Humanities and the director of the Middle East Research Center at Ariel University; to Dr. Eyal Lewin for days and nights of fruitful debates; to Dr. Hanna Gendel-Guterman who helped me with statistics and SPSS, without whose help I would have been lost; to Prof. Albert Pinhasov, the head of the Authority for Research & Development at Ariel University; and to my senior research assistant, Ms. Roni Shulman, who again had to "suffer" my schedule and missions.

My beloved wife, Mrs. Yael Keinan-Cohen, comforts me with her anonymous support and assistance and, besides devotedly taking care of me, is also a valued partner in my discussions of issues and the shaping of minds and targets. My precious wife—I look forward to many years of informative and inquisitive discussions regarding children, food, housing, and, especially, Islam, Shi'a, and Middle Eastern history. Orianne and Yair, my children, are always the source of my spirit and happiness in a generation of shaping identities and I am happy that they are part of my identity and hope that I too will be part of their identities.

In the book of Proverbs 4:7, it is written: "First of all is wisdom. Acquire wisdom and with all you possess acquire understanding." Leading a group of both prominent and young promising scholars is a blessed mission but requires much responsibility. I cannot guarantee that there have been no errors here and there but the pursuit of wisdom has been worth the effort. These scholars should be applauded for their efforts and professional work. Any criticism regarding their work should be directed towards me.

Introduction

Ronen A. Cohen

In the thirty-five years since the emergence of the Islamic revolution and the establishment of an Islamic theocracy in Iran the regime has created a seemingly stable political order that few dare to challenge. Compared to other countries in the region that have been shaken by dissent, violence, and even civil wars the Islamist theocracy ushered in by Ayatollah Ruhollah Khomeini has presented the image of being a unified society of the faithful leading a life of steady devotion to the spirit of its founder. Under the official, laudatory Islamic identity construct, however, there are deeper dynamics that have generated varied forms of expressing individuality and group character. In addition to the traditional ethnic minorities that are often in variance with the regime, certain social and cultural strata, religious groups, human rights groups, and other elements of civil society have constructed themselves or undergone reconstruction—even expressing opposition to the officially sanctioned Islamic definition of the self. While the process of creating new, often counterrevolutionary identities, began during the 1990s, it has intensified since the Arab Spring which has become a symbol for the awakening of individual and collective imagination.

This book offers a variety of articles written by young, prominent scholars from different fields that capture the varied dimensions and complexities of these new and proliferating identifies. While they use different methodologies, all the contributors agree that much of the process has been driven mainly by the post-revolutionary generation that grew up in the shadows of the uniformity imposed by the founding fathers of the Islamist order. That such diverse identities could flourish in the face of the cultural monolith reinforced by state coercion is a testimony to the resilience and creativity of the identity-formation project and a challenge to the regime as it struggles to hold on to the vestiges of the tattered revolutionary imagination.

Creating an identity, shaping it, reconstructing it, denying it, exposing it, and even inventing it all have sociological elements that are driven by many rooted and theoretical/creative factors. An identity is flooded by influences and all of these are built up on the foundations of characters of the self, of the commonality of values, religion, history, culture, and environmental circumstances. If one uses Judith Butler's concepts of sex, gender, and performativity then the meaning of human activity is found in its being a repetition of common and known patterns that symbolize, or are meant to symbolize, social meaning. While the self is built upon practices of culture, and these give it significance and meaning, it is the participation of the individual in these behavioral conventions that creates his/her identity.

Moreover, the distinction made between individual, natural values-facts (man/woman), and gender as a whole collection of social roles and values that are in correlation with the natural identity has created a real pathway that has made the call for gender liberalism and equal rights possible. Thus the natural basis for creating an identity is not enough since the real influences upon the creating of an identity are the environmental cultures. The self favors the use of these cultural foundations and is supported by the individual's identity that gives it meaning, shape, and desire. Even so there is an inconsistency in Butler's thesis that shows that there are several limitations the individual has while creating his/her identity in cultural terms.

If this method is adopted to define the identity of a nation, would it give us the same results? Can we assume that what is relevant to one who seeks to emancipate himself through struggling in the battle between the natural basics and the cultural environment is also relevant to, for example, a religious Islamic nation whose cultural basics are at war with its religious identity? Does Iran represent some kind of special case study in which a religion (Islam) is imposed on a nation whose cultural foundations are stronger (Persia) than its previous religious identity (Zoroastrianism)? Does social/private identity have to be divided by ritual repetition and the natural basics in order to make it possible for social norms and cultural/religious basics to be orchestrated as the elements of a normal and acceptable social life?

The social construction approach in sociology argues that identical social categories are not ongoing, essential, and stable products that have always existed "out there" but are the product of historical and social processes that construct these categories. Social interactions in concrete social contexts make it possible for society to recount collective narratives that form the imagined past shared by the members of the group and produce a system of symbols, significances, labels, and narratives that establish a shared significance for members of the group and other groups with which it interacts. The process of establishing collective identities can take a long time but, ultimately, is assimilated in the personal identities of the individuals in the group until it is impossible for the individual to imagine himself and his social environment without them. In this way the collective acts as if the existing social structure is natural, obvious, and has historical continuity.

The process of socializing individuals into the society in which they live is carried out through the adoption and transference of the same social, class, religious, national, and sexual categories, and distinguishing between them and the norms, symbols, and the daily practices that are agencies for these categories. Thus, for example, the gender division of male and female or the ethnic division of blacks and whites are charged with a variety of things that are imagined to be significant and natural and which share a past but, in practice, these social categories are fluid, brittle, and changeable; and the social significances given to these identities change in different periods of history. Thus, in contrast to essentialist approaches, the social construction approaches argue that collective identities are the product of historical circumstances, technological development, and social encounters and are not natural but are strengthened by symbols and daily repetitive social practices. At the same time, however, the approach does not maintain that these identities are absolutely the planned product of an elite that has material interests as maintained by the Marxist approach. The approach similarly maintains that the establishing process produces fairly stable identities that have significance and that do not constantly change every day on the basis of interaction between the individuals. Thus, although the collective identities are daily maintained by the practices of individuals the individual person cannot regularly or easily change his identity and, in a certain sense, is "trapped" in a collective identity and the social context in which he lives. The process of socialization and the "gatekeepers" who mark the boundaries of the categories make any transition between the categories difficult and regiment the individual into constructed identity categories.

More than this, recent research into the field of national identity formation shows that, in cases where national identity is unconsolidated, heterogeneous collectives in the name of a sound common culture, are negatively contrasted against a profound image of the Other and tend to construct their national identity based on cultural criteria, while the nation-defining cultural characteristic is increasingly strengthened as the negation of the perceived image of the estranged Other. [1]

In this collection of essays we have tried to provide the readers with insights concerning identities in the crisis in Iran that relate to cultural, political, and religious influences and aspects. When identity experiences difficulties, whether they be of a personal or environmental nature there is an opportunity to rebuild and create a new form of this identity. When we are talking about national identity the problem seems to be impossible, but we do have the ability to delineate several fundamentals that will help us understand Iran as well as the sources and development of its identity.

Obviously the Iran of 2014 is much different from that of 1979 but to say this about a theocratic regime is not something obvious. The same theocratic regime is, indeed, governing this amazing country but we can certainly say that the people of 1979 moved this nation into a new reality that has led to their children and grandchildren in 2014 to be living in a different atmosphere than previously, with different dreams, different revolutionary thoughts, habits, private-social relations, relations between the self and God, and, of course, a different identity.

Part one of this book, "Historical and Current Perspectives on Persian, Islamic, and Contested Religious Identities," opens with a chapter by Dr. Harold Rhode, a distinguished and experienced expert who has served as an advisor on Middle Eastern and Islamic affairs in the Office of the Secretary of the U.S. Department of Defense. In his interesting chapter, "The Unending Battle between the Persian and Islamic Identities of Iran," he draws a wide-ranging but clear line between "Iranian-ness" and the Shi'a religion. Each of these significantly influences Iran's national identity and, of course, the self of each individual citizen of the nation. Iran, a proud and glorious empire that existed for eleven hundred years was defeated and overtaken by Arab Muslim nomads who stormed out of the Arabian desert. Iran, Rhode writes, being a great civilization, looked down upon these Arab Muslims and was unable to even imagine being defeated by these primitive nomads. He asks how this proud and ancient culture came to grips with its defeat. How did the Persians deal with the onslaught of the Arabic culture and language? Why did they not succumb to the Arabic culture like their neighbors to the West? If the Iranians, in fact, developed all sorts of methods to placate their rulers by publically showing fidelity to them while privately maintaining their core values, how could that have been the reason for them adopting Shi'ism? And if it was, why did the people in other areas of the Arab empire not become Shi'ites?

Dr. Rhode provides us with a brief yet refined story about the fascinating battle between these two cultures which he traces in order to demonstrate that the unending conflict between these two cultures has not, and probably never will be, resolved.

In chapter two we meet Ms. Ladan Zarabadi, who gives us an overwhelming description of how the Iran of today has taken its history and Islamized it. In her chapter, "National Identity or Political Legitimacy: The Reconstruction of the City of Bam," Ms. Zarabadi says that the identity of a nation is often a cultural matter that has been undergoing severe challenges from political powers over time, as they have constantly attempted to reinterpret national identities and transform cultures in order to legitimize their authority and authenticity. In the other words culture, as a dynamic phenomenon, has been influenced, formed, transformed, and occasionally exploited by political powers in such a way as to urge nations to believe, validate, and approve of them. This means that the culture develops a political hue in which history and culture are considered to be the means of establishing legitimacy to certain political actors who attenuate the real essence of the nation's historical memory by accentuating a few parts and ignoring other parts of it.

She initially examines the interplay between political powers and national identity in a given society and goes on to argue that history, culture, and consequently national identity are influenced, formed, or transformed by political powers in order to enhance the legitimacy and authenticity of their political system.

The chapter explores how the reconstruction of the historical-cultural complex of the city of Bam in Iran can be exploited by a political power to establish a new sense of identity and redefine it in order to obtain legitimacy. The process of misrepresenting culture and national identity is thus examined as a case study in the context of Iran during the last century.

Part two, entitled "An Islamic-National Identity and Nuclear Program," opens with Prof. Ofira Seliktar's chapter: "The Islamic Identity Project: Between Coercion and Voluntarism." Professor Seliktar writes that social-identity theory defines social identity as a person understanding that she belongs to a social category or group. Indeed, a social group is composed of individuals who share a common social identification but who come to see themselves as members of one category or group (the in-group) in comparison with another (the out-group).

One's religious identity is, however, a specific type of identity formation that is related to the individual's concept of self, and one's membership in a religious category may exist regardless of participation in religious practices or actions. By drawing on cultural anthropology, social theorists have been able to point out that this identity is based on a shared system of meaning drawn from metaphysical and ethnic beliefs. Some scholars argue that religious identity is a key to the development of the concept of self and, because of its appeal to the transcendent and rootedness in texts and practices, it may actually be stronger than other forms of group identity.

Seliktar emphasizes the point that tensions between national and religious identities have shaped modern history and that it has been the clash between religious identity and secularism that has taken center stage. Secularism is grounded in rational-legal legitimacy norms that make numinous claims redundant, and the ascent of a democratic authority system that gives members of a national collective the right to choose their rules is the most celebrated result of the secularization of religious group identity.

Once in power, Ayatollah Ruhollah Khomeini laid the foundation for a numinous authority system based on the doctrine of *Velayat-e Faqih,* the divine rule by a religious guardian. Khomeini saw such a rule as indispensable for the creation of a *republic of virtue*, which is an Islamic polity and society based on Quranic principles. Only in such a system, it was argued, can individuals, who are considered to be morally deficient by nature, be perfected, thus assuring their salvation. The Ayatollah and other revolutionary leaders justified such religious despotism because of the need to block the emergence of flawed and nondivine perspectives. At the same time, they were mindful of the democratic ferment that toppled the shah and, operating within this complex and rather convoluted political system, the Khomeinists set out to impose a new Islamist group identity which involved all three levels of identity shaping: cognitive, attitudinal, and behavioral. By censuring public discourse—notably in the education system and the media—the regime hoped to mold attitudes and create appropriate behavior. The inherent difficulties inherent in the social engineering of the magnitude required to fit the "republic of virtue" coupled with the vestigial form of democratic discourse, however, turned the Islamist identity project into an uphill battle.

With this impressive and sophisticated outlook, Prof. Seliktar's article analyzes the stages of the project from 1979 to 2014 according to the three dimensions—cognitive, attitudinal, and behavioral—in order to trace its development, and the concluding section lists the factors that have contributed to its seemingly unfortunate failure.

In part two there is also Mr. Farhad Rezaei's chapter "Iran's National Identity and the Nuclear Program: A Rational Choice Theory Analysis." Mr. Rezaei is a promising scholar who provides us with unique and rare insights into Iran's nuclear program and its importance in the rebuilding of the nation's identity around this project. Mr. Rezaei's theoretical yet well-documented case study and his critical abilities help us understand the Islamic Republic's ambition for nuclear power.

Rezaei argues that, as proliferation theory postulates, factors other than strict security calculations can prompt countries to embrace a nuclear weapons program, and national identity and pride are among the things most often mentioned in this context. Accordingly, national elites use their nuclear projects to enhance their legitimacy by creating a new unifying identity for their countries often described as a new "civil religion."

Rezaei maintains that Iran's nuclear program fits this notion and his article contends that, in addition to widely perceived security threats, the Islamist elite has seized upon the nuclear project to construct a new national identity. By merging traditional Persian culture, Islamist elements, and a universalist-oriented scientific creed, the regime hopes to enhance national pride and its own legitimacy. The resistance of the clerical establishment to the idea of abandoning proliferation can be partially explained by its fear of losing public support.

The increasingly painful sanctions imposed by an international community determined to roll back Iran's nuclear program poses a serious challenge to a nuclear-program-based identity. Sanctions have eroded the standards of living of the population and have left the regime vulnerable to economic upheavals. Sanction literature holds that if the cost of sanctions exceeds the perceived benefits of the nuclear program, the public may discard this high-cost component of its national identity. While it is not yet clear whether the elite is ready to give up the program there is a real possibility that rank-and-file Iranians may withdraw their support in exchange for an improved lifestyle.

Last in this section is Dr. Moshe-hay S. Hagigat. Dr. Hagigat's chapter, entitled "Overcoming 'the –isms': Iranian's Role in the Modern World, from the Perspective of Mahmūd Ahmadi-nezhād," is a byproduct of Hagigat's PhD dissertation directed by Prof. Ze'ev Maghen. It is like a breath of fresh air since it is mainly based on Persian literature and gives us the real dimensions of Ahmadi-nezhād's national ideology and identity. What is important is that the dissertation deals with Mahmūd Ahmadi-nezhād's Islamic identity from his own point of view and the relevance of that identity today—a period of time in history that he believes is critical for both individual Muslims and the Muslims as an *Ummah*.

Ahmadi-nezhād's religious doctrine is the cornerstone of all his doctrines, including the political and economic doctrines as well as all the other various views which he holds. In his speeches Ahmadi-nezhād treats the subject of religion as a sort of invisible "Archimedean point" on which he relies for his other viewpoints. In each idea he adheres to, in each position he takes—from the smallest and lightest to the most serious—Ahmadi-nezhād always turns to religious, Shi'ite-Islamic ideas, and it is from them that he draws expression. Hagigat claims that, at the same time, Ahmadi-nezhād also makes mention of the various ideas and theories originating from the West and, derisively dismissing them by referring to the dominant contemporary conceptions or paradigms as "the –isms" (*ism-ha*), he shows how he considers them to be outdated, comprising something that most people have a need to abandon.

In the last part of this book, entitled "Sexuality, Beauty, and Social Networking: Between the Private, Self, and the Public Sphere," my article, "The Identity Designers of the Self in Sexuality, Beauty, and Plastic Surgery in Iran," claims that the Islamist revolution of 1979 has heightened the historic tensions that exist between two contradictory identity components: the strict implementation of Shi'ite Islam and the veneration of Persian history and language. Ever since the Persians adopted Sunni Islam—which they subsequently changed to Shi'a Islam during the Safavid rule in the sixteenth century—there has been a struggle between the Shi'a way of life and the Persian identity of Iranian society. While Islamic, especially Shi'a, theology pushes individuals to achieve the high standards of piety deemed necessary for salvation, Iranian society's ethnocultural and linguistic anchors are steeped in elements from a more earthy, even sexually charged, pre-Islamic period whose proponents have fought to preserve with its original identity. With neither the Islamic or Persian elements gaining any clear victory the resulting identity that has been formed is a blend of often contrasting values expressed on the level of the self.

My chapter analyzes how the self-image of the Iranians, as reflected in their understating of gender, beauty, and sexuality, has tried to integrate the conflicting elements of their sociocultural milieu. It is noted that these three factors are part and parcel of a more universal culture but they have also been infused with certain Persian cultural markers. Even this native Persian version, however, which is overlaid with a patina of traditional modesty, has been harshly attacked by the regime which finds all manifestations of gender, beauty, and sexuality threating to the strict mores of Islam. At the same time the guardians of the revolution have failed to create a system that has been able to impose—neither through persuasion or coercion—a uniform religious identity for society. The resulting identity is a symbiosis formed between the Islamic Shi'a religion and Persian culture, between the past and the present and between what is forbidden and what is permitted. By tracing the attitudes towards gender, beauty, and sexuality the process of identity formation in contemporary Iranian society is deconstructed, and the analysis made assesses whether the amalgamated identity poses any serious challenge to the regime.

The last chapter in the section that closes this book is the brilliant article by Dr. Raz Zimmt, of Tel Aviv University, on Iran's social media and its influences on the private and collective identity—"Iranians Against the 'Other': Iranian Identity in the Social Network Era." For Dr. Zimmt, the increase in the use of social networks and the continuing control of the traditional communications media by the regime has transformed these networks, and mainly Facebook, into central arenas of activity for carrying on social, political, and civil struggles in the Islamic republic. The network has developed as a relatively free channel of communication that has made possible discourse, the creation of contact, and the exchange of messages both between Iranian citizens and overseas entities.

Not surprisingly the research dialogue about the social networks in Iran over the last decade, and especially since the riots of 2009, has emphasized the use made of these networks for the purposes of political protest, mainly by those who have been demanding change, the reformists and the opponents of the regime. While one cannot ignore the potential that exists in the social networks for political purposes and the advancement of political protest, the focus placed on the potential for protest has, to a great degree, led to the ignoring of additional central issues that characterize the dialogue about the networks.

Close observation of public dialogue concerning Iranian social networks has shown that they are often used for mobilizing the broader, public, and advancing struggles that are viewed by the Iranian public as being of greatest national value. In cases where Iran faces external challenges, the network dialogue tends to express a shared national identity that rises above the differences in political views that characterize Iranian society. The responses of Iranian browsers often reflect a feeling of national pride and a mobilization to defend national symbols, especially in cases where they find themselves facing the "other"—non-Iranians—whether they are Westerners, Arabs, or anyone else.

Zimmt's chapter examines how the social networks have become an arena that makes it possible for the Iranian public to express its national identity and unite around a shared, all-Iranian goal. The article uses different case studies to provide examples of the patriotic dialogue that has developed over recent years on the social networks in the Islamic Republic.

FINAL NOTE

This collection of chapters all in all aims at finding answers to the questions about the puzzling character of the Iranian identity—and is a small yet confident attempt to provide an updated and realistic, but also an adequate and comprehensive, overview of this developing issue. Totally covering this issue in all its relevant aspects is impossible, especially in one short book, but the abovementioned excellent writers have made a great effort to present the readers with clear and focused, easily understood writing in which each contributor has offered insights from his or her field of expertise.

The general message conveyed by these chapters is that identity, especially when it is faced with fundamental tensions as in the case of Iran, is a phenomenon that is constantly developing via factors involving the private-self and common-social factors. The real tension lies between Persian culture, which represents the glory and pride that arise from its history, and the Shi'a religion, which is a suppressive, gloomy, and obligating religion, and this tension is somehow dealt with by the Iranian people. At first sight this irrational and often unwelcome connection made between Shi'ism and Persianism seems to be unrealistic and doomed to eternal failure or, at least, to conflict. Perhaps this is so, but it has worked for the last five centuries and, as a small compensation, to us at least, this struggle has never stopped being interesting and challenging.

NOTE

1. For more details and theories regarding nation-building's ideologies, see Yuri Teper and Daniel D. Course, "Contesting Putin's nation-building: The 'Muslim other' and the challenge of the Russian ethno-cultural alternative," *Nations and Nationalism*, Vol. 20, No. 4 (2014), 721–41.

Part I

Historical and Current Perspectives on Persian, Islamic, and Contested Religious Identities

Chapter One

The Unending Battle between the Persian and Islamic Identities of Iran

Harold Rhode

The two great forces that have shaped the Iranian/Persian world[1] during the last fourteen hundred years have been the Islamic and Persian cultures and neither force can be understood in the Western sense of territorial nationalism. Both are, in essence, ethnocultural loyalties and, until the twentieth century, had little connection with the territorial concept of Iran and its twenty-five-hundred-year-old monarchy. Since most of the population converted to Islam more than one thousand years ago, the prime identity of most Iranians has been Islamic. Non-Muslims, regarded as outsiders, have therefore been excluded from playing active political and social roles in the affairs of the country.

At the same time Persian culture, the culture of the settled population—most of whom resided in the central plateau—has had a great impact on both Iranian Islam and the non-Persian ethnic groups living in the country. Most of these non-Persian ethnic groups, many of whom were Turkic nomads who constantly invaded the Iranian central plateau from the northeastern steppe area, have traditionally lived in the area surrounding the central plateau.

Historically, the goal of the ruling class was to try to settle these nomadic tribes and "Persianify" them. Persian culture was regarded as superior, and attempts were made to suppress and eradicate other "inferior cultures"—meaning the non-Persian cultures.[2] Various regimes encountered great opposition to this policy, especially in areas which were almost completely non–Persian-speaking, such as Turkish Azerbaijan and Kurdistan.

Ethnically and religiously Iran is a mixture of many peoples who, during the course of history, have migrated to the Iranian plateau. Although the deposed Shah's government claimed that the majority of the people of Iran was ethnically Persian, no reliable statistics exist which can prove this claim to be true. For example, Tehran was considered to be ethnically Persian but, in reality, a large part of the city's population is Azerbaijani Turkish, some of whom know little, if any, Persian. When asked about this situation government officials and some Iranian intellectuals would answer that there have never been any Turks in Iran—only Turkish-speaking Iranians or Turkish-speaking Persians, who were forcibly linguistically "Turkified" over the centuries.

At the same time another force, Islam, played a major role in Iran. Islam and Persian culture managed to coexist in an uneasy framework where supporters from both of these forces did their best to impose their will on supporters of the other. This uneasy coexistence has been the source of many upheavals in Iran since the Islamic conquest of the Persian Empire more than fourteen hundred years ago. Up until the time of the Islamic conquests, the proud and glorious Persian Empire had existed for eleven hundred years but it was defeated and overtaken by the Arab Muslim nomads storming out of the Arabian desert. Iran, a great civilization, viewed these nomads with contempt, and simply could not accept the fact that these primitive nomads had defeated their illustrious civilization.

How did this proud and ancient culture come to grips with their defeat by the Muslim Arabs? Iran has, in fact, been wrestling with this problem for more than fourteen hundred years and has still not managed to resolve it. Since that time, there has been an ongoing massive cultural battle between Iranian culture and Islam, with Iranian culture sometimes having the upper hand while, at other times, the Islamic culture prevailed. This battle between these two cultures has been like mixing oil and water which, in the end, simply doesn't worked. The main goal of this chapter is to describe this battle and demonstrate that the unending conflict between these two cultures has not yet been resolved and probably cannot ever be resolved.

In the biblical book of Esther, Persia—also known as Iran—is described as a great empire in which 127 nations lived which extended from today's Ethiopia to India. We do not know exactly when the story described took place nor for that matter if the events described are even true but, from the story, we can deduce that Persia was already a great empire long before the Arabs appeared on the world stage. A myriad of ancient Persian sources describe that empire and its culture and civilization and, from what these sources indicate, ancient Persia was a proud, confident, and highly developed urban civilization. Ancient Greek sources also inform us about the numerous clashes between the Hellenic peoples and Persia.

We need to understand the impact of the Arab Muslim defeat of Iran, which occurred approximately eleven hundred years after the Persians established their first empire, in this context. In 636 CE at Qādisiyya, in today's southern Iraq, the Arab desert nomads from Arabia defeated the Persian

Empire and brought with them a new religion, Islam, which would in time supplant Zoroastrianism, Iran's ancient religion. How could these desert no-mads have defeated the mighty Persian Empire? One of the reasons is that in the approximately twenty years beforehand, the Persian and Byzantine em-pires had been engaged in exhausting battles which weakened both of them to the point where it was relatively easy for Arabs to defeat Persia.

That victory at Qādisiyya[3] shook the Persian culture and confidence to their very foundations. How could an inferior, as the Persians saw it, nomad-ic culture defeat the glorious and highly sophisticated Persians?[4] The Per-sians simply could not fathom this idea and, up until today—more than fourteen hundred years later, the Persians have still not come to grips with this cultural and political defeat which altered their lives and culture forever. That battle between Islam and Iran, between Persian culture and Arab Islam, still rages in the hearts and minds of Iranians/Persians everywhere. In today's modern Iranian culture, both play particular roles but they live together in an uneasy existence. The bottom line is that, no matter how hard they try, the Iranians do not seem to be able to devise a strategy in which these two forces can peacefully coexist and, since the defeat of the Sassanid Empire, Iranian history has never been able to square this circle.

HOW DID THE PERSIANS DEAL WITH THE ONSLAUGHT OF ARABIC CULTURE AND LANGUAGE? WHY DID THEY NOT SUCCUMB TO THE ARABIC CULTURE LIKE THEIR NEIGHBORS TO THE WEST?

How did this ancient empire, with its long and highly developed culture, deal with the Arab conquests? Very few sources are available to inform us about the first three hundred years of Arab/Islamic rule in Iran but, from what we can surmise, Persian culture seems to have gone underground and, in contrast to what happened in the west which constitutes today's Arab world, Persian culture found ways to survive. Within one hundred years of the Arab con-quests, the territory of today's Arab world underwent a process of "Islamifi-cation" and "Arabization" in which the local cultures conquered by the Arabs rather quickly submitted both to Arab rule and Islam and mostly abandoned their pre-Islamic and pre-Arabic languages and cultures.

What explains the resilience of Persian culture as opposed to the cultures of those groups who submitted? To begin with, Persia/Iran had a confident culture which ruled many other peoples. The countries that today constitute the Arab world, on the other hand, had become used to being conquered and, throughout history, had learned to adapt themselves to the will of their con-querors. Iran, on the other hand, was a conquering nation and had had a long tradition of ruling over others. Iran's borders certainly expanded and contracted but the core of the Persian Empire stayed the same for approximately eleven hundred years. It had lost battles but it had only been conquered once—by Alexander the Great.

Like many other empires throughout history, Persia had great difficulty accepting defeat. It retreated into itself and never gave up its basic cultural awareness. During the early years of Islam individual Persians tried to adapt to the new Arab-Islamic reality but, despite the fact that, according to Islam, all Muslims are brothers and equal, in reality, Arab tribal identity was paramount among the early Muslims. This means that non-Arabs and people who did not belong to the more important Arab tribes were ignored by the system. But the nomadic desert Arabs desperately needed the skills of the settled peoples they had conquered and a system was devised in which individuals became appendages to particular Arab clans. The system, known as the *Mawā li* system,[5] enabled Persians to become associated or aligned with particular Arab clans and tribes and, although this gave them the status they craved, it also meant that these Persians had to convert to Islam and often even adopt an Arab identity.

Although this system worked for individuals, it could clearly not work for an entire people. With time, other systems were developed to mitigate this problem. Probably the most important and earliest large scale approach was to try to infiltrate Islam and, indeed, to conquer it from within. How did they do this? Some of the earliest and most interesting events were those involving the Abbasid revolution in 750 CE. During the previous one hundred years, the Muslim world had been ruled from Damascus, by the Umayyads, one of the most important Arab-Muslim clans that had originated in Mecca. From 660 CE through to the mid-eighth century, Islam had expanded all the way across North Africa into Spain and eastward into today's India. This was an enormous part of the then known world and this vast swath of territory was ruled from Damascus.

In 750 CE, Abu Muslim of Khorasan, in today's northern Iran, led a rebellion against the Umayyads, overthrew them, and installed in their place a descendent of another Arab Muslim of Mecca origin: 'Abbās (who was the prophet Muhammad's uncle). They moved the capital of the Islamic Empire to Baghdad, a city founded in 762 CE possibly where a city called *Bagdata*[6] had once been and in an area that was much more under the influence of Persian culture. Even the name of that city, Baghdad, is Persian (meaning "God gave").[7] By watching the development of that city, which was soon to become one of the most important cities of that era, we can see the gradual overtaking of Arab culture by Persian culture. To be sure, the Arabic language and Islam reigned supreme, but one could make an excellent case claiming that these were a facade behind which Persian culture ruled the roost.

Over time the Persians showed the Arabs how to rule over a huge empire using methods Persia had developed and refined for more than twelve hundred years. Senior bureaucrats in Baghdad wrote books on how to rule in order to teach their nomadic desert Arab rulers.[8] Persian art and culture also became the rage in Baghdad.

Meanwhile the Persians tried to find other ways to bridge the gap between the Persian and Islamic cultures and, in the process, developed highly creative methods. For example, a tradition was instituted in which the daughter of the last pre-Islamic Sassanid ruler of the Persian Empire, Yazdegird II, married the third Imam Hussein Ibn Ali.[9] Their son was supposedly Zayn al-'Ābidīn, the fourth Shi'ite Imam, Ali Ibn Hussein and, if this is true, it means that the following Shi'ite Imams, that is, the fifth to twelfth Imams, were descendants of Zayn al-'Ābidīn and of Iranian royal blood. I have personally been told that this is the traditional "proof," (*hujja*) that Shi'ism's central figures, the Imams who are directly descended from Muhammad, are Iranian; and this, many Iranians say, also proves that Shi'ism is an Iranian religion. The only problem with this theory is that it appears only to have been "discovered" many years after Iran succumbed to Islam and has little historical evidence to support it. Even if it is true, Islam is passed on via the father, which would mean that the son of the above-mentioned marriage, though having an Iranian mother, would still be an Arab. Moreover, according to Iranian custom, kingship is also passed down through the father. These facts, however, are largely overlooked because they do not fit into the Iranian/ Persian narrative which says that, because of the aforementioned marriage, the Shi'ite Imams are Iranians.

Another way Iranians developed in order to deal with this seemingly impossible task of coming to grips with Iran's defeat was to invent a flowery language that had all the features of today's political correctness. This was called *ta'ārof* and was done in order to make the listener believe that he would get exactly what he wanted even though the speaker had absolutely no intention of giving it to him.[10] The Persians learned to tell their new Muslim rulers exactly what they wanted to hear because it gave the Persians time to develop strategies to circumvent their rulers' wishes. Sadly, in order to escape the harsh reality of life, they also developed another way to address this problem: the extensive use of opium.[11]

THE PERSIAN LANGUAGE AND THE IRANIAN IDENTITY

Language was another key tool used to retain Persian culture and identity. As mentioned above, within one hundred years most of what we know today as the Arabic-speaking world abandoned pre-Islamic languages in favor of Arabic. What happened in Iran was different. We have few sources of information about the earlier centuries of Iran under Islam but we do know that the written Persian language reemerged in Samarkand and Bokhara—two Persian cultural centers in today's Uzbekistan—and became the written language of culture and writing in that area. Written Persian also reemerged farther south in what is today's Iran and, in this way, the language was preserved by the people and by the local cultural powers.

Several questions arise. First, what was so different in Persian culture that stopped Persians from succumbing to linguistic Arabization like their neighbors to the west? Second, what was the nature of this new language? Was it Islamic or post-Sassanid Persian? And third, were attempts made to purify Persian by not using any Arabic words? This would have been an almost impossible feat given the pervasive nature of Islam and its Arabic-language base.

Persia was a strong and proud empire with an ancient and confident historical tradition that had ruled many peoples and had developed powerful institutions to do so. The Arab world, on the other hand, had, by the advent of Islam, suffered many both political and religious invasions. This constant change weakened them culturally and made them more susceptible to linguistic and religious imperialism. For example, though many living in what is today's Arab world were Christian, their Christianity was different from that of the Byzantine Empire, which constantly tried to impose Byzantine Christianity on them. Many of the Islamic religious principles were more similar to those of the Muslims than to those of the Byzantines who were steeped in Hellenic culture. In short, this region was nowhere as culturally and linguistically confident as the Persian Empire to the east. [12]

THE EARLY INTERACTION BETWEEN
PERSIANS AND THEIR NEW ARAB MASTERS

From what little we know, during the first approximately 120 years after the Arab conquest of Persia, the Persians did their best to find ways to preserve their language and culture. The Arab Muslim conquerors, on the other hand, did their best to try and impose Arabic as the language of the Islamic Empire. For example, al-Hajjāj bin Yūsuf was incensed that Persian was prevalent in the court and ordered that only Arabic be used as the language of government throughout the empire. [13] Others, such as Abu al-Faraj al-Isfahāni [14] and Abū Rayhān al-Bīrūnī, [15] have also mentioned vicious, anti-Persian cultural attacks as well. Nevertheless, unlike their neighbors in the region that is today's Arab world, the Persians resisted and refused to accept Arabization willingly.

Persia, besides being an empire, was also a culture which had struck deep roots in the peoples it had ruled over the eleven hundred years of its existence. Customs such as *Nowruz,* the Iranian New Year which starts on the first day of spring and the six-day celebrations that precede it, became so deeply embedded in the areas which Persian culture dominated that they were celebrated by the locals long after the Persians ceased to rule them. Seeing that Persian culture was so prevalent among these peoples, it stands to reason that this culture, no matter what external and powerful influences might try to overwhelm it, would continue to survive below the surface.

That is exactly what happened in the region that is the Iran of today and the area to Iran's east. What we do know is that the post-Islamic Persian language that emerged was a new "Islamic" Persian that was heavily influenced by Arabic and Islam, yet remained distinct from Arabic. The grammar remained almost exclusively[16] Persian but, over time, Arabic vocabulary deeply penetrated this new version of Persian. Moreover, the Persians abandoned their pre-Islamic script *Pahlavi*, which was much more suited to Persian than to the modified Arabic script which the Persians used to write their new Islamic dialect of Persian.

Although the Muslim Persians used this new hybrid language, there were attempts to write this new language without using Arabic words. For example, in his *magnum opus*—the *Shahnameh*—Ferdowsi, who wrote in what we could call early modern Persian, went out of his way to use as few Arabic words as possible. This is a huge feat given the fact that this epic poem contains over fifty thousand couplets. What motivated him and other writers to do this? This epic poem—as well as others written by Hafez and Sa'adi—was an attempt to preserve Persia's ancient pre-Islamic history and traditions in the face of the onslaught of the Arab-Islamic culture.

Later, the aforementioned, well-known Persian spiritual and mystical poets Hafez (1325/26–1389/90 CE) and Sa'adi (1210–1291/92 CE), two of the greatest poets of the classical Iranian literary tradition, wrote odes to wine (which was strictly forbidden in Islam) as well as other non- or anti-Islamic subjects. Both tried to use as much Persian vocabulary as possible and, in a polite manner; belittled certain aspects of Islamic culture and the Muslim clergy. Like Ferdowsi, this was their way to denigrate the Arabs and Islam, while emphasizing the greatness of pre-Islamic Iran.

These writers, along with many others, simply refused to accept the Islamic concept of *Jāhiliya*, that is, the period of ignorance (in Arabic, all pre-Islamic history), meaning that anything that existed before Islam was at best irrelevant, useless, and of no value. These writers did a fine job trying to preserve the ancient Persian culture in spite of Arab-Islamic attempts to obliterate it. These writers were the beginning of a long tradition of trying to prevent Persian culture from being overwhelmed by Arabic and Islamic culture, a battle which still rages to this day.

How does this linguistic battle manifest itself today? Under the Pahlavi dynasty (1925–1979), there was a major attempt made to replace Arabic words with ancient, pre-Islamic Persian words and to invent words for modern concepts based solely on Persian roots. A few examples illustrate this point: 1) The word for "kitchen"—*matbah*—in Arabic, a word long in use in Iran, was replaced by the word *ashpaz-khaneh*; 2) The Arabic word *ālān*—meaning "now," also used for many centuries in Iran, was replaced by the "pure" Persian word *aknun*; 3) The Arabic word *tashih* followed by the Persian auxiliary verb *kardan,* meaning "to tell the truth," were replaced by the Persian "*dorost kardan.*" Were these old and new words, however, accepted by the masses? The answer is part of the struggle between these two cultures and is exemplified by the fact that, when Khomeini established the Islamic Republic, he consciously tried to use Arabic words instead of the many Persian words that the late shah and his father had tried to inculcate into Persian.

At the same time, however, one of the ways that young Iranian university students tried to protest Khomeini's re-Arabization of Persian was to study pre-Islamic Persian, called *Avestan*. Given the indirectness and formal politeness of Persian culture, it is not surprising that Iranians are ingenious at finding ways to express their opposition to their regime in any way possible. Language, it appears, has evidently been a potent tool in the battle to keep Persian culture alive. Interestingly, Iranians today are still passionately concerned about purifying—that is, de-Arabicizing—their language, and publish detailed lists of "pure Persian" words to be used instead of Arabic ones.[17]

RELIGION AS A TOOL IN THE BATTLE BETWEEN PERSIAN CULTURE AND ISLAM

Religion itself has also been a useful tool in the battle between Iran and Islam. Prior to the sixteenth century Iran was largely Sunni with a few pockets of Shi'ism and, at that time, Iran, like all of its surrounding neighbors, was ruled by Turkish/Turkic[18] dynasties, almost all of whom were Hanafi Sunnis represented by the Ottomans to the west, the Shaybanids to the north (the forebears of the modern Uzbeks), and the Mogul Empire to the east. How then could Persia, which was constantly looking for ways to separate itself from the "inferior" cultures of the Arabs and nomadic Turks, differentiate itself from its surrounding neighbors; and how could it gain allies in the region of its major adversary, the then-mighty Ottoman Empire?

An example of how Persia fought to separate itself from the surrounding people was Shah Esma'il, an Azeri Turk who ruled Iran from Tabriz—the capital of Iranian Azerbaijan in northwestern Iran. He tackled this problem brilliantly, going on to conquer all of what is present-day Iran and the surrounding areas, and founded the Safavid dynasty which ruled Iran between 1501–1722. In order to separate Iran from the surrounding Turkic Sunni empires, he adopted Shi'ism as the state religion, thus effectively differentiating Iran from the surrounding Sunni Hanafi empires. We again have few sources to explain how, but we know that, within one hundred years, the Iranian plateau and its northwest had become overwhelmingly Shi'ite.[19] The Iranians developed all sorts of methods to placate their rulers, publically showing them fidelity but privately maintaining their core values. If placating the rulers was the reason these people adopted Shi'ism, why then did people in other areas of the empire not become Shi'ites as well?

In essence, Shi'ism, as it came to be understood in Iran, was perfectly suited for the post–Arabic Conquest Iranian character. Iranian Shi'ism has a strong sense of persecution because of its constant invocation of Ali, his sons, and their suffering—but at the hands of whom? Just as members of Muhammad's family—from whom Shi'ism develops—were persecuted by the people who later became known as Sunnis, so too, were the Iranians being persecuted and discriminated against by the Arabs. As a persecuted minority branch of Islam, Shi'ism developed highly elaborate and effective means of dealing with the dominant and aggressive Sunnis. It developed *taqiya* to a fine art. *Taqiya*, which appears in the Quran, means that you are able to dissimulate by telling people who might hurt you anything that will help you preserve your existence. This means that you may lie, obfuscate, or do whatever else is necessary in order to maintain your essence. Indeed, that is exactly what Iran needed to do to survive as a separate cultural entity.[20]

Did the people of Iran initially adopt Twelver Shi'ism (*Ithna-'ashariya*) because their rulers demanded it? What little we do know is that the rulers dispatched preachers throughout the country, but we know little of the details. Whatever the case, Twelver Shi'ism enabled Iran to survive culturally. It is sometimes hard to distinguish between what is culturally Iranian and what is culturally Shi'ite, which is why Iranians often say that Shi'ism is an Iranian religion that both differentiates them from the surrounding peoples while, at the same time, allowing them to be Muslims—but in their own unique way. This has constituted the Iranian attempt to blend Iran and Islam into one unique cultural entity.

Adopting Shi'ism also proved useful for finding allies abroad. For example, when Shah Esma'il adopted Shi'ism in 1501, most of eastern Anatolia, which was part of the heartland of the Ottoman Empire, was populated by people whom we today call Alevis, who are religiously much closer to Shi'ites than Sunnis.[21] In fact their religion is very close to Twelver Shi'ism which is radically different from Sunni Hanafi Islam, the religion of the Ottoman rulers. Some of these Alevis migrated to Iranian Azerbaijan, but the majority remained in eastern Anatolia and instantly became a fifth column against the Ottomans, who viewed Shi'ism as an existential enemy. The Alevis of eastern Anatolia formed an alliance with Shah Esma'il against the Ottoman rulers. The Ottomans, who in 1511–1513 had concentrated their troops in today's Syria, had planned to march southward and conquer Mamluk Egypt but, given the rise of Shi'ism in the east, they had no alternative other than to move their troops eastward in order to defeat both their Alevi[22] fifth column and the Persians and their Alevi allies. This move created a logistical nightmare but, in 1514, the Ottomans defeated Shah Esma'il who was forced to flee deep into Iran's heartland and move his capital from Tabriz to Esfahan.

THE PERSIAN LANGUAGE AND CULTURE AND ITS INFLUENCE ON ITS NON-PERSIAN SUNNI NEIGHBORS AND FELLOW SHI'ITE ARABS

Language again is a window into the heart and soul of Iran and its neighbors. Until Shah Esma'il's time any self-respecting Ottoman—and the other great Turkic rulers to Iran's north and east—had to learn Persian, which was considered to be the most sophisticated language and culture of the area. In fact, most of the correspondence extant in the Ottoman archives between the Ottomans and the Safavids shows an interesting twist. The Ottomans wrote to the Safavids in Persian, the language of culture, but the (Azeri Turkic) Safavid rulers of Iran responded in Turkish. This was a fascinating situation in which the rulers of the Ottoman (Turkish) Empire wrote in the language of Persia while the rulers of Persia wrote to the Ottomans in their own language—Turkish.

This episode, however, also illustrates how powerful and seductive Persian culture and language was throughout most of the Muslim world. Besides the Ottomans who were, at least on their paternal line, descended from nomadic Central Asian Turks, other great Muslim empires, such as the Mogul Empire in India, adopted the Persian language and culture as their own. Thus we can see that the Persian culture was resilient and made its mark throughout much of the Muslim world that stretched from the Bosphorus all the way to China. This was not the case with the Sunni Arabs. Persian never became a language used by the upper classes, especially after Iran became Shi'ite.

Things were different, however, among the Arab Shi'ites; who, no matter how much they tried to maintain their unique identity as Arab Shi'ites, they had great difficulty in doing so. Consider, for example, the enormous Persian cultural influence in Iraq, as can be seen at the Shi'ite shrines in *Kadhimiyah* in Baghdad and in the Shi'ite "Vatican" (i.e., the Iraqi cities of Najaf and Karbala).

Many Iranians often claim that "Shi'ism is an Iranian religion" and these same Iranians look down upon their Arab and Turkish/Turkic neighbors. They have invented all sorts of epithets for these neighbors—especially the Arabs—both Sunni and their fellow Shi'ite Arabs—and have labeled them

Mush-Khor (i.e., rodent eaters) and *Marmulak-Khor* (i.e., lizard eaters). Arabs, especially the Shi'ite Arabs, resent Persian cultural imperialism and respond, "If you break open the bone of a Persian, shi*t comes out" [in Arabic: *idha tiksar 'admu, titla' khara*]. Persians also look down on Turks and call them donkeys (in Persian: "*Tork-e Khar*").

Persian cultural superiority, in short, trumps everything. It matters more than Islam, whether Shi'ite or Sunni. Consequently, it is so strong that whatever forces get in its way, it often finds ways to either co-opt and incorporate them into Iranian/Persian culture. Or it lies in waiting until it can find a way to merge with and dominate whatever culture or country is in its way.[23]

THE SAFAVIDS: BLENDING PERSIAN CULTURE AND ISLAM

After Shah Esma'il adopted Shi'ism, he and his descendants imported Shi'ite scholars, largely from Jebel 'Amil in today's Lebanon,[24] to teach them Shi'ism. These scholars translated Shi'ite texts into Persian and then, in later years, wrote other material in Persian so that the Persian-speaking masses could have access to it.

Until the Safavid era the Ottoman Sunni upper class made sure that its children learned Persian which they considered the most sophisticated language. But once Shi'ite texts were available in Persian, the Ottomans felt threatened by the idea that if their children learned Persian, they might be tempted to become Shi'ites—and this was anathema to the Sunni Muslims who ruled the Ottoman Empire. As a result the Ottomans stopped allowing their future ruling class to learn Persian, until these future leaders reached the age of sixteen when, it was hoped, their Sunni identity was sufficiently ingrained so that they would not be influenced by Shi'ite texts. This shows how powerful and important the influence of Persian culture was on others who did not live under Iranian Shi'ite domination.

It was Shi'ism, in short, that enabled Iran/Persia to separate itself from the surrounding peoples and survive. Shi'ism and Iranian culture insulated that land from the surrounding areas and helped maintain the Iranian/Persian identity.

PERSIAN ATTEMPTS TO ASSIMILATE NON-PERSIAN PEOPLES INTO PERSIAN CULTURE

Unrelated to Shi'ism, Persian culture continued to have a magnetic and almost seductive effect on the surrounding Sunni countries and drew people from India, Central Asia, and today's Chinese Xinjiang province into its cultural orbit.

Iran continued to dispatch emissaries, this time mostly under the guise of Shi'ism, to convert people to its newly found religion. Historically, especially during the pre-Islamic era, Persians constantly had tried to domesticate the surrounding peoples, mostly nomads, by culturally "converting" them into Persians. They were so successful at this that they managed to convince the Azerbaijani Turks that they were originally Persians who had been forced to speak Turkish in the early 1400s by Tamerlane, who is supposed to have cut out four hundred thousand tongues of the people who refused to speak Turkish.[25] These "pure" Persians speak Azeri today and, although they maintain their ethnic Azeri identity, many among them believe that they are the true Persians.[26] It is truly remarkable that the Iranian Persian culture has succeeded, without much violence, in convincing an entire people that their natural language should be Persian. This was a source of endless puzzlement and disappointment for the Soviet Azerbaijanis who gained their independence in 1991. The former Soviet Azerbaijanis were sure that their southern Azeri brothers, who lived in Iran and who numbered more than three times the number of Azeris in independent Azerbaijan, would want to join them in forming one Azeri state. But after meeting these Iranian Azeris, the former Soviet Azeris were crestfallen when they discovered that most of the Iranian Azeris they met referred to themselves as Azeri Iranians—that is, first and foremost as Iranians. The Soviet Azeris had lived under Russian rule since the end of the Russo-Iranian war in 1828, and seemingly had lost their "Iranianness" and begun to think of themselves solely as Azeris.[27] On the other hand, Iranian culture had so enveloped the Iranian Azeris that they came to believe that being Iranian was more important to their basic identity than being Azeri. In time almost all the rulers of Iran, irrespective of their origin, became thoroughly "Persianized." Such is the power of Persian culture.

The Qajar dynasty (1785–1925 CE) was also Azeri Turkish but, apart from the initial rulers, few of their upper class used Turkish. It is interesting to note that many Azeris who later served in very high positions under the Pahlavi shahs were also Azeri, and strongly identified themselves as such, but many of them barely knew any Azeri Turkish and had become thoroughly "Persianized," both linguistically and culturally. At the same time, however, they also strongly identified as Iranians—and not as Turks.

What does it mean to be Azeri to these "Persianized" Azeri Iranians? Looking at the National Front, an Iranian opposition group that existed under the Pahlavis, provides interesting insight. When this group expressed its opposition in political terms, was something deeper occurring? In fact many National Front members belonged to the Qajar ruling class. They were the descendants of the ethnically Azeri Turkish Qajars and belonged to its ruling class but, culturally, had been the Persian rulers of the previous dynasty. This author's personal experience with National Front members indicates that almost none of them spoke their ancestral Azeri language; thus they were no longer Azeri Turks, even though their ancestors had been. Persian language and culture are so powerful and enticing that the National Front Members, along with so many other non-Persian speaking Shi'ites, were very willing to abandon their past in favor of what they viewed to be a far superior Persian culture.[28]

ATTEMPTS TO LEAVE ISLAM—BAHAISM

The ability of Iranians/Persians to adapt to change was, and still is, visible in the nineteenth, twentieth, and twenty-first centuries. In the nineteenth century, the new "religion" of Bahaism developed in Iran and was anathema to traditional Islam because of one of the classical principles of Islam that holds that their prophet Muhammad was the "Seal of the Prophets" (in Arabic: *Khatim al-Anbiya*). This means that there would be no more prophets after Muhammad. Bahais, however, claimed that prophecy never stopped and that their leader, Bahaullah, was a modern-day (i.e., nineteenth-century) prophet. As Bahaism—a peaceful religion according to which all people are brothers—spread in the nineteenth century, Iran's Shi'ite rulers and religious establishment felt that this new creed was a mortal threat. As Bahaism succeeded, more and more people embraced this new religion. This again, is an example of the quintessential Iranian tactic of converting to the religion of the most powerful in order to protect Persian essence. When the Qajar rulers, however, defeated the Bahais, Iranians who had followed Bahaism began returning to Islam. This experience is deeply engrained in the Iranian Shi'ite religious psyche and is why today's the Iranian Islamic Republic's leaders so passionately loathe Bahaism.[29] They see Bahaism as a threat to Islam, and given the nature of Iranian culture, they have every reason to believe that it is.

Bahaism was indeed an existential threat to Iranian Shi'ite Islam when it was militarily powerful because of the malleability of Iranian culture. It is therefore not surprising that, today, a significant number of Iranians in the diaspora—most notably in the United States and the Netherlands—have left Islam and have converted to Christianity, the major religion of both countries.[30]

CONCLUSION

Whither Iran? Will Iran remain Muslim? What will happen to a post-Islamic Republican Iran? What are the questions facing the Iranian people?

It is not surprising that a favorite food in Iran is the onion, a vegetable which typifies the essence of what it means to be an Iranian. The onion's many layers protect its core, just like the many layers of external adaptations Iranians have created over fourteen hundred years preserve the very core of their being—Persian culture. In this context, Islam is just one layer among the many layers that make up what it means to be Persian. The type of Islam Iran eventually chose helped it retain its core values and protect itself against the surrounding non-Persian peoples. This is truly an amazing accomplishment because almost all of the ancient cultures of their neighbors to the west succumbed to Arab Islam.[31] Islam, however, even Shi'ite Islam (and it doesn't matter how much Iranians claim Shi'ism to be an Iranian religion), is really still a foreign body grafted onto the body of Persian culture, and it is still not, and probably will never be, totally at one with Iran.

What does this tell us about the future? Will Iran remain part of the Muslim world? So many Iranians inside this country hate the Islamic establishment with a passion. They blame the religious authorities for everything that is wrong with their country and, to be sure, there are those forces which believe that their religious leaders do not represent the "true Islam," whatever that means. Nevertheless, although it is hard to gather exact details, there seems to be some subterranean conversion to Christianity going on inside Iran, and reliable reports from longtime observers of Iran have reported that about five thousand people per month are quietly converting to Christianity inside Iran. They are doing this quietly because it is dangerous for these converts to reveal themselves; conversion from Islam is punishable by death. Early Christianity was also an oppressed religion and people often hid the fact that they had become Christians. As such the early Christians might well be models for Iran's hidden Christians today.

Could Iran's ancient, pre-Islamic religion—Zoroastrianism—offer a way out for Iranians? There are only two hundred thousand adherents left in Iran, but elsewhere many more exist. For example, the Parsis in India still belong to that faith. Since interest in Iran's pre-Islamic culture goes hand in hand with Zoroastrianism, could there be a revival of that religion in Iran? Almost all of Iran's pre-Islamic culture was Zoroastrian and this is something that has captivated many Iranians. *Nowruz*, the Iranian New Year and the ceremonies that lead up to it, are Zoroastrian in origin, as are the *ying-yang* (hot-cold) aspects of the culture. Are Iranians tired of Islam? Has Iran's Shi'ite religious establishment alienated the people? The problem for Iranians who are interested is that Zoroastrians do not accept conversions and demand that both parents must be Zoroastrian in order for a child to be a member of that religion. Could there, however, be ancient texts, not yet unearthed, which demonstrate that once there were other ways to become a member of the religion? After all, the first Zoroastrians could not have been born to Zoroastrian parents. If such a thing were possible could Iranians revert to some sort of pre-Islamic form of their ancient religion and culture?

Iran is in flux. Its relationship with Islam has always been uncomfortable. Islam and Persian culture can probably best be summed up as a mixture of oil and water. One can mix them forever, but in the end, given their nature as distinct entities and left to their own devices, they cannot blend together into one entity. Persian culture, no matter how much Shi'ite leaders such as Ayatollah Khomeini tried to suppress it, has proven to be resilient, so that when attacked, it seems to retreat into the background, waiting for an opportunity to reassert itself when the forces of Islam prove weak.

If the past is prescient, the struggle between Iran and Islam will continue far into the foreseeable future and, given the upheavals that the entire Muslim world is experiencing, whether Iran will remain Muslim or choose some other path is anyone's guess.

NOTES

1. We use the term "Iranian world" to indicate not only Iran within its present borders, but also Central Asia and beyond, where Persian culture has had an enormous cultural impact for millennia.

2. Interestingly, this is why Iran and China have so much in common. Both are highly urbanized and sophisticated cultures. They both had to deal with constant nomadic invasions and each developed similar ways of absorbing those nomads. Their message was, in short, "Please come in and rule us. You are very welcome to do so as long as you assimilate into our culture and adopt our ways." Two of the Mongol leaders who were Genghis Khan's grandsons, for example, ruled large empires. Kubla Khan started the Yuan dynasty which ruled China and he and his descendants underwent a process of sinofication while another grandson of Genghis Khan—Hulagoo—ruled Iran as a culturally Persianified Muslim.

3. For an in-depth description of the Persian defeat at Qādisiyya, see D. Gershon Lewental, "Qādisiyyah, Then and Now: A Case Study of History and Memory, Religion, and Nationalism in Middle Eastern Discourse." For a summary of this dissertation, see: http://dissertationreviews.org/archives/4499.

4. Harold Rhode, "Sources of Iranian Negotiating Behavior," *The Resilience of Iranian Culture Following Arab Conquest*, jcpa.org, pp. 4–5.

5. For more on the Malawi system, see the *Encyclopedia of Islam*, http://reference-works.brillonline.com/entries/encyclopaedia-of-islam-2/malawi-COM_1423?s.num=0& s.f.s2_parent=s.f.book.encyclopaedia-of-islam-2&s.q=malawi.

6. Nevertheless, a third-century scholar Rabbi Hanna Bagdata is mentioned in the Talmud. The great European Jewish scholar Rashi (1040–1105 CE) equated Bagdata with Baghdad. This might be true, but we have no other evidence to corroborate this claim.

7. *Bagh*, "God," *dad*, "gave," the past tense form of *dadan*, "to give."

8. For a description of how the Persians explained the methods of kingship to the Arabs, see Nizam al-Mulk, *Siyasat nameh*, that is, "Book of Government" or "Rules for Kings."

9. See Moshe Gil, "Ha-Mifgash Ha-Bavli (The Babylonian Encounter)," *Tarbitz*, Vol. 48.

10. For more on how ta'ārof works, see "Persian Culture," Part One, http://www.youtube.com/watch?v=9ZTnBMQjr0A; "Learn Persian (Farsi) with Chai and Conversation—About Tarof (Taarof), an Iranian tradition," http://www.youtube.com/watch?v=u5oX2n1-diA, retrieved: October 5, 2014; Christopher De Bellaigue, "Talk Like an Iranian: As the author learned in Tehran, yes sometimes means no," August 22, 2012, http://www.theatlantic.com/magazine/archive/2012/09/talk-like-an-iranian/309056/, retrieved: October 5, 2014.

11. For a history of opium use in Iran, see: Rudi Matthee, *The Pursuit of Pleasure: Drugs and Stimulants in Iranian History, 1500–1900* (Princeton, NJ: Princeton University Press, 2005).

12. For more on the Byzantine-Persian wars before the rise of Islam, see Harald Sigurdsson, "Battle of Dara Byzantines defeat Persians," June 6, 2012, http://burnpit.us/2012/06/battle-dara-byzantines-defeat-persians, retrieved: October 5, 2014.

13. Richard Nelson Frye, et al., "The Arab Conquest of Iran," in *Cambridge History of Iran*, Vol. 4 (London, 1975), p. 46.

14. Kitab al-Aghani, Vol. 4, p. 423.

15. *The Remaining Signs of Past Centuries* (Arabic: *Kitāb al-āthār al-bāqiyah `an al-qurūn al-khāliyah*), completed in 1000 CE, pp. 35–36 and 48.

16. Ferdowsi started writing the *Shahnameh* is 977 CE and completed it in 1010 CE. For more details about Ferdowsi's *Shahnameh* project see Djalal Khaleghi-Motlagh, "Ferdowsi, Abu'l Qāsem-i.Life," *Encyclopædia Iranica* (January 26, 2012).

17. For an example of this, see "Parsi-begoo," uploaded on the net from Belgium. Moreover, the choice of the name of the language "Parsi" and not "Farsi" says it all. Arabic does not have the sound "p." In its place, Arabs have historically used "f." That is how the name of the language "parsi" became "farsi."

18. The distinction between the words "Turkish" and "Turkic" was invented in the nineteenth century. Turkish was used for anything describing the Ottomans while Turkic was used for the rest of the Turks of the world. This division was more an attempt by outsiders—mainly the Tsarist Russians—to divide the Turks in separate entities for political reasons but, culturally, this was largely a distinction of little difference. Turkish, for example, uses the word "Turk" to describe all Turks wherever they live.

19. Often, when a king converts to a particular religion, many of his people do so as well but this is not always the case. We simply do not know the details here.

20. For more on the concept of Taqiya, see Harold Rhode, "The Sources of Iranian Negotiating Behavior," www.jcpa.org, pp. 11–12, and Moojan Momen, *An Introduction to Shi'i Islam* (Yale University Press, 1985), pp. 39, 183.

21. In the early 1970s, before much of the mass migration of the cities of western Turkey, this author traveled extensively in areas of Turkey which were then largely Alevi. He asked many of the Alevis there whether they preferred their daughters to marry someone from Tabriz (meaning an Iranian Shi'ite) or a man from Istanbul (then meaning a Turkish Sunni.) What was clearly implied here was whether they would have preferred their daughters to marry a Sunni or a Shi'ite. Almost without any hesitation they responded, "A man from Tabriz."

22. The Alevis of Turkey and the 'Alawis of Syria are different sects. Indeed, they both venerate 'Ali but Alevis in Turkey have many central Asian practices and Shamanist practices. The 'Alawis of Syria do not share these practices.

23. For more on the Persian domination of Shi'ism, see Harold Rhode "Review on Laurence Louër's *Shiism and Politics in the Middle East*," (London: Hurst, 2012), http://www.israelcfr.com/documents/8-1/8-1-7-HaroldRhode.pdf.

24. For more on how these Lebanese Shi'ite clerics influenced Iran during the Safavid period, see Roschanack Shaery-Eisenlohr, *Shi'ite Lebanon—Transnational Religion and the Making of National Identity* (New York: Columbia University Press, 2011), and Stefan Winter, *The Shiites of Lebanon under Ottoman Rule, 1516–1788* (Cambridge: Cambridge University Press, 2010).

25. There is no historical evidence that this actually happened. But from this author's extensive travels in Iran, and from numerous conversations with Iranian Azeri intellectuals, it is clear that many believe this myth. Legend very often triumphs over truth in the Middle East.

26. Alireza Asgharzadeh, "Azerbaijan and the Challenge of Multiple Identities: In Search of a Global Soul," GLORIA Center, IDC Herzliya, December 2, 2007, http://www.gloria-center.org/2007/12/asgharzadeh-2007-12-02/, retrieved: October 6, 2014; "Ahmad Kasravi Azerbaijani Linguist," March 23, 2011, http://ahmadkasravi-iranhistory.blogspot.com/2011/03/ahmad-kasravi-azerbaijani-linguist_3301.html, retrieved: October 5, 2014.

27. See the 1828 Treaty of Turkmenchay—where Iran ceded to the Russians several areas that Iran had controlled in the southern Caucasus for centuries.

28. This is very similar to what happened in China. Historically, many non-Chinese people have ruled over China, but Chinese culture—like Persian culture—has had a smothering effect so powerful that many of its ruling classes—the Manchus for example—simply abandoned their non-Chinese (Han) cultural origins and assimilated into Han Chinese culture. Like Iran, the Chinese were very willing to accept this people who accepted Chinese culture.

29. For more on this subject, see Ronen A. Cohen, "The Hojjatiyeh—From Anti-Baha'i and Anti-Revolutionary Movement to the Real Creators of the Islamic Revolution in Iran," *The New East—Journal of the Middle East and Islamic Studies of Israel (MEISAI)*, Vol. 51, (Summer 2012), pp. 69–92.

30. Curiously, we do not witness significant numbers of converts from Sunni Islam to other religions among Muslims in the West.

31. So did the Ottoman Empire to a very large extent, which did its best to submerge Turkish culture in favor of a Sunni Islam often based on the classic ruling principles of pre-Islamic Iran.

Chapter Two

National Identity or Political Legitimacy

The Reconstruction of the City of Bam

Ladan Zarabadi

The identity of nations often involves cultural issues and severe challenges posed over time by political powers, who have perpetually attempted to interpret national identities and transform cultures in order to legitimize their authority and authenticity. In other words, culture as a dynamic phenomenon has been influenced, formed, transformed, and occasionally exploited by political powers to enhance the legitimacy and authenticity of a particular political system. This means that culture attains a political quality, in which both history and culture are considered to be a means for legitimizing political actions. In fact, they may attenuate the real essence of a historical memory by accentuating some parts, while ignoring others.

The use of architecture, urban design, and planning is one of the best instruments for gradually reshaping the existing built environment and, accordingly, defining a new sense of identity. Civic, political, and governmental leaders often attempt to establish their own version of what they consider to be national identity, through the design of new monuments, complexes, or even cities. In other words, the manipulation of the built environment is a grandiose way of redefining identity. National identity is a term tied to the concepts of nation and nationalism. In his essay "Nation and Nationalism" Ernest Gellner defines nationalism as a "theory of political legitimacy."[1] The works of architecture and urban design are used by the prevailing powers in particular nations as powerful symbols that define their identities and demonstrate their power in a tangible way so as to achieve legitimacy.

This chapter initially examines the interplay between political powers and national identity in a given society. It explores how the reconstruction of a historical-cultural complex can be a means used by political power to establish a new sense of identity and redefine it in order to obtain legitimacy. In this chapter, the misrepresentation of culture and national identity in the context of Iran during the last century will be analyzed. While the concept of interaction between politics and national identity may not be a new and unprecedented phenomenon, what is crucial is how this interplay takes place in different political systems and varying situations. The main focus of my argument is how Iranian national identity has been gradually and subtly changing under the policies of the Islamic Republic. To clarify this process, I will briefly explain two events that took place in different contexts: one in New York City and the other in Shiraz, Iran, prior to the Islamic Republic emergence. The second part of the chapter focuses on the reconstruction of the old city of Bam (located in Kerman Province, southeast of Iran) as a case study—especially after the earthquake of December 2003, which placed Bam in a more critical situation. The most important questions regarding the topic of this research are why and how the renovation and reconstruction of the old city of Bam could be a means for political legitimacy instead of being a mirror of Iran's national identity.

RESEARCH METHOD

In this chapter the concept of identity is first briefly analyzed using the theories of Pierre Bourdieu. Next, an investigation is made into Iranian identity and its challenges during the recent century under the governance of two different political powers and their influence on the national identity of Iranians. The next step is identifying the influences of these two extremely different views in their representation of national identity with regard to the material world. The reconstruction of the Citadel of Bam (the Old City—a historical complex), which is located in the southeast of Iran, has been selected for this case study. The three most important resources of information used for the main part of the research will be the Comprehensive Management Plan (CMP) of Bam, the website of the Cultural Heritage Organization of Iran, and ancient Persian literature. The CMP was produced and published in 2008 by The Iranian Cultural Heritage Organization, Handicrafts and Tourism Organization, and the UNESCO Tehran Cluster Office with support from the UNESCO JAPAN funds-in-trust for World Cultural Heritage.[2] The CMP consists of a set of plans, constraints, and suggestions designed to reconstruct the entire city of Bam including the old city from 2008 to 2017.

THEORY OF IDENTITY

The philosophy of Zoroastrianism was the major factor in shaping the cultural identity of Iranians prior to the advent of Islam. After the Arab conquest, Iran was ruled under the Islamic ideology for almost two centuries. Nevertheless, Persians kept innumerable aspects of their original Zoroastrian identity and tried to adapt the new Islamic identity to what they already possessed. In spite of all attempts at adaptation and consistency between Islamic and pre-Islamic culture, a dramatic divergence between these two views gradually took place. One group considered themselves to be more attached to pre-Islamic Persian culture and its civilization, while the second group tended to follow Islamic values and ideology. The former prefers the interests of Iran over those of Islam, while the latter prefers to improve and expand the Islamic ideology and stay attached to its values. There has been an ongoing conflict between these two groups to dominate and establish their identity. The separation between the views and perspectives of these two groups has been so conspicuous in the last century that each group has tried to establish its own political culture and compete with the other to obtain or retain power. Saeid Zahed, an Iranian scholar of sociology, has examined the phenomenon of Iranian identity and has added one more category to the above competitors: the group that supports Modernism.[3]

Reza Shah (King Reza Pahlavi), the first king of the last dynasty of Iran (Pahlavi), based his authority on Aryan identity and promulgated its superiority over the Semitic race. His son and successor Mohammad-Reza Shah (King Mohammad-Reza) found the modern ideology of the West meaningful and attempted to use this ideology to modernize Iran. He founded a Perso-Western identity, which made it possible for him to form an alliance with the United States.[4] Finally Ayatollah Khomeini, the Islamic leader, founded his political system based on sharia (*Shari'a*) law and introduced an Islamic identity into Iranian culture.

To theoretically expand the notion of identity, I would like to analyze this concept through Pierre Bourdieu's theory. In Bourdieu's theory, he presents valuable components such as habitus and fields of capital, which I will be examining in order to explain my argument. Habitus is a way of understanding the world which is constructed based on everyday experiences and social practices since early childhood. Habitus is a noncognitive disposition and, instead of being consciously understood, it is internalized and embodied within individuals over time. Bourdieu also has a particular view of the relationship between body and space, which he sees as a cyclic structure through which we adapt our world and are adapted by it.[5] In relation to architecture and the built environment, members of a society tend to translate their social spaces into physical spaces and these physical spaces, then, reproduce the social spaces and practices. Clear examples that show the different divisions of habitus (such as gender, class, ethnicity, and age) are seen in spaces such as kitchens, suburbs, cafes, playgrounds, and classrooms.

According to this pattern the habitus of Islamists can be found in the belief system of sharia which is reinforced and reproduced by developing physical spaces that promote and enhance this habitus. They do not attempt to revive non-Islamic ideologies or practices nor do they care about these practices. On the other hand, the habitus of those who love non-Islamic Persian cultures can be found in the concept of its great civilization and pre-Islamic history. Thus they improve and expand their choices according to the related practices and do not attempt to promote Islamic views, because they do not see Islamic practices and culture as something that belongs to them. The Persian-Iranians who were dominant in the Pahlavi period established practices and activities based on their canon of history while Islamic-Iranians, who were dominant after the Islamic Revolution of 1979, founded their choices based on the principles of Islam and their social world. Accordingly, different habitus (in this case civilization versus religion) indicate different structures of practices and necessitate the (re)construction of different physical spaces.

Another invaluable concept presented by Bourdieu that relates to my argument is fields of capital. A field is a physical or abstract space or a container, in which social values are practiced. The concept of capital is considered on different levels, from economic to cultural, as well as social and symbolic. I focus particularly on the cultural and social levels, which relate strongly to my argument. Cultural capital is the accumulation of views, behaviors, knowledge, and skills obtained over time through education and upbringing.[6] It can be defined as a subject or view inherited from the ancestors. Cultural capital can be manifested into a tangible form such as food or clothes or in terms of an educational degree. Social capital is considered mostly as a resource based on social relations and the network of a community or society. In a simple and clear way, the main difference between these two forms of capital is their scale—with cultural capital being mostly individual, while social capital relies on interaction and collective practices. That means social capital is shaped through social interactions and practices, which makes it distinctive from cultural capital defined in an individual scale. Social capital, on its highest level, inspires a sense of solidarity and community and is mainly embedded in the built environment, which objectifies and reinforces the social and cultural values and concepts, such as community centers, university departments, mosques, churches, night clubs and sport centers.[7] Symbolic capital is the most controversial part of this category and is a form of honor that often denies that it is a powerful form of capital. This capability of exercising power with symbolic capital is applicable when this denial exists as a mask; otherwise it cannot be identified as a capital. Based on Bourdieu's definitions there may not be rigid boundaries between these capitals and they can also be converted to one another. Thus, the cultural capital of those who devote themselves to Islamic values is obtained through Islamic practices, especially the practice of *Shi'a* ideology since the sharia laws provide them with power and status throughout the nation. The followers transform their cultural capital into social capital in order to support Islamic ideology and preserve and promote their identity. This is accomplished through (re)constructing Islamic centers such as mosques, and *Tekyeh*s or by promoting Islamic performing arts like *Tazieh*. On the other hand, the cultural capital of those who appreciate Persian legacy is made up of their historical heritage, their civilization and the Zoroastrian messages and values. They develop their cultural capital on those foundations and transform it to social capital through cherishing, promoting, and fostering their ancient ideology, which is different from an Islamic identity in terms of social practice.

IRANIANS' NATIONAL IDENTITY

Following the outline provided thus far, I will divide the national identity of Iranians during the last century into two major categories: before the Islamic revolution in 1979 (the Pahlavi Era) and after the revolution (the Islamic Republic period). Among numerous scholars who have studied the history of Iran, Nikki Keddie provides valuable insights in her essay "Understanding the Enigma" where she discusses these two main periods of Iranian history. In 1925 Reza Shah took power over a traditional Iran that had a religious *Shi'a* identity. Reza Shah was a Muslim but he carried out many social reforms and attempted to divorce Islamic preconceptions from politics. He paid special attention to the original Aryan ethnicity of Iranians and admired pre-Islamic Iran, which was more consistent with the Western way of life and modernization. He praised this ancient originality by introducing cultural practices and architectural buildings as a representation of Persian culture. Many Islamic groups, however, opposed him and his reforms and considered him to be a follower of Western, non-Islamic culture.[8] His son, Mohammad-Reza Shah, also followed similar policies, albeit slightly more autocratically. During the 1960s the shah implemented a reformation which was called "The White Revolution" that made drastic changes such as land reforms, the introduction of women's suffrage and secular education all over Iran. This revolution was intended to distance Iran from the sharia laws and Islamic ideals. Emphasis was placed upon returning to "the Great Persian Civilization" by promoting the national identity as a dominant identity. This created an inconsistency followed by a struggle between the followers of Persian culture and Islamic groups. The Islamists opposed the Pahlavi Kings and considered their regime to be an illegitimate government since there was, according to them, a large gap between Pahlavi practices and sharia laws. Consequently, after the Islamic Revolution, the period of the Islamic Republic officially began in 1979.

Based on Bourdieu's theories, the practice of *shi'a* ideology and the laws of sharia are the cultural-capital reproduction of Islamists, by which they can obtain legitimacy, power, and status in the nation. In order to establish, support, and promote their own identity Islamists needed to convert their cultural capital into a social capital. They attempted to accomplish this through construction and reconstruction of places such as mosques, *Tekyehs*, religious gatherings, and instituting and promoting practices such as *Taziehs* (Islamic performances of mourning for Hussein). These religious institutions promoted the Islamic ideology and provided opportunities for Islamic leaders like Khomeini to communicate their ideology and found a powerful unity.

The sociologist Saeid Zahed introduced three different kinds of identities based on Manual Castell's theory: Project Identity, Resistance Identity, and Legitimizing Identity, the third of which is the subject of this discussion. Zahed, quoting Castell, points out that a Legitimizing Identity is "introduced by the dominant institutions of society to extend and rationalize their domi-nation"[9] which is evident in both the Pahlavi and the Islamic Republic peri-ods. Based upon the ideas of Bashiriye, Zahed describes three phases of the Islamic Republic. During the first phase the populist ideology rejected other ideologies; during the second, a constructive ideology was introduced as a revision of the populist ideology; and during the third phase a democratic ideology replaced "rejecting others" with "looking for others."[10] He analyzes the first phase as a period in which Islamists emphasized certain Islamic concepts such as the Islamic *Ummah*, the Muslim nation, and Islamic unity in order to establish and promote a new identity for the nation, and some "Is-lamic entrepreneurs believed that returning to the Islamic identity was the main road to emancipation."[11] This insistence on an Islamic identity attenuat-ed a part of Iran's historical identity as well as its relationship with other nations and, in some ways, isolated Iran.

Intellectuals and modern Islamists also played an important role in the formation of the Islamic system. Ali Shariati believed that "nationalist ideas polluted *Shi'ism*; Islam does not need to be justified by love of land and history. This was the background to the anti-nationalist policy of the Revolu-tion."[12] Shariati believed that the ancient Persian identity was something that belonged to the past and was not relevant to the current time. He considered an Iranian national identity to be meaningless to most people while an Islam-ic identity was alive and the essence of life for a nation that was seeking justice, asking for rights, valuing martyrdom, and struggling to live a life with values.[13]

In the second period, after the Iran-Iraq war, some political groups wished to reconstruct and enhance Iran's international relations, however all the changes were based on the first decade's identity. Nematollah Fazeli, an Iranian anthropologist, believes that revolutionary antinationalism declined at that time and a new form of Islamic nationalism was born, which could be used as a barrier against what the leader of the revolution called a cultural invasion from the West. [14]

This idea for the second period was not sufficient to solve the socio-cultural problems and, consequently, a new type of democratic discourse emerged which was not completely compatible with the dominant identity. President Khatami posed the notion of pluralism and defined the concept of a civil society as grounds for the acceptance of diverse identities. [15] As Zahed points out, Bashiriye did not predict what would happen in the future. He goes on to express his belief that this reformist movement, which was led by Khatami, was "slowing down and Islamic identity was waxing although not as much as during the first decade." [16] It is unreasonable to expect a functional democracy to emerge from a system based on a well-defined religious framework, since no drastic changes took place during Mahmud Ahmadinejad's or Hassan Rouhani's presidencies.

Bashiriye considers identity to be a cultural matter and believes that the authoritative modernist policy was not the answer since it caused tension among other elements of Iranian identity and became a source of inspiration for the Islamic Revolution. After the Islamic Revolution similar mistakes were made, and they created another crisis. Zahed considers the role played by "policy makers" and their multifaceted interests to be very important for the formation of Iranian identity, since each aspect needed to be identified and assigned its own proper value. Taking all the above points into consideration, Iranian identity can be seen as something that falls into three main categories each separately affected by: Iranian, Islamic, and Western or modern civilization. As Zahed also confirms, the Pahlavi version of national identity consisted of only two resources—Iranian and modern—which was not a sufficiently effective solution, since it caused the oppositional movement by the Islamists. Emphasis placed upon the Islamic dimension of an Iranian identity by the Islamic Republic was also not the answer. The solution for the establishment of a true national identity for Iranians is a combination of all three. The relationship between these three notions is well-explained by Zahed when he says:

> Ancient Iranian civilization is the standpoint for Iranians. They recognized themselves as different ethnic groups living in the plateau of Iran several thousand years ago. This civilization is the foundation of their identity. They have chosen Islamic ideology on the basis of that foundation and have made it a reasoned and reasoning aspect of their identity. Thus, new cultural influences should establish some relationship with this ideology: adjusting if necessary. [17]

HISTORICAL SITES: A POTENTIAL PLACE FOR
ACHIEVING POLITICAL LEGITIMACY

Considering the explanations given above we can find that the history and identity of the Iranian nation are a combination of pre-Islamic and Islamic periods; however, based on Castell's classifications of identity, it has only been the Islamic period that has brought the Islamic state of Iran legitimacy and political stability. Accordingly, the state promotes *Shi'ism* and declares it to be the only part of the Iranian identity that is worthy of consideration. This is done by revising Iran's concrete, tangible history and by reminding people of the prominent memories of Islamic events and heroes while diluting other parts of the identity by purposely ignoring their existence. The introduction of these selective restorations creates a false form of culture that reflects a distorted and incomprehensive national identity which in turn, can be exploited by political forces to gain approval and enhance their legitimacy.

In order to illustrate the above I will present an example from the late Pahlavi period which demonstrates the way the political system used a historical site to enhance its stability and legitimacy.

Talinn Grigor has investigated the politics of the nationalist monarchical government of the Pahlavi dynasty shown in the use made of the royal complex of Persepolis in 1976 and its aftermath. In 1971 the buried remnants of a royal city, including royal palaces, residential zones, and their exquisite decorative embellishments and motifs from the Achaemenian dynasty (the first Persian dynasty), were discovered by some national and international specialists near Shiraz. "That complex and Cyrus the Great's tomb were unanimously selected to be the place of a national festival in 1976"[18] since it would represent the beginning of Iranian authenticated history. Magnificent military parades in ancient attire, theatrical performances, technologies, splendid furniture and decor, and the manufacture of fireworks as an ancient custom that Iranians inherited from the pre-Achaemenian era, were all efforts to "prove that Iran could and had transcended its 'Orientalist traditions' while still remaining true to its heritage."[19] The second half of the celebration was changed from Shiraz, the ancient Oriental capital, to Tehran, a modern western capital, specifically to the Shahyad Monument and Museum and thereafter to the modern Aryamehr Stadium. This changing of locations and traveling from the distant past (Shiraz and Persepolis as symbols of the ancient past of Persia) to the present (Tehran as a symbol of a modern city and modernity), indirectly represented a continuity in the monarchy from the past to the present and into the future.[20]

Although theatrical performances displayed historical and cultural realities and demonstrated intangible historical values, they, in general, did not succeed in presenting any true and comprehensive national identity on stage. Although a historical past was exploited as a deed in order to approve the monarchic despotism and confirm the continuity of it, the process that was employed to preserve the past and appreciate its history was not sophisticated enough to reveal a national culture and identity.

The abuse of history, neglecting and reshaping historical sites, takes place in various ways and in different geopolitical contexts. Ned Kaufman expounds an event, which overlaps with the main discussion of this chapter. The story occurred in "New York's eighteenth-century African Burial Ground, located north of City Hall, [which] originally covered about five acres and held perhaps 20,000 burials, mostly of slave and free blacks."[21] This zone was to be the site of a new federal office tower; but when it was excavated, well-preserved skeletons were uncovered. Local politicians, archeologists, and African-American activists formed a coalition to save the burial ground but the federal government ignored it and continued building. The only power that influenced and ceased it was an African-American congressman, toward the end of his term in office, who oversaw the federal agency project. He warned the agency that its funding would be at risk if it continued to disregard the burial ground. Thereafter, the building process stopped, the rest of the site was filled and leveled with clean soil, and the federal government promised to install an interpretive center and build a permanent memorial for the site.[22] Through its rediscovering, the site "has become a place of study, pilgrimage and the observance of various traditional religious and cultural rituals"[23] in order to demonstrate a segment of New York's history.

Discovering the burial ground and revealing the history behind it seemed unpleasant for the state. Although this event referred to a period of history and indicated the situation of a group of people, the government resisted the site's preservation. Regardless of sociopolitical-power equilibrium and the consequences of survival of the site, the state obviously leaned towards keeping a part of history covered for its own benefit and credibility. A forgotten piece of the puzzle was placed back in the history of African Americans of the United States; however, not all historical puzzles are lucky enough to hold their place in the history of a nation due to political, social, and economic coercion.

The old city of Bam is one of the most significant sites that has a potential to become easily distorted by the wrong policies of reconstruction and preservation. Certain aspects of its identity have been lost as a result of its use as a means for the government to secure legitimacy. The questions that need to be asked are: why does the reconstruction and renovation of the old city of Bam matter to the government and how can the reconstruction of Bam be used as a means to legitimize political authority in Iran? To answer these questions it is essential to know the history of Bam and its cultural landscape.

BAM OVER TIME

According to archeological discoveries, the area of Bam was first occupied during the Neolithic-Chalcolithic period and this continued until the nineteenth century CE. The residence of the regional ruler was located inside the citadel and the barracks were in use until 1932, making this complex old enough to include buildings constructed by many different cultures. The old city of Bam included the main citadel, the caravansary and the residential areas, the Jame Mosque, the *sahib az-zaman* (the Master of Time) well, the *tekyeh* of Bam (a place for religious theatrical performances), the *Zurkhaneh* (an ancient kind of gymnasium), a few castles, many temples that were mostly located next to water sources and also the private houses of some of Bam's famous residents. As is evident, the old city of Bam did indeed contain a variety of buildings from different periods of time.

There are many buildings in Bam that are very old but still well-preserved, even if their origins refer to pre-Islamic periods; and an example of this is the Great Mosque (Jame Mosque). A crisis arose when the earthquake of December 2003 occurred in Bam and destroyed almost 80 percent of the city. This devastating earthquake provided the foundation for what probably has been a selective reconstruction of the old Bam in several different ways—ways which seem to have resulted in another disaster.

PRESERVATION OF BAM—THE CRITERIA OF RECONSTRUCTION AND A BRIEF EXPLANATION OF THE PRESERVATION PROJECTS OF BAM

Pilot projects. Eskandar Mokhtari[24] and his colleagues have publicized the necessity of a restoration plan for the Bam Citadel. Mokhtari, in an essay, recounts a few pilot projects that have been executed so far: the barrack, the stable, the Sistani House, the bazaar, the Second Gate, Tower 1, the Mirza Na'eem School, and work done to fortify the adobe walls and Tower 32.[25] He states that these buildings have mostly been small projects (like the Prophet Mosque of almost eighty square meters) or parts of a larger building.

The mausoleum of *Mirza Ebrahim*. The Tomb of *Mirza Ebrahim* is one of the properties in the immediate vicinity of the *Arg-e Bam*. This building, which was ruined as a result of the earthquake, was attributed to the *Safavid* period (sixteenth century). Mirza Ebrahim was the father of *Mirza Na'eem*, who was the mentor of a religious (*elmiyya*) school (*madrasa*) of the same name close to the mosque within the Arg. This complex is being reconstructed by ICHHTO[26] because of its social value and importance to the local community.[27]

Qanat (Kariz). One of the most important structures that need to be re-built is the *qanat (kariz)* an ancient, practical irrigation and water system which was the main reason and key component for recording Bam as a World Heritage site. According to the CMP reports and confirmation of the Islamic Republic, repairing the damaged active *qanats* was immediately be-gun after the earthquake for two reasons: first, this water system served as an example of the interaction between human and nature, which was a major point of interest for UNESCO, and second, this system was still capable of functioning for the irrigation of agricultural crops.

The Congregational (Great) Mosque. According to the evidence provided by the CMP, the Great Mosque (Jame Mosque) has been dated back to the eighth century CE and is one of the oldest mosques in Iran. The mosque, one of the places that was in use prior to the earthquake, is thought to have been built over a Zoroastrian fire temple, since its original form faced due east. Its internal arrangements were reconfigured in a way that *mihrab* (the focal point of praying) was placed on the southwest side of the mosque (facing Mecca).[28]

Tekyeh. Another place that was fully restored right before the earthquake, which survived the disaster was *Tekyeh* of *Arg-e Bam.*[29] A *Tekyeh* is a building in which religious theatrical performances (*tazieh*) are held in order to show the scenes of the martyrdom of *Hussein,* the third Imam of the *Shi'as.* These dramas may last up to ten days and the audiences are profound-ly involved in them, with processions of people accompanying the theater troupes as they pass through the streets of the old city. Prior to the earth-quake, and even afterwards, the *Tekyeh* of Bam continued to be used as a venue for meetings, conventions, and religious festivals such as *Ashura* peri-od.[30]

Castles, Citadels, and Temples. There are castles like the *Dokhtar* ("girl") castle that are remnants of the pre-Islamic era that contain three motifs in the form of three spears which depict the late *Sasanid* era. On a hill to the north of *Dokhtar* castle there are the remnants of two temple walls that were in the vicinity of the castle that survived because the damage caused by the earth-quake was not very severe. According to CMP reports the most significant damage caused to the building was mostly because of climate fluctuations over time, the lack of preservation, and insufficient maintenance of the com-plex. In addition to all this lack of attention and in spite of efforts made by the Cultural Heritage Organization of Iran to save the zones around the castle from illegal construction and inappropriate development, there is some evi-dence that shows that the slope of *Qal'eh Dokhtar (Dokhtar* Castle) was being used for motorcycling, which damaged this vulnerable area. On the hill to the north of *Dokhtar* Castle there are also ruins of two walls of a fire temple which is thought to have been associated with the castle.[31]

It seems, according to the evidence, that the process of selecting and prioritizing which buildings to preserve and emphasizing the quality of their reconstruction might not have been random. As pointed out at the beginning of the article, and based on Bourdieu's theory, Islamic practices, especially those related to Shi'a ideology and Islamic laws, represent the cultural capital of Islam. In order to transform cultural capital to social capital and institutionalize Islamic values, it is necessary to support Islamic ideology and promote the Islamic identity. Mosques, *tekyehs*, and the houses of religious mentors are places that embody Islamic concepts and present concrete images of Islamic values. Accordingly the maintenance and preservation of old Islamic centers is a policy adopted by the Islamic government to strengthen cultural capital and institutionalize a renewed identity—an identity which may not be very alien but is not yet comprehensive enough to be called a "national identity." Based on Castell's classification, this new identity would be a "legitimizing identity" that provides an opportunity for Islamic political powers to increase their legitimacy and control the social systems. As previously noted, most of the well-preserved major projects—such as the Mosque and *tekyeh*, which were rigorously preserved and in use prior to the earthquake—are somehow related to Islamic values. [32]

The earthquake and its aftermath in the restoration of Bam. Prior to the earthquake, although it had been affected by natural erosion and decay, ancient Bam was still standing. After the earthquake Bam's became much more critical due to the scale of destruction. The subsequent need for reconstruction increased the probability of selectivity and, consequently, the misrepresentation of a true comprehensive national identity. In other words the necessity of a comprehensive reconstruction was considered to be greater than before the earthquake.

Another important point in the debate over national identity is the importance of anthropological assets—those that can be identified as a country's intangible heritage. These intangible assets are rooted in the people's collective memories and are related to the myths, stories, and anecdotes that are expressed in the people's daily lives. Below is the CMP's list of priorities with respect to preserving these intangible assets.

ANTHROPOLOGICAL ASSETS

Craft traditions and skills. This tangible heritage includes craft traditions and skills such as stylized embroidery, "night tent" blanket textiles, coin and mirror work, palm products, and a particular carpet-weaving design. It also includes some traditional occupations such as those of the *Moqanni* who digs and maintains *qanats*, the *Mirab* who is responsible for allocating water, the *Abyar* who irrigates the crops and, finally, the experts who use adobe construction. These should be taken into account in order to preserve them as a part of the culture and history of Bam.[33]

The intangible cultural heritage. This category is one of the most important parts of cultural heritage and is based on social values which are vulnerable to exploitation by political powers. According to the CMP:

> The government of the Islamic Republic of Iran is party to the 2003 UNESCO convention for the safeguarding of the intangible heritage, which aims to protect the social values of the community. These include the traditions, customs and practices, the aesthetic and spiritual beliefs and the artistic expressions and language. An intangible heritage is therefore the non-physical characteristic, practices, representations, expressions and knowledge and skills that define a civilized group. These include oral traditions and expressions including language as a vehicle of the intangible cultural heritage, music, dance, drama and other performing arts, social practices, rituals and festive events, knowledge and practices concerning nature and the universe, food and clothing and traditional craftsmanship.[34]

Literature, art, social practices, and experiences are issues that are vulnerable to attempts at distortion and alteration.

The "culture of anthropology" versus the "political culture." Nematollah Fazeli, an Iranian anthropologist, articulates the differences between notions of the "culture of anthropology" and those of a "political culture." By knowing the differences between these two ideas we can figure out what probable barriers exist in the way of the proper preservation of anthropological assets. He explains that "anthropology by nature is a critical awareness of cultural life";[35] in fact anthropology, by its very nature, contains self-criticism and is associated with making comparisons between cultures and posing questions that have no certain answer. Anthropology can be contrasted with ethnocentrism in that it does not recognize superiority between different cultures and posits that no culture can claim to be exclusively sacred and surpassing. In the discourse of anthropology we accept that "cultures are humanly constructed and can thus be humanly changed in more reasonable and human directions."[36] Another trait of anthropology is tolerance. When the object of anthropology is to study, analyze, and "demonstrate diverse cultures, it should accept and tolerate this diversity." And finally, anthropology creates uncertainty and does not look for a decisive answer; instead it provides "a ground for tolerating ambiguity."[37]

Fazeli quotes Parvin and Vaziri in his book about the Islamic Republic's symbolic framework which must contain: "absolute submission to the interpretation of Islam according to the rule of *Velayat e Faqih*, spiritual materialism, the internalization of the values of clerical ideology, [and] Islamic unidimensionalism [which means] Islam as the only acceptable world view."[38]

After the eight-year Iran-Iraq war, Iran entered into a new situation in which revolutionary antinationalism decreased and a new Islamic nationalism was created.[39] For instance, "from the state point of view, nationalism is a device for creating a sense of cultural resistance against the penetration of anti-Islamic values propagated through the globalization process."[40] This new Islamic definition of nationalism was employed to prevent a so-called "cultural invasion" and has been promoted by the government together with the idea of "nation" being mostly based on Islamic commonalities. By presenting such a definition of "nation," the nation's historical assets not included in the Islamic arena could be easily ignored as national or cultural assets.

Evidently, there are fundamental differences between the natural character of the culture of anthropology and the political culture of the Islamic Republic of Iran and its symbolic framework. For instance, one would not expect the local music of *Dohol* whose birthplace was Bam to be preserved. Can one ever be sure that research about music and dance, the wearing of clothes and fashion, stories and anecdotes are even possible if they go beyond the symbolic framework as defined by the state? To clarify the role state policies play in preserving a country's intangible heritage I will describe two different stories and how widespread they are among the people.

There is a well near the Great Mosque of the old city of Bam that is called "the Master of Time Well" and it has an important ritual significance. It is believed that by throwing money into the well and whispering into it, people can talk to the last twelfth *Shi'a* Imam (the *Mahdi* or the Master of Time). He disappeared in 874 CE in *Samera* which is located in what is currently central Iraq, and it is believed that he is still alive. He is beseeched to intercede for people going to heaven after dying and for the granting of other benefits. While appealing to the Imams is common in *Shi'ism* even Sunni visitors are interested in visiting the mosque and the well.[41] The government supports this ritual indirectly since there is another mosque and well near the city of *Qom* which has the same characteristics.

On the other hand there is a mythical story related to the Parthian period that is about a battle between *Ardeshir Babakan*, a Parthian[42] king, and *Haftvad* a local ruler near Bam. This story is even referred to in the *Shahnameh* of Ferdowsi, the most prized epic of Persian Literature. *Shahnameh* is composed of epic poems in which we can see the pre-Islamic history of Iran in a symbolic and metaphoric way. Mohammad Mehryar explains this story based on *Shahnameh*'s poems on the Iranian Cultural Heritage Organization's website and also uses other resources to ensure the credibility of the story of *Shahnameh*.[43] According to Ferdowsi, Haftvad, after his victory, founded a citadel that might be an earlier foundation of the Bam Citadel. Ferdowsi has combined the story of Ardeshir's campaign with an amazing legend, followed by the story of Akhtar (the star of luck), the daughter of

Haftvad who made her father rich by raising a special worm.[44] The story of the worm (*kerm*) became so eminent that it influenced the name of the region (Kerman).[45]

The story continues and reveals other aspects of the history of silk production and the second battle between Ardeshir and Haftvad, the victory of Ardeshir and the transferring of Haftvad's wealth to his territory. As Mehryar points out, this story has also been confirmed by the *Tabari*, history and it has been said that Haftvad's wealth that was later transferred to Ardeshir, was made from the production of silk. There is a blocked gate in the eastern governmental quarters that is called *Kod-e-Kerm* or *Kot-e-Kerm* (the House of Worms) and it is thought that this is evidence of the Haftvad story.

Both the CMP and the Islamic Republic have also confirmed the story of Haftvad and *Kot-e-Kerm* and their relation to silk production. They have proclaimed that "the legend of Haftvad and *Kot-e-Kerm* together with its association with the development of silk production and weaving are important and should be featured in the interpretation of the property as a valuable intangible cultural heritage asset of Bam."[46]

The obvious questions that need to be asked are: Is the *Haftvad* story important enough to be promoted and introduced to the people by the government? Who evaluates the importance of the story and based on what criteria? Will the story about the "Well of Master of Time" that has been tied with *Shi'ism* also be defined as equally important as the Haftvad or *Kote-e-Kerm* story that is mentioned in ancient literature in the *Shahnameh* of Ferdowsi and affirmed by other historical resources? Since there are noticeable differences between the Islamic Republic's canon of belief and the nature of the objects of modern anthropology, it is hard to believe that there will be a proper preservation of these anthropological assets.

CONCLUSION

This chapter, using the Citadel of Bam as a case study, has tried to reveal the possibilities that exist for misrepresenting a cultural heritage in the process of its reconstruction and renovation in order for a government to attain political legitimacy and legality. Two main issues were analyzed: first, the tendency of political powers to abuse a country's historical heritage in order to heighten their level of legitimacy and second, their need to achieve this by redefining cultures through the strengthening of some parts of their cultural and historical heritage and disregard for others. One way they achieve this gradual cultural change is selective and prioritizes which sites of a historical heritage area should be reconstructed and it seems that buildings that call to mind political values will be selected or be given first priority. Each political system has its own symbolic framework and sets of values and the Islamic

Republic has been formed based on Islamic values which have been defined by the political system in power. Thus, any place which is more adapted to Islamic values and reminds people of the government's legitimacy will be given priority for reconstruction. This process does not happen only in the renovation of tangible history but can also be seen in the revitalizing of the more intangible aspects of history including memories, stories, anecdotes and most anthropological assets. In this situation cultures are exploited by political powers and gradually lose contact with their origins which leads to a comprehensive change in national identity or to a limited, handicapped identity—and all of this is done in order to benefit the government.

NOTES

1. Lawrence Vale, *Architecture, Power and National Identity* (New Haven, CT: Yale University Press, 1992), p. 45.

2. Iranian Cultural Heritage. *Bam and Its Cultural Landscape World Heritage: Property, Comprehensive Management Plan* (Tehran: Iranian Cultural Heritage. 2008), p. ii, http://whc.unesco.org/en/list/1208, retrieved: October 6, 2011.

3. Saeid Zahed, "Iranian National Identity in the Context of Globalization: Dialogue or Resistance?" *Center for the Study of Globalization and Regionalisation (CSGR),* No. 162/05, (2004), p. 10.

4. Shahin Ayazi, "Persian Iranian Versus Islamic Iranians: 1979 Social Movement of Iran." (Master's Thesis, University of San Francisco, May 2003), p. 45.

5. Kim Dovey, "Silent Complicities: Bourdieu, Habitus, Field," in *Becoming Places: Urbanism/Architecture/Identity/Power* (New York: Routledge, 2010), p. 32.

6. Ibid., p. 33.

7. Ibid., p. 34.

8. Nikki Keddie, "Iran: Understanding the Enigma: A Historian's View" (Lecture presented at Teachers' seminar at UCLA, Los Angeles, California, 1998).

9. Zahed, p. 8.

10. Ibid., p. 20.

11. Ibid.

12. Nematollah Fazeli, *Politics of Culture in Iran: Anthropology, Politics and Society in the Twentieth Century* (New York: Routledge, 2006), p. 139.

13. Zahed, p. 20.

14. Fazeli, p. 169.

15. Zahed, p. 21.

16. Ibid., p. 22.

17. Zahed, p. 23.

18. Talinn Grigor, "Preserving the Antique Modern: Persepolis '71," *Conservation Information Network 2,* No. 1 (2005), p. 25.

19. Ibid., p. 26.

20. Ibid., p. 27.

21. Ned Kaufman, "Heritage and the Cultural Politics of Preservation," *Places* Vol. 11, No. 3 (1998), p. 60.

22. Ibid.

23. Ibid., p. 61.

24. According to their article, the technical team has introduced themselves as the following: Eskandar Mokhtari: Director (RPBCH), Mahmoud Nejati: Deputy of Research and Technical Consultant (RPBCH), Shirin Shad: Manager of Technical Office (RPBCH). RPBCH is the acronym of Recovery of Bam Cultural Heritage.

25. Eskandar Mokhtari, "Lesson Learned from Recovery Project of Bam's Cultural Heritage (RPBCH)," p. 8, http://www.iitk.ac.in/nicee/wcee/article/14_01-1021.PDF, retrieved: June 21, 2014.

26. ICHHTO is the acronym of "Iranian Cultural Heritage Handicrafts and Tourism Organization."

27. Iranian Cultural Heritage, p. 17.

28. Ibid., p. 16.

29. Ibid., p. 16.

30. Ibid., p. 17.

31. Ibid., p. 19.

32. Ibid., p. 17.

33. Ibid., p. 35.

34. Ibid., p. 36.

35. Fazeli, p. 160.

36. Ibid.

37. Ibid., p. 161.

38. Ibid.

39. Ibid., p. 165.

40. Ibid., p. 169.

41. Iranian Cultural Heritage, p. 16.

42. Parthian was one of the ancient empires ruled Persia before the Sasanid Empire.

43. Mohammad Mehryar, "Arg-e Bam." *Iranian Cultural Heritage Organization*, http://www.ichodoc.ir/scripts/wxis.exe, retrieved November 2011. Arg-e Bam." *ichodoc.ir*. http://www.ichodoc.ir/argebam/, retrieved: October 6, 2011.

44. M. Zandiye, K. N. Mohammad-Poor, and H. R. Rezaee, "The Totemic Signs of Simorgh and Dragon in Shahnameh." *Journal of Basic and Applied Scientific Research* Vol. 2, No. 1 (2012), p. 793.

45. Ibid.

46. Iranian Cultural Heritage, p. 36.

Part II

An Islamic-National Identity and Nuclear Program

Chapter Three

The Islamic Identity Project

Between Coercion and Voluntarism

Ofira Seliktar

Well before taking the reins of power in February 1979 Ayatollah Ruhollah Khomeini proclaimed that the goal of the Islamist revolution was to turn Iran into an Islamic republic.[1] His major work, *Velayat-e Faqih* (The Governance of the Jurist) asserted that religious guardianship was vital for the creation of a *republic of virtue*, an Islamic polity and society based on Quranic principles. Specifically, Khomeini claimed that individuals, considered deficient by nature, could be perfected—thus assuring their salvation if properly guided by the state.[2] In other words a strict theocracy was needed in order to create pious individuals ready to live according to the moral code of the Quran.

While theologically appealing, the shaping of such an identity proved to be an uphill battle, not least because religious characteristics are known to compete with other markers of self-identification. Whatever the early expectations, Khomeini and other revolutionary leaders soon realized that considerable social engineering and brutal state coercion were required if they wished to mold the planned Islamic individual. Facing increasing social resistance, the regime leaders had to scale back their ambitious religious identity project and allow a more pluralistic one to emerge, only to later again adopt a more restrictive and punitive mode of social engineering.

Basing itself upon a thematic-historical approach this chapter analyzes the oscillations that took place between the coercive and voluntaristic impulses that underlay the Islamic identity project. The first of five sections provides a short methodological survey of group identity formation with special application to Iran. The second section analyzes the unfolding of the Islamic identity project during the first decade after the revolution. The third section

41

discusses the efforts, known as the Islamic Reformation, to liberalize the religious code under President Mohammed Khatami. The fourth section examines the hardline backlash against efforts to promote a more voluntary Islamic identity. The concluding section appraises the future of the Islamic identity project.

RELIGIOUS IDENTITY AND SOCIAL IDENTITY: THEORIES OF IDENTITY FORMATION

Social identity theory defines social identity as a person's understanding that he or she belongs to a social category or group and, indeed, a social group is a composed of individuals who share a common social identification. As societies have progressed from being primordial to modern, the tribal, kinship-based *gemeinschaft* identity has been replaced by the inclusive *gesellschaft* national identity. In either case individuals come to see themselves as members of one category or group (the in-group) in comparison with another (the out-group).

Religious identity is a specific type of identity formation related to the individual's concept of self. By drawing on cultural anthropology, social theorists point out that this identity is based on a shared system of meaning drawn from metaphysical and ethical beliefs embedded in the religion (or belief system) of a group. Some scholars argue that religious identity is key to the development of the concept of self; and since it appeals to the transcendental and is rooted in texts and practices, religious identity may be stronger than other forms of group identity. At the same time membership in a religious group may exist regardless of one's participation in religious practices or actions and this makes for a complex relationship between beliefs, officially sanctioned forms of piety, and related behavior.

Tensions between national and religious identities have shaped modern history, but it has been the clash between religious identity and secularism that has emerged as the quintessential marker of modernity. Secularism is grounded in rational-legal legitimacy norms that make numinous claims questionable or redounded. More to the point, secularism has brought about the separation of state and religious intuitions, liberating the individual from state-enforced religious beliefs and practices. The separation of state and church in Western Christianity is the hallmark of modernity, giving individuals the free choice to set their level of observance; and democracy, a political system that protects individual liberties, prevents the government from interfering with such personal choices.

With state coercion removed, the shaping of, for instance, a Christian identity has relied on human agency, that is, voluntary action taken by individuals based on free will, performed free from state constraints. In taking the first steps towards religious voluntarism the Protestant Reformation denounced the Catholic state-church establishment for wielding coercive powers which prevented the exercise of free will, and subsequent theological elaborations led to the concept of spiritual rebirth aligned with God through free choice. As a matter of fact the contemporary born-again movement is predicated upon a personal commitment to living according to relevant moral precepts. Paradoxically, the United States—where the separation of church and state is almost complete—has the highest proportion of individuals who profess a voluntary form of piety as the core of their religious identity.

Clearly the experience of the Muslim world has followed a very different pattern since only a minority of Muslim countries has any viable separation of state and religion. The rest feature a spectrum of state-enforced adherence to sharia laws—with Saudi Arabia and Afghanistan under the Taliban constituting pure theocracies. To what extent a truly voluntary formation of piety exists under strict public enforcement can be only speculated on.

Theories of religious identity formation indicate that one's degree of personal piety is influenced by societal discourse, and the shaping of such discourse to bolster normative beliefs has been a critical part of religious endeavors throughout human history. Role model theory explains why controlling discourse is so crucial; since roles that guide behavior—both public and private—are reinforced by feedbacks from discourse. When the feedback is positive convictions tend to stay strong while discourse at odds with religious norms is known to weaken religious belief.

These theories are pertinent to our being able to understand Ayatollah Khomeini's Islamist identity project. Under the Pahlavi dynasty the state tried to balance the conflicting demands of modernization with the tenets of Islam, but secularization took an inevitable toll on personal piety with the better-educated, urban sector increasingly abandoning traditional indicators of Islamic identity while hard-core believers were relegated to rural areas and urban slams inhabited by newly arrived peasants. Even so, leading religious authorities at the time, such as Grand Ayatollah Seyyed Hossein Borujerdi and Grand Ayatollah Mohammad Kazem Shariatmadari, were quietists, though adverse to secularism, and did not call for either the replacement of the shah or for the creation of a theocracy with a disciplinary power to shape Islamic identity.[3] Ayatollah Khomeini, however, a highly activist Grand Ayatollah who spent decades harshly condemning the secularization of Iranian society, considered it of utmost importance to "return" his countrymen to a pure Islamic identity through the disciplinary power of state. As one analyst put it the Iranian revolution "imagined *Homo Islamicus*, the ultimate Islamic person."[4]

LAUNCHING THE ISLAMIC IDENTITY PROJECT:
SHAPING DISCOURSE AND BEHAVIOR

More than a million people turned up to greet Ayatollah Khomeini upon his arrival in Tehran on February 1, 1979. Referred by his followers as the Imam, Khomeini became the Supreme Leader in the new regime, but this seemingly totalitarian position belied a far more complex reality. Khomeini's Islamic Revolutionary Party (IRP) was part of a broad coalition that over-threw the shah under the banner of democracy and individual freedom. The Iranian media, kept on a tight leash under the Pahlavis, enjoyed an unprece-dented renaissance during which hundreds of new publications appeared that reflected all streams of thought in the society. The free discourse, however, alarmed the Islamists since it espoused themes deemed antithetical to Islamic identity, not to mention that it gave competing political factions a forum for expression. On August 8, 1979, because of the resultant pressure, the revolu-tionary prosecutor banned the leading left-wing newspaper, *Ayandegan.* On August 20, forty-one opposition papers were closed and on September 8 the two largest newspaper chains in the country, *Kayhan* and *Ettelaa't,* were expropriated and transferred to the Foundation for the Disinherited, one of the many parastatal organizations that answered to the Supreme Leader.[5]

The regime's efforts to shape the discourse through radical censorship generated considerable resistance and led to the creation of the *Pasdaran*, the Revolutionary Guards,[6] a parastatal military force loyal to the Supreme Leader. Subsequent violent repression threatened the gradualist-stealthy strategy being used to gain power that Ayatollah Mohammed Beheshti, a close aide to Khomeini, and the head of IRP had developed. Beheshti, a practical politician whose understanding of mass control was shaped by North Korea, concluded that only a massive unleashing of the state's discipli-nary power could control the discourse. Not willing to pay the cost to legiti-macy of totalitarianism and worried about negatively affecting gradualism, the Islamists settled on a mixed political system. The 1979 Constitution allowed for a popular vote to a legislative body, the *Majlis*, to take place, but a number of clerical bodies controlled much of the political process. The Guardian Council approved candidates and made sure that legislation passed by the Majlis was compatible with the principles of Islam and the constitu-tion.

While the constitution provided a veneer of democratic legitimacy it made it harder for the regime to shape the discourse. The ever-resourceful media learned to play the game with the censors and publications that were closed routinely opened under new names. Unofficial social networks in the pre-Internet era were only modestly efficient but, even so, alternative news that was critical of the regime was widely available, along with rumors and conspiracy theories—that, ironically, the Khomeinists had also used to discredit the shah.[7]

Eliminating media messages deemed inimical to Islamist values was only one part of the identity project. The other part entailed purging the culture of pre-Islamic markers. The ancient "lion and sun" emblem in the national tricolor flag was replaced with a symbol of the Islamic crescent and Allah's name. The official name of the Majlis was changed from the "National Consultative Assembly" to the "Islamic Consultative Assembly" and learning Arabic became mandatory in secondary and tertiary education. The hardline clergy wanted to replace Iran's solar calendar with the Arab lunar calendar and banned the pre-Islamic celebration of *Chahar Shanbeh Soori* (a fire festival of the Iranian people involving symbolic fire rituals).[8] The popular *Nowrouz,* an ancient celebration of the Persian New Year, was reduced to three days while the regime pushed for additional Muslim-themed festivals. As had happened with the media, there was a public reaction against the Islamic dictates and, in the case of *Nowrouz,* an open defiance of the authorities. The unflagging popularity of the Persian past was a clear signal that the Islamist identity project was encountering resistance.

Restructuring individual behavior proved particularly hard since the sharia-compliant lifestyle outlawed gambling, pornography, alcohol consumption, and most live music and dancing. Gender segregation in public became increasingly enforced along with a restrictive dress code. On March 7, 1979, in a move that shocked many, the Revolutionary Council issued an edict requiring women to wear the *Chador*. The coercive power of the state was subsequently codified in article 102 of the Islamic Punishment Law enacted in 1984 and in the amendment of article 638 of the Islamic Criminal Code whereby "women who appear in the public thoroughfare without the Islamic covering will be subject to 10 days to two months' imprisonment or up to 74 lashes."[9]

Ironically, during the mass protests against the shah, many secular women wore the *Chador* as a political symbol but the new law provoked tumultuous demonstrations. Rushing to calm the waters, Ayatollah Beheshti invoked tradition, history, and opposition to "colonialism and imperialism" to justify the dress code. In his view, wearing the *Chador* gave women "national character" and made them "dignified"; while the ban on the veil under the Pahlavis was an effort to "embarrass women and draw them into lightheaded loose behavior," a hallmark of the "colonialist policies" of the monarchy.[10]

Beheshti failed to mention that the Islamic rationale came as little surprise to observers of the political scene who knew that urban, secularized women nursed resentments about the new Islamist identity. Azar Nafisi, a prominent political dissident and author explained that, although veiling during the anti-shah demonstrations was an important symbol, it was voluntary. Its mandatory imposition, however, was "a powerful sign of the clergy's power." Indeed, as Nafisi observed: "the veil, in Iran, is an instrument to show that the government has gained power to impose its own dream on women. Since there remains no choice for women in such a political context, the veiling limits their freedom of choice and affects their identity."[11]

More than any other lifestyle requirement the *Chador* became a symbol of defying the government. Squads of the "Propagation of Virtue and the Elimination of Vice," special police units established to supervise Islamic-compliant behavior, patrolled the streets to find offending women. Displaying strands of hair or shortening garments was punished with fines, flogging, or jail sentences. The special force was also given the task of seeking out incidents of alcohol consumption, the possession of satellite dishes (a common practice among Iranians dissatisfied with the officially sanctioned fare on TV stations), and unchaperoned outings by young people, among other "infractions." The newly created Ministry of Culture and Islamic Guidance issued a steady stream of detailed rules and guides for Islamic-compliant behavior. Aiming for an even higher level of personal piety, Ayatollah Khomeini published his *Resaleh Towzih al-Massaeel* (A Clarifications of Questions), a compendium of three thousand problems intended to guide the layman towards a more pious life including personal hygiene and ritual purity for men and women.

In addition to the demands for a change in lifestyle was Khomeini's insistence that *Homo Islamicus* should adopt a proper view of the distributive justice system. During his exile in Iraq the Ayatollah had become acquainted with the writings of Ali Shariati, a philosopher and polemicist who sought to combine the precepts of Islam with classic Western socialism. The highly popular Shariati called for a return to a genuine Islamist identity based on the egalitarian society enshrined in the Quran and representative of the simple living of Mohammad. Khomeini, who prided himself on his modest lifestyle, insisted that material goods, defined as the products of a corrupt and materialistic Western civilization, should be shunned. Khomeini wanted all ordinary Iranians to embrace a frugal lifestyle and expected the clerical class to be models of this behavior for the masses.[12]

If the regime hoped to create a new "Islamic person" through a mix of state coercion and voluntary acceptance, it was bound to be disappointed. In spite of the steep fines and corporal punishment, women tried to defy the "virtue squad," turning the streets of Tehran and other urban centers into battlegrounds. Khomeini's efforts to dictate personal piety standards backfired, giving rise to a robust industry of jokes and other forms of humor. For instance, sellers of *Kitab-e Shakhsi-ye Ayatollah Khomeini*—a booklet compiled from the most outlandish advice offered by the Supreme Leader, did a brisk business in Tehran and the clerics' appetite for the good life was the subject of equally robust lampooning with the cartoonist Nikahang Kowsar making a career of depicting clerics as men with prominent girths driving around in large Western cars. [13]

Faced with public defiance, the regime increased the coercion by reviving the thuggish Basij and adding it to the original *Hezbollah,* reconstituted in 1995 as the *Ansar-e Hezbollah,* and this proved to be effective in harassing and intimidating protesters. Under Minister of Interior Ali Mohammad Besharati, the ninety-thousand-strong militia turned into the regime's enforcer of its disciplinary power, overseeing security in large urban centers, patrolling university campuses and other potential troublemaking spots. The Revolutionary Courts, known for their liberal use of the death sentence, were incorporated into the judiciary system that filled the prisons to overflowing. Sundry "miscreants" accused of violating the tenets of Islam were incarcerated along with the Communists and the Mojahedin-e Khalq (MeK), who were treated with extreme brutality.

That so much coercion was required to uphold Khomeini's "republic of virtue" disturbed some of the original leaders of the revolution, with Grand Ayatollah Hussein Ali Montazeri, whom Khomeini picked as his successor, offering a spirited opposition. Montazeri, imprisoned for years by the shah, argued that, in some ways, the Islamic Republic had been exceeding the repression of the monarchy: "The denial of people's rights, injustice and disregard for the revolution's true values have delivered the most severe blows against the revolution. Before any reconstruction [takes place], there must first be a political and ideological reconstruction. . . . This is something that the people expect of a leader." Soon afterwards Montazeri was dropped as the heir apparent and, following further protests, spent the remainder of his life under house arrest in Qom. [14]

On the other side of the divide were hardliners associated with the Haqani School in Qom, the stronghold of the archconservative Ayatollah Mohammed Taqi Mesbah-Yazdi. Described as the philosopher of "radical Islam," Mesbah-Yazdi vehemently rejected all forms of democracy, stating that an "Islamic republic" is a contradiction in terms since a truly Islamic government makes people's opinion superfluous. He believed that "the republican component" was established in Iran as a concession to secular forces and should be "stripped" away to leave the true essence of the "Islamic system." In other words people's opinions tarnished Islamic purity since, in his view, "It doesn't matter the Iranian equivalent of the French *Ecole Nationale d'Administration*, spread these views through a network of alumni in state and parastatal positions. Mesbah-Yazdi's archconservative weekly *Parto-Sokham* was said to have ties to the Revolutionary Guards and the intelligence services. [15]

The fierce clashes within the clerical establishment have been part and parcel of the negotiated political order that has evolved since the revolution. To recall, the 1979 Constitution provided for a rather mixed system of governance in which, in addition to tolerating both state and parastatal groups such as the Revolutionary Guards, influential clerics based in Qom and provincial cities had their own followers who were often equipped with private militias and independent sources of revenue. The resulting political system was somewhat chaotic, fluid, opaque, and marked by bitter internal debates that occasionally made it into the public arena. Clearly, the questioning of the wisdom of applying overwhelming coercion to the Islamic identity project was among the most crucial debates taking place in the inner circle with far reaching implications for the regime.[16]

Typical of the negotiated order was the struggle that took place between the followers of Montazeri and Mesbah-Yazdi which ended in a complex compromise in which Ayatollah Ali Khamenei, a regime stalwart and former president, was appointed Supreme Leader in 1989. Lacking the clerical standing required for the position and the personal charisma of his predecessor, Khamenei was a cautious politician who believed in balancing groups in ways that pitted one against the other. He also brought executive skills to his new post creating a dense network of personal emissaries who served in the state bureaucracy. More to the point the new Supreme Leader relied on the Revolutionary Guards and the militias to control societal discourse and behavior. Khamenei's stewardship of the tools of coercion was put to the test when Ayatollah Mohamed Khatami, a leading liberal, won a landslide presidential election in 1997.

THE ISLAMIC REFORMATION:
A VOLUNTARY APPROACH TO ISLAMIC PIETY

The credentials of the new president Mohammad Khatami as a moderate were impressive since during his tenure as the Minister of Culture and Islamic Guidance (1983–1992), he relaxed lifestyle laws and suspended some forms of censorship. In his book *From the World of the City to the City of the World,* Khatami posited that "popular consensus and social contracts" are the only source of legitimacy in a society, and this was a subtle but clear repudiation of the concept of *Velayat-e Faqih.*[17]

It was the philosopher Abdul Karim Soroush, however, who inspired Khatami to subject the Islamic identity to a critical examination. Soroush, often called the Martin Luther of Islam by both his supporters and critics, postulated that true faith requires a voluntary human agency, when he wrote that "true believers must embrace their faith of their own free will—not because it was imposed, or inherited, or part of the dominant local culture. To become a believer under pressure or coercion isn't true belief."[18] This also means that the believer "must . . . remain free to leave his faith."[19] Khatami also borrowed liberally from the writings of Dariush Shayegan, a prominent philosopher and the head of the Center for a Dialogue of Civilizations at Tehran University before 1979, who urged Iran to adopt many of the political features of Western liberalism while instituting a nonimitative dialogue exchange.[20]

Though couched in universal terms, Soroush's writings offered a critique of the endless rules and regulations enforced by the disciplinary power of the regime. He suggested that, far from creating genuine piety, the system was a breeding ground for religious hypocrisy. To create the free space needed for a true profession of faith, Soroush urged the relaxation of the strict limitations placed on public discourse and the liberalization of the highly regulated behavior in the public arena. Soroush was joined by a number of Islamist intellectuals and political activists who developed an interest in human rights and democracy and who became known as the *Kiyan* circle—named after the periodical they published. Faeza Rafsanjani, the daughter of Ayatollah Ali Akbar Hashemi Rafsanjani, headed a group of women who advocated placing curbs on the notoriously intrusive "Squads for the Propagation of Virtue" and liberalizing the lifestyle requirements.

To implement these demands, President Khatami lifted censorships, and this triggered a journalistic revival akin to what took place during the immediate postrevolutionary period. His Minister of Culture and Islamic Guidance, Ata'ollah Mohajerani, proclaimed a policy of "leniency" in arts and culture which led to the releasing of controversial music albums and the screening of movies critical of conservative Islam. Abdullah Nouri, Khatami's Minister of the Interior, arguably the most vocal advocate of the Islamic Reformation and the editor of its flagship publication, *Khordad,* advocated human rights and the freedom of expression in order to build a democratic and modern Islamic polity. Gholamhosein Karbaschi, the progressive mayor of Tehran, where the Islamic Reformation was particularly popular, implemented many of these measures thus providing a role model for other urban centers. The reformists could also count on the support of the Majlis where their representatives soundly defeated the conservative forces of Ayatollah Khamenei.

Thrown into confusion by the strength of the reformist movement and, parenthetically, the widespread rejection of the coercive Islamic identity, the inner circle of the Supreme Leader, the Revolutionary Guards, and other conservatives engaged in an intense internal debate. Ruling out the outright suppression of the democratic forces, they settled on a three-pronged strategy. First, in what some observers described as a virtual "constitution coup," they transferred a substantial chunk of executive power to the Office of the Supreme Leader (*Rahbar*). Second, the Guardian and Expediency Councils and the judiciary began to work in tandem to limit the government and roll back the free press and civil society. Third, both the Ministry of Information and Security (MOIS) and the Revolutionary Guards began to use violence against reformers. [21]

The conservatives' counterattack devastated the reformist movement and the Rahbar's Office takeover left Khatami with little power and influence. Under the archconservative Ayatollah Mahmoud Hashemi Shahroudi, the judicial branch strengthened the power of the Legal Office (*Edareh-ye Hoqu-qi*) and created the Research Center in Jurisprudence—a move to bolster the novel doctrine of "judicial review." Utilizing the new legal tools, Shahroudi, acting through his protégé Saeed Mortazavi, dubbed the "butcher of the press," closed many of the reformist newspapers and prosecuted reformist activists and politicians. Mayor Karbaschi was arrested on trumped-up charges of corruption, but this was preceded by the arrest of Abdullah Nouri who was sentenced to five years in prison. Scores of lesser known reformists shared the same fate and the prison population increased to levels not seen since the revolution.

A combination of forces from the Revolutionary Guards, MOIS, *Ansar-e Hezbollah* and assorted vigilante groups soon unleashed a wave of violence against the reformists and in April 1998 the newly appointed head of the Revolutionary Guards, Major General Yahia Rahim Safavi, declared his intention to "break the pens and cut out the tongues" of intellectuals and journalists. Soon after, a number of dissident writers were murdered or went missing and the highly respected politician Darius Forouhar and his wife were killed in a grisly manner in their home. Dubbed the "chain killings," the murders were sanctioned by Ghorbanali Dorri-Najafabadi, the MOIS chief, and carried out by the Special Operations Committee under Mohammed Pourmohammadi. In March 2000, an assassination attempt left the prominent reformist Saeed Hajarian crippled and, according to some accounts, there were some eighty unexplained murders during this period. The judicial unit of the Devotees of Pure Muhammadan Islam (*Fedayeen-e Eslam-e Nabi-e Mohammadi*), an extremist group, was said to have issued a *fatwa* allowing the killings of "hypocritical persons" as "corrupters on earth," but some suggested that it was Ayatollah Mesbah-Yazdi who authorized the murder of the dissidents. [22]

Ansar-e Hezbollah, Basij and other assorted vigilante groups were highly effective in breaking up reformist events, burning down liberal bookstores and assaulting prominent liberal figures. Some of the auxiliary organizations, such as the Hezbollah Cultural Front, the *Shalamche* Cultural Group, the Shahid Avini Culture Group and the Mawoud Cultural Front, were sponsored by the Revolutionary Guards and/or prominent hardline clerics. Massoud Dehnamaki, the editor of two radical Islamist publications, acted on behalf of the Revolutionary Guards and the Ayatollahs Ahmed Jannati, and Mesbah-Yazdi to run their own vigilantes and the Habibollah Asgaroladi's Islamic Coalition Society (renamed the Islamic Coalition Party) invested its own resources into the battle against the reformers.[23] Elements from Ansar-e Hezbollah, Basij, and the vigilante group *Guruh-e Feshar* provoked a bloody confrontation at Tehran University on July 8, 1999. Dubbed the "Iranian Tiananmen," it prompted widespread international condemnation which was virtually ignored by the hardliners.[24]

To further embarrass the reformists the Revolutionary Guards directed their Basij forces to increase the monitoring of lifestyle regulations which was a bold challenge to Khatami's promise to ease cultural restrictions. Vigilantes increased the harassment of women and men whose public behavior was deemed to be noncompliant, and there was even an increase in raids made on private residences suspected of breaking the sharia laws. For all those who hoped for voluntary piety, as per Soroush, the crackdown sent a clear message that the Islamic identity project would be fully enforced via the disciplinary power of the state.[25]

Although traditional Islamists' strongholds in the rural regions and among the urban poor were supportive, the massive violence created a strong backlash. The internal intelligence unit of the Revolutionary Guards tasked with monitoring public opinion commissioned secret polls that indicated wide disenchantment with the Islamic Republic—a conclusion also reached by the Majlis-affiliated National Society for Public Opinion. When some of the results were leaked the Khatami-appointed head of the Iranian News Agency (IRNA) Abdullah Nasseri was accused of publishing false results and was forced to admit to "human error." The regime was particularly embarrassed because Abbas Abidi—one of the radicals who seized the American embassy in 1979 but who had now turned reformer—had previously published similar results in his *Salam* magazine.[26]

Naturally, the Guardian Council declined to approve any reformist candidate for the presidency, but hardline politicians, including Khamenei's preferred candidate, fared poorly. Facing an almost certain defeat the Supreme Leader and the Revolutionary Guards were forced to place their faith into the hands of a relatively new political movement, the Principalists.

THE PRINCIPALISTS' REMAKE OF THE ISLAMIST IDENTITY: NEW TOOLS FOR OLD GOALS

In 1955, after observing the clerics' increasingly struggle to prop up Islamic values, a group of political activists founded the Society for the Devotees of the Revolution (*Jamiyat-e Isargaran-e Enqelab-e Islam*) or *Isargaran*. Mahmoud Ahmadinejad, the then little-known mayor of Tehran, was one of its cofounders, along with veterans of the Iran-Iraq war—many of whom were Revolutionary Guard commanders, former prisoners of war, and the relatives of those killed in the war. Ahmed Tavakkoli, the revolutionary prosecutor once famous for imposing sharia-based sentences like stoning for adultery, became the public face of Isargaran. Tavakkoli, a Majlis member who founded the *Resalat* newspaper, was one of the first to call attention to the erosion of Islamic values and advocated a "fundamentalist" (*Osulgiri*) remedy that represented a return to Khomeini's original vision; but to avoid confusion with clerical fundamentalism, *Isargaran* followers often used the label "principalists." In 1996, Mohammed Reyshahri, the former MOIS chief, forged another Principalist group, the Society for the Defense of the Values of the Islamic Revolution (SDVIR) (*Jame-e Defa'e-e az Arzesha-ye Enqelabi-e Islami*). Like Ahmadinejad, Reyshahri, known as the "butcher of Tehran" for his role in the postrevolutionary reign of terror, was extremely concerned about the waning revolutionary ardor. Not incidentally the Coordination Council of Islamic Revolutionary Forces (*Shura-e Hamahangi-ye Niruha-ye Enlqelab*), an organization that boasted a long list of ranking past and present Revolutionary Guards commanders, placed Islamic purity at the top of their agenda.[27]

Unlike the clerics who worked largely through mosque-based networks, the Principalists penetrated into civil society. Ahmadinejad, for instance, launched his political career by joining the Islamic Association of Students in Science and Technology, one of the Islamic societies that had been created within every professional field to compete with the secularists. More to the point, the Principalists came to dominate many of these associations, creating an Islamic civil society which acted as a counterpart to the clerical establishment which at this point was perceived as the embodiment of the state. They contended that the clerical establishment had lost its legitimacy because of their corruption and obsession with power. In particular, they attacked the *aghazdehs* (children of the clergy) whose lavish lifestyles and extravagant exploits were widely known.[28]

Upon entering office in 2005 Ahmadinejad set out to purify the way Islamic values were being expressed according to the standards of Ayatollah Khomeini and Ali Shariati. Ahmadinejad reiterated that social equality and humble living were core values of Islam and, not only sported shabby clothes, but refused to move to the official presidential residence, preferring his own modest house in an unfashionable suburb of Tehran. Unlike Khomeini, however, the new president had more reservations about the viability of *Homo Islamicus*. Instead he turned to the idea of a new national identity to bolster the flagging legitimacy of the regime and structured it around a defiant, muscular foreign policy that was anchored in the nuclear project. This was considered not only to be Iran's entrance ticket to the club of scientifically developed nations but also to act as a blow to "American nuclear hegemony." As a matter of fact Ahmadinejad tried to turn the nuclear project into a new civil religion, replete with elaborate rituals, mass celebrations, and even especially commissioned music.[29]

The popularity of the nuclear project notwithstanding, President Ahmadinejad and the Principalists did not fare any better than the clerics in bolstering the legitimacy of the regime but, to the contrary, they were beholden to the philosopher Ahmad Fardid, who was considered the "Soroush" of the radical right. Influenced by Martin Heidegger, a defender of the Nazi ideology, Fardid came up with a novel synthesis of Fascism and Islam. He argued that the *Velayat-e Faqih* was actually a fusion of the idea of the Mahdi with Heidegger's concept of the strong leader, the Fuehrer. In what one analyst called a "complicated feat of philosophical reasoning," Fardid argued that democracy and human rights are a noxious example of Western liberalism and preached the redeeming value of political violence. Although Soroush declared Fardid to be an "intellectual fraud," his writings struck a chord with Ayatollah Mesbah Yazdi who proclaimed that "we must do away with the shameful strain whereby some people imagine that violence has no place in Islam." The weekly magazine of *Ansar-e Hezbollah*, entitled *The Blood of Hussein,* embraced the fascist-Islamist philosophy and popularized it among the rank and file.[30]

Philosophy aside, by 2007 both Ahmadinejad and the Supreme Leader determined that the vigorous suppression of dissent was needed to stave off an Iranian version of the civil revolutions that had undermined communism in Eastern Europe. Khamenei's new chief of the Revolutionary Guards, Major General Mohammed Ali Jafari, was an expert on the subject of political subversion and asymmetrical conflict, having taught at the War University of the Revolutionary Guards and reputed to have studied the "velvet and color revolutions" in Eastern Europe. In 2008, to beef up the coercive power of the regime, the Guards fully incorporated the Basij and thus gained control of internal security, the policing of lifestyle issues, and the suppression of dissidents.

Much as on previous occasions, the violence perpetuated against civil society, moved some former revolutionary stalwarts to question the regime's ways. Mahdi Karroubi, a veteran politician who had unsuccessfully opposed Ahmadinejad in 2005, urged the elimination of the morality police and the liberalization of lifestyle restrictions, notably in regard to the Islamic dress code for women. Mir Hussein Mousavi, a former prime minister and an ex-confidant of Ayatollah Khomeini, likewise urged a more liberal approach to human rights, joining forces with Karroubi and Ayatollah Khatami. He subsequently cofounded the Green Movement to contest the 2009 elections against Ahmadinejad. Although less philosophically inclined the Green Movement leaders borrowed Soroush's argument that a true Islamic identity cannot be imposed by violence meted out by the Guards and their shadowy militias.

Compelling as these arguments were to the advocates of voluntaristic identity formation, this was not the case with the Supreme Leader and the

Revolutionary Guards who had few incentives to relax their hold on the population. A new round of secret internal polls indicated that the Greens were most likely to defeat Ahmadinejad and, even worse, that liberal sentiments were spreading to the once solidly conservative rural population—where Karroubi had a considerable following.

Despite Ahmadinejad's stormy relationship with the Supreme Leader, Khamenei and the Revolutionary Guards decided to support his reelection. The results, announced two hours after the polls closed on June 12, 2009, favored the incumbent but were widely dismissed as a fabrication. Months of protest followed but the regime held fast and, during protests that took place following the vote, members of the Basij force beat and killed Green supporters in Tehran and the provinces.

Unsurprisingly, Ahmadinejad's second term was marred by harassment and violence against opponents of a magnitude not seen since the Reign of Terror. According to the International Campaign for Human Rights in Iran (ICHRI) "freedom of assembly is all but non-existent, hundreds of people are illegally detained, freedom of expression is at its lowest point in years, torture and ill-treatment in prison are rampant, and rising numbers of executions have made Iran the world's largest executioner on a per capita basis." The Campaign published a list, compiled by Nobel Peace Prize laureate Shirin Ebadi, of forty-three lawyers who had either been imprisoned or harassed since the June 2009 election. Among them was the distinguished human rights lawyer and founding member of the Defenders of Human Rights Center, Abdolfattah Soltani. [31]

To many observers the violent suppression of human rights was indicative of a deeper failure of the Islamist identity project. One expert derided the Iranian revolution for its "utopian claim that promised to engineer a new human being." Another stated that "it is possible to argue that, the Islamic Republic's program of social engineering has failed. There are indications that the ideological state is struggling to authenticate its 'Islamic' mandate and cannot effectively filter the mediums of thought to its own favor." Following the election scandal, "it leaves the regime with one choice and that is tightening its control." [32]

By 2011, Iran's human rights record triggered widespread international condemnation. In March 2011, the Human Rights Council in Geneva created a mandate for a special rapporteur to monitor and report on the human rights situation in Iran. Ahmed Shaheed, former Foreign Minister of the Maldives, who was appointed Special Rapporteur, was denied access as the continuation of a 2005 decision to bar United Nations experts. Compiled from personal testimonies and independently corroborated, a March 2013 report by a UN special rapporteur cited "widespread and systemic" torture, harassment, arrest and attacks against human rights defenders, lawyers, and journalists. [33]

The brutality of the regime mattered little to Ahmadinejad who was still obsessed with ushering Iran into the nuclear club of nations. While the president was known to be oblivious to political reality, the Supreme Leader and the Revolutionary Guards, however, were worried about their fast-eroding legitimacy. The polling unit of the Guards and broad-based anecdotal evidence indicated that Iranian society had become less amenable to coercion-based social engineering. This was so much so that the authorities decided on a new voluntary approach. With little fanfare they introduced a marriage-counseling program that emphasized Islamic values for couples: "religiousness, good deeds, piety, following Shi'ite leaders, obeying God, devout worship, obeying the rule of the mullahs (*Velayat-e Faqih*, or guardianship of the jurist), and following religious orders and duties." Couples who participated in the program were given special marriage certificates. One observer noted that, sensing that the disciplinary power of the state had failed to produce the desired Islamic identity, the despairing clerics had turned to raising a generation of truly pious citizens from scratch. [34]

The growing impact of the stopping of nuclear proliferation by the international community was making the leadership even more anxious, the percentage of families living in poverty had risen from 22 percent to more than 40 percent during Ahmadinejad's eight-year term, while the rial lost 50 percent of its value in the course of 2013 alone. Restrictions on trade meant that the government could not import western drugs and medical supplies and the price of food, especially milk, bread, fruit, and vegetables skyrocketed. Once a neopatriarchal state accustomed to paying off its citizens with oil proceeds the regime now found itself facing high inflation and widespread unemployment on top of there being severe shortages of imported goods including medicines. Without being able to offer the public the carrot of economic benefits, applying the stick of Islamic coercion was becoming more problematic, as the authorities began to realize in the period preceding the 2013 presidential election. [35]

Most worrisome to the clerics was the huge resurgence of the reformist camp and, although Khatami himself could not run for a third term, his surrogates were more than ready to take on the challenge. In a preemptive move, the Guardian Council disqualified all serious reformist candidates leaving the field open to Mohammed Baqer Qalibaf, a former commander in the Revolutionary Guards and mayor of Tehran, Hassan Rouhani, a former head of the Supreme National Security Council (SNSC) and Saeed Jalili, another former SNSC chief. Jalili, favored by Ayatollah Khamenei, however, was trailing badly behind Baqer Qalibaf who seemed to be leading, according to polls taken two weeks before the election. On Election Day, Hassan Rouhani won by 18,613,329 votes, comprising 50.7 percent of the vote. The number was just above the 50 percent needed to avoid a runoff, triggering speculations that the Supreme Leader and the Revolutionary Guards, had decided on a "slight adjustment," in favor of Rouhani whom they considered the lesser of two evils. Indeed, immediately after the election, some in the Supreme Leader's camp pointed out that, as a cleric and a revolutionary stalwart, Rouhani shared the Islamist values of the regime.[36]

Though not their first choice, the Green Movement leaders hoped that Rouhani would press on with liberalization. During the campaign he had pledged to relax lifestyle restrictions imposed by the Haqani School representatives in the judiciary and the security apparatus. The new president promised to release the activists jailed following the 2009 election protest, notably Mir-Hussein Mousavi and Mahdi Karroubi, who were still under house arrest.

Like Khatami, the new president quickly found that there were serious limitations to his power. His Ministry of Culture and Islamic Guidance issued permits for books that had previously been banned and lifted the ban on the country's feminist *Zanan* magazine. Music bands and musicians holding public concerts, banned under Ahmadinejad, were allowed to resume their activities. Both Rouhani and his Minster of Communication, Mahmoud Vaezi, vigorously defended the right of Iranians to use the Internet and the social media which were communication channels that had helped him get elected.

The conservative establishment retaliated with a show of force. The judiciary, under Ayatollah Sadeq Amoli Larijani, the brother of Saeed Larijani, continued with its policy of imposing stiff sentences for Islamic noncompliance that, in the age of Internet, had come to include "offensive" posting on Facebook. A spokesman for the judiciary accused Rouhani and Vaezi of acting "unlawfully" by refusing to carry out the directives of the Committee for Determining Criminal Web Content (CDCWC) that would block access to Internet sites. Arguably, Rouhani was least effective in tackling human rights abuses especially the high number of executions. According to human rights groups, during the first year of Rouhani's tenure 746 prisoners were executed (the government put the figure at 319) but only 38 were declared political prisoners. The president was not able to release Karroubi and Mousavi from house arrest and, to add insult to injury, the judiciary imprisoned a number of prominent journalists and had some flogged.[37]

To those familiar with the workings of the negotiated political order, Rouhani's problems were hardly surprising. His main mandate was to negotiate a nuclear agreement with the international community in order to lift the sanctions they had imposed on Iran. Ayatollah Khomeini made this part very clear, going so far as to restrain the Revolutionary Guards from criticizing the president but the Supreme Leader, a conservative himself, was not likely to support Rouhani's efforts to put the Islamist identity project on a more voluntary footing. On the contrary, Khamenei and other hardliners had repeatedly declared that a Khatami-style Islamist Reformation was an existential threat to the regime.

CONCLUSION

The Islamic Republic of Iran is not the first ideological regime to have tried to engineer a hand-tailored identity for its citizens. The once celebrated *Homo Sovieticus* is just one of the many projects that failed to take root and shriveled, taking the Soviet Union with it.

Since religiosity is an organic part of core identity, the shelf life of *Homo Islamicus* may last much longer than comparable projects in the past. The regime can count on "true believers" who support the theocratic state and the coercion needed to manufacture the "republic of virtue." Although estimates are difficult to come by, this sector is a sizable demographic factor that has not only congregated around the extensive clerical network but, as noted, has penetrated civil society. As for those who oppose the theocracy, the regime has put its hope in a carefully calibrated formula of coercion, intimidation and economic enticements. The complex balancing of all these forces has created a pattern of movement between coercion and voluntarism in the process of shaping the Islamic identity and, barring a dramatic change, either exogenous or endogenous, the Islamic identity project is expected to continue for the foreseeable future.

NOTES

1. Khomeini was principally interested in an Islamic state and only acquired an interest in a *republic* in 1978 largely under the influence of people like Ibrahim Yazdi and Sadegh Ghotbzadeh.

2. Rouhollah Mosavi Khomeini, *Velayat-e Faqih* (Government of Jurisprudence), (Tehran: Tanzim va Nashr-e Asar-e Imam Khomeini, 1993).

3. Majid Tehranian, "Communication and Revolution in Iran: The Passing of a Paradigm," *Iranian Studies* Vol. 13, No. 1–4 (1980), pp. 18–22.

4. Arshin Adib-Moghaddam, *On the Arab Revolts and the Iranian Revolution: Power and Resistance Today* (New York: Bloomsbury, 2013), p. 26.

5. Arshin Adib-Moghaddam, "Iran, Bazargan and the Provisional Government," *The Library of Congress Country Studies*, July 4, 2002, http://workmall.com/wfb2001/iran/iran _history_bazargan_and_the_provisional_government.html, retrieved: August 22, 2014.

6. Its full name is: *Sepāh-e Pāsdārān-e Enqelāb-e Eslāmi*—Army of the Guardians of the Islamic Revolution.

7. Ofira Seliktar, *Failing the Crystal Ball Test: The Carter Administration and the Fundamentalist Revolution in Iran* (Westport, CT: Praeger, 2000), pp. 96–102.

8. For more details regarding *Chahar Shanbeh Soori*, see Abbas Milani, *Tales of Two Cities: A Persian Memoir* (Washington, DC: Mage Publishers, 1996).

9. UNODC, "Islamic Criminal Code, Approved by Law Affairs Committee of the Islamic Consultative Assembly (Parliament)," in *Tehran, 1363* (1983), https://www.unodc.org/tldb/ pdf/Islamic_Penal_Code_in_Farsi.pdf, retrieved: July 12, 2014.

10. Azadeh Namakydoust, "Covered in Messages: The Veil as a Political Tool," *The Iranian*, May 8, 2003, http://iranian.com/Women/2003/May/Veil/p.html, retrieved: June 5, 2014.

11. Farah Shilandari, "Iranian Woman: Veil and Identity," *Gozaar.org*, September 7, 2010, http://www.gozaar.org/english/articles-en/Iranian-Woman-Veil-and-Identity.html, retrieved: June 5, 2014.

12. Seliktar, *Failing the Crystal Ball Test*, pp. 61–62.

13. Fred Halliday, *100 Myths about the Middle East* (Berkeley: University of California Press, 2005), p. 24. Geneive Abdo and Jonathan Lyons, *Answering Only to God: Faith and Freedom in 21st Century Iran* (New York: Henry Holt, 2003), p. 40. Shilandari, "Iranian Woman: Veil and Identity."

14. Baqer Moin, *Khomeini: Life of the Ayatollah* (New York: Thomas Dunne Books, 2000), p. 264.

15. Afshin Molavi, *The Soul of Iran: A Nation's Struggle for Freedom* (New York: W. W. Norton & Company Inc., 2010), p. 105.

16. Ofira Seliktar, "Reading Tehran in Washington: The Problem of Defining the Fundamentalist Regime in Iran and Assessing the Prospect for Political Change," in Joseph Morrison Skelly (ed.), *Political Islam from Muhammad to Ahmadinejad: Defenders, Detractors, and Definitions* (Santa Barbara, CA: Praeger, 2010), pp. 163–81.

17. Mohsen M. Milani, "Reform and Resistance in the Islamic Republic of Iran," in John L. Esposito and R. K. Ramazani (eds.), *Iran at the Crossroads* (New York: Palgrave, 2001), p. 99.

18. Robin B. Wright, *Dreams and Shadows: The Future of the Middle East* (New York: Penguin, 2008), p. 268.

19. Robin Wright, "Islam and Liberal Democracy: Two Visions of Reformation," *Journal of Democracy*, Vol. 7, No. 2 (1996), pp. 69–72.

20. Wright, *Dreams and Shadows*, p. 268. Wright, "Islam and Liberal Democracy," p. 73.

21. Ofira Seliktar, *Navigating Iran: From Carter to Obama* (New York: Palgrave Macmillan, 2012), pp. 105–10.

22. Ziba Mir-Hosseini and Richard Tapper, *Islam and Democracy in Iran: Eshkevari and the Quest for Reform* (New York: I. B. Tauris, 2006), p. 32. Saïd Amir Arjomand, "The Rise and Fall of President Khātami and the Reform Movement in Iran," *Constellations*, Vol. 12, No. 4 (2005), pp. 506–9. Saïd Amir Arjomand, *After Khomeini: Iran Under His Successors* (New York: Oxford University Press, 2009), p. 263. Abdo and Lyons, *Answering Only to God*, p. 179. Ray Takeyh, *Hidden Iran: Paradox and Power in the Islamic Republic* (New York: Times Book/Holt, 2006), p. 192. Vali Nasr and Ali Ghessari, *Democracy in Iran: History and the Quest for Liberty* (New York: Oxford University Press, 2006), p. 216. Kenneth R. Timmerman, *Countdown to Crisis: The Coming Nuclear Showdown with Iran* (New York: Crown Forum, 2005), p. 214. Farhang Rajaee, *Islamism and Modernism: The Changing Discourse in Iran* (Austin: University of Texas Press, 2010), p. 174.

23. Abdo and Lyons, *Answering Only to God*, pp. 179, 220–21. Asef Bayat, *Making Islam Democratic: Social Movements and the Post-Islamist Turn* (Stanford, CA: Stanford University Press, 2007), pp. 116–17. Robin Wright, *The Last Great Revolution: Turmoil and Transformation in Iran* (New York: Vintage Books, 2001), pp. 73–75, 105. A. William Samii, "Candidates and Quitters," *Iran Report*, Vol. 3, No. 38 (October 9, 2000), http://www.globalsecurity.org/wmd/library/news/iran/2000/38-091000.html, retrieved: July 12, 2014.

24. Abdo and Lyons, *Answering Only to God*, pp. 179, 220–21. Bayat, *Making Islam Democratic*, pp. 116–17. Wright, *The Last Great Revolution*, pp. 73–75, 105.

25. Hooman Majd, *The Ayatollah Begs to Differ: The Paradox of Modern Iran* (New York: Doubleday, 2008), pp. 28–29.

26. Stephen C. Poulson, *Social Movements in Twentieth-Century Iran: Culture, Ideology, and Mobilizing Frameworks* (London: Lexington Books, 2005), p. 262. Kasra Naji, *Ahmadinejad: The Secret History of Iran's Radical Leader* (Los Angeles: University of California Press, 2008), pp. 188–89.

27. Bill Samii, "Iran: A Rising Star in Iran Politics," *Radio Free Europe/Radio Liberty*, November 7, 2005. Farideh Farhi, "The Antinomies of Iran's War Generation," in Lawrence G. Potter and Garry G. Sick (eds.), *Iran, Iraq and the Legacies of War* (New York: Palgrave Macmillan, 2004), p. 104–7. Walter Posch, "Prospects for Iran's 2009 Presidential Elections," *Middle East Institute Policy Brief*, No. 24 (June 2009), http://www.mei.edu/sites/default/files/publications/Posch2.pdf, retrieved: May 14, 2014. Olivier Roy, Antoine Sfeir, and John King, *The Columbia World Dictionary of Islamism* (New York: Columbia University Press, 2007), p. 152. Buchta Wilfried, *Who Rules Iran: The Structure of Power in the Islamic Republic* (Washington, DC: The Washington Institute for Near East Policy, 2000), p. 18.

28. Akbar E. Torbat, "Financial Corruption in Iran," *Information Clearinghouse*, March 2, 2013, http://web.calstatela.edu/faculty/atorbat/docs/Corruption%20in%20Iran.pdf, retrieved: May 14, 2014.

29. Farhad Rezaei, *Nuclear Proliferation and Nuclear Rollback: The Case of Iran* (PhD thesis, University of Malaysia, KL, 2014), pp. 199–204.

30. Naji, *Ahmadinejad*, pp. 98, 107–8.

31. ICHRI, "Hold Ahmadinejad Accountable for Iran's Human Rights Crisis During UN Visit," *International Campaign for Human Rights in Iran*, September 14, 2011, http://www.iranhumanrights.org/2011/09/ahmadinejad-accountable-for-human-rights-crisis/, retrieved: June 5, 2014.

32. Arshin Adib-Moghaddam, *On the Arab Revolts and the Iranian Revolution* (New York: Bloomsbury Academic, 2013), p. 40. Afshin Shahi, "Iran's New Wave of Social Engineering," *Open Democracy*, September 29, 2010, http://www.opendemocracy.net/afshin-shahi/irans-new-wave-of-social-engineering, retrieved: June 5, 2014.

33. HRW, "UN: Expose Iran's Appalling Rights Record," *Human Rights Watch*, September 21, 2011, http://www.hrw.org/news/2011/09/21/un-expose-iran-s-appalling-rights-record, retrieved: June 5, 2014. ICHRI, "Hold Ahmadinejad Accountable," September 14, 2011, http://www.iranhumanrights.org/2011/09/ahmadinejad-accountable-for-human-rights-crisis/, retrieved: June 5, 2014.

34. Majid Mohammadi, "Zealous Militants in Citizens' Bedrooms," *Gozaar, Freedom House*, July 2, 2010, http://www.gozaar.org/english/articles-en/Zealous-Militants-in-Citizens-Bedrooms.html, retrieved: June 5, 2014.

35. Rezaei, *Nuclear Proliferation and Nuclear Rollback*, pp. 275–78.

36. Ibid., pp. 290–93.

37. Saeed Kamali Dehghan, "Noam Chomsky Calls on Iran to Release Imprisoned Journalist Marzieh Rasouli," *The Guardian*, July 12, 2014.

Chapter Four

Iran's National Identity and the Nuclear Program

A Rational Choice Theory Analysis

Farhad Rezaei

Proliferation theory postulates that factors other than strict security calculations can prompt countries to embrace a nuclear weapons program, and national identity and pride are among the things most often mentioned in this context. National elites can use a nuclear project to enhance their legitimacy by creating or bolstering a new unifying identity and, in some cases, nuclear proliferation is placed at the core of such a nationalist identity, often described as "civil religion."

Iran's nuclear program certainly fits this notion. This chapter contends that, in addition to widely perceived security threats, the Islamist elite in Iran has seized upon the nuclear project to construct a new national identity. By merging traditional Persian culture, Islamist elements, and a universalist-oriented scientific creed, the regime hopes to both boost national pride and its own legitimacy.

The increasingly painful sanctions imposed by the international community, however, have posed a serious challenge to the nuclear-program-based identity. Sanctions have eroded the standards of livings of the population and left the regime vulnerable to economic upheavals. The professional literature holds that if the cost of sanctions exceeds the perceived benefits of the targeted behavior then rethinking both the program and its role in identity building is in order. While it is not yet clear whether the elite is ready to give up proliferation there is a real possibility that the Iranian public may withdraw its support in the hope of achieving an improved lifestyle. The nuclear civil religion, which is a sophisticated construct designed to bolster the legitimacy of the regime, has begun to lose its allure because of the increase in the economic "misery index" associated with the nuclear program.

The article has five sections. The first reviews the theories of nuclear proliferation and nuclear rollback through sanctions. The second discusses the clerical establishments' use of the program to shape an Islamist national identity. The third section analyzes the efforts of the Principalists, a secular hardline opposition to the Ayatollahs, to fashion a civil religion around the nuclear project. The fourth explains the revival of the nuclear civil religion by Principalists. The concluding section uses rational choice theory to evaluate the impact of sanctions on the nuclear component of Iranian identity.

NUCLEAR PROLIFERATION AND ROLLBACK: INSIGHTS FROM THE RATIONAL CHOICE THEORY

Since the dawn of the atomic age the proliferation of nuclear weapons has threatened world security. Political leaders, scholars, and scientists have expressed concerns about the spread of weapons of mass destruction, prompting a major research effort to uncover the causes of proliferation and propose solutions for its rollback.

The dominant International Relations (IR) theories—realism and neorealism—can serve as platforms for launching propositions about proliferation and scholars working within both the realist and neorealistic tradition may thus offer a series of possible propositions regarding the behavior of states in general and cooperation and conflict behavior in particular. Both realists and neorealists postulate that states acquire nuclear weapons because their security demands it. Since the international system is said to be anarchic,[1] countries may believe that they need to deter potential attackers, and acquiring a nuclear capability may enhance their security through deterrence: it signals that the cost of aggression toward them would exceed the potential benefits of such an action. Assuming that countries are rational players, would-be aggressors might be dissuaded from acting by performing a simple cost-benefit analysis.[2]

Kenneth Waltz, considered the "father" of neorealism, used this argument to assert that obtaining a nuclear capacity is a highly rational act on the part of a state. Moreover, in his view, ethical concerns have little influence in the "dog-eat-dog" international environment. Consequently, every state has to be prepared to do what is necessary for its interests as it defines them. Anarchy is a state in which all can, and many, play "dirty pool" and strategic interdependence and the absence of morality mean that each state, if it wishes to be effective (or secure), must be prepared to play according to the rules set by the "dirtiest" player.[3]

The nuclear powers of the Cold War era: the United States, Great Britain, France, the Soviet Union, and China, however, have tried to prevent others from joining the "nuclear club" via the Non-Proliferation Treaty (NPT) which was launched in 1968 and went into effect in 1970. The treaty recognized the inalienable rights of states to use nuclear energy for peaceful purposes but went to great lengths to prohibit the transfer or acquisition of nuclear weapons and related technologies. For countries willing to abide by the NPT, the United States offered the Seeds of Peace—a modest program of nuclear technology for peaceful uses.

Proliferation apart, Cold War strategists could rely on the theory of Mutual Assured Destruction (MAD) to avoid a nuclear Armageddon. Conceptualized by Thomas Schelling, the construct postulates that, given the catastrophic cost of a nuclear conflagration, rational actors would refrain from launching an attack on a nuclear-armed adversary. Though some critics have questioned the Schelling theory, MAD has been credited with keeping the nuclear peace during the so-called First Nuclear Age.

The end of the Cold War and the appearance of new nuclear contenders have, however, raised serious doubts about the soundness of the NPT regime. In a vigorous debate over what was dubbed the Second Nuclear Age, scholars have pointed out that the non-proliferation treaty was not robust enough to prevent a variety of countries from developing their own nuclear arsenals. It has been assumed that these new actors have benefited from the so-called free ride to nuclear know-how which has made the cost of acquiring and expanding nuclear weapons capability lower, and that this now outweighs financial and other risks.[4]

More worrisome are the doubts about whether Second Nuclear Age players possess the type of rationality needed to sustain MAD. In particular, analysts have focused on the heightened sense of nationalism of the new crop of nuclear pretenders. Emerging from colonial rule in the late 1940s, leaders of these countries came of age in the atomic era and, for them, nuclear weapons have represented more than being mere security-military instruments as envisioned by Waltz. Second Nuclear Age experts hold that such leaders have planned to turn the bomb into the center of nation-building projects to reinforce national identity and cohesion. Closely related to this is the notion that the nuclear endeavor can act as a convenient shortcut to regional hegemony or even world status—which is something that some of them are known to crave.[5]

Drawing on numerous case studies Scott Sagan, a leading nuclear strategist, has concluded that factors other than strict security calculations may prompt countries to embrace nuclear weaponry. Sagan argues that domestic politics and other nonsecurity factors can prompt states to pursue nuclear weapons especially since leaders tend to view them as symbols of national prestige, modernity, and identity for the state.[6] These so-called secondary drivers—national identity, prestige, and political currency—are not merely casual afterthoughts since, used in conjunction with the security language, they inform proliferation decisions. Clearly, the Seeds for Peace program and other NPT incentives—based on rational-utilitarian considerations—do not seem to have satisfied elites beholden to secondary-driver considerations.[7]

The synergy between the political and emotional needs of elites and the bomb would have been hard for the theorists of the First Nuclear Age to imagine; but Second Nuclear Age experts, expanding on Sagan, have taken a serious look at the psychology of the elites who support proliferation. Jacques E. C. Hymans's psychological theory of nuclear proliferation, for instance, has provided important insights, and this largely overlooked work asserts that the National Identity Conception (NIC) of leaders has influenced their decision to acquire nuclear weapons. The NIC itself has, in turn, been shaped by the leaders' awareness of how their nation compares to others on the international status ladder—an evaluation called "key comparison other" (KCO). Simply put, leaders with an inflated NIC who crave international status are the most likely to develop a nuclear vision and a matching commitment to implement it.[8]

Even the most determined nuclear visionaries, however, have to reckon with the costs of launching and maintaining a nuclear weapons project in defiance of the nonproliferation regime. In order to dissuade would-be proliferators the NPT architects developed a rollback plan based on economic sanctions which, like nuclear rationality sanctions, are predicated on a cost-benefit calculus based on the idea that by raising the cost of "doing business" the targeted country will eventually desist from its activities. The literature indicates that certain categories of countries—oil dependent, rentier states among them—are particularly sensitive to international sanctions. Put differently, the high cost of acquiring a nuclear weapons capability may alter the leaders' NIC since their desire to proliferate and have a nuclear program must be balanced with the danger of economic collapse and the loss of political power.[9] Needless to say, eroding the economic power of a proliferator will adversely affect the KCO analysis.

NUCLEAR WEAPONS AS A NATIONAL IDENTITY ENHANCER UNDER THE SHAH: THE CIVIL RELIGION PERSPECTIVE

According to Max Weber building national identity is an evolutionary process since, in a tribal society, or *gemenischaft*, ties were based on kinship. In the more advanced *gesellschaft*, societies-turned-countries, cultural and linguistic markers have provided the necessary cohesion. The more diffuse bonds in the *gesellschaft* community require a constant supply of unifying symbols like the flag, an anthem, or national history—to mention just a few.

Rituals surrounding national symbols are said to deepen the *gesellschaft* ties, notably in the case of polycentric countries made up of different and, occasionally, antagonistic *gemenischaft*-derived units. Jean-Jacques Rousseau suggested that this type of nation-building identity amounts to civil religion—an effort to sanctify a coherent body of civic elements to create a religious-like bond to the state.

Sociologists differ in defining the parameters of civil religion since they intersect and overlap with patriotism and nationalism, but most agree that in countries with strong sectarian traditions, civil religion provides the glue that binds the disparate communities. It is interesting that, even where religious identity does not divide the country into hostile camps, attempts to form a civic super-identity have been noted. Taking a cue from Alexis de Tocqueville, Robert N. Bellah claimed that the American civil religion provided a much-needed bonding among immigrants. In yet another permutation, secular elites may use civil religion in nation-building as a counterpart to a deeply entrenched religious tradition. For example, two Israeli social scientists found that the secular Socialist-Zionist pioneers created an elaborate civil religion by sanctifying carefully chosen national and Zionist symbols.[10]

Faced with a strong competition from Shi'a Islam, the Shah of Iran set out to create a competing civil religion based on adoration of the monarchy, reverence for modernism, respect for science, and anticommunism. The shah made little secret of his ambition to see Iran join the club of developed nations by the end of the twentieth century, a forecast that Robert E. Looney, an economic advisor to the government, strongly agreed with. To stand by this timetable, the shah embarked on a vigorous campaign to recruit top scientists and industrial experts from the United States and Europe.[11]

Supported by the United States, the Iranian nuclear program was the crown jewel in plans to modernize and industrialize the country. Iran was an early beneficiary of the Seeds for Peace program; but the shah was vastly more ambitious and not only wanted to build nuclear power plants but occasionally hinted at acquiring a nuclear arsenal that would reflect Iran's hegemonic vision in the region. According to some sources, in 1974 the shah declared that Iran would have nuclear weapons, "without a doubt and sooner than one would think." The agreement with the United States made it easier for American companies to transfer nuclear technology to Iran and, more significantly, the Iranians decided to finance a uranium-enrichment plant in the United States.[12]

All along, the shah emphasized that nuclear power was Iran's entry ticket to the developed-countries club. The Atomic Energy Organization of Iran (AEOI), established in 1973, was the poster child of modernization—one of pillars of the emerging civil religion of Iran. Highly ambitious for a beginner, the AEOI announced plans to create 23,000 MW of electricity generated from nuclear power stations. Akbar Etemad, the former head of the AEOI, revealed that the shah was convinced that Iran's technological prowess would not only elevate the country to the much aspired position of advanced nations, but also elevate his military to regional superiority. Presiding over a rentier state, the shah clearly counted on the increase in oil revenues in the early 1970s to accelerate the development process and put the new civil religion on a firm footing.[13]

THE ISLAMIC IDENTITY PROJECT OF THE AYATOLLAHS: THE NUCLEAR PROGRAM TO THE RESCUE

By the mid-1970s the Iranian economy had run into a number of obstacles. Revenues from oil had decreased, inflation had increased, and social unrest had mounted. To quell the upheaval, the government alternated between coercion and compromise but, after a year of demonstrations and strikes, the monarchy collapsed in early 1979. Much to the surprise of the world, Ayatollah Rouhollah Khomeini, until then a little known Grand Ayatollah who had spent decades in exile in Najaf, Iraq, took power on February 1, 1979. Nothing in the background of the aging cleric had prepared him to deal with foreign policy in general and nuclear weapons in particular. As a matter of fact Khomeini condemned the nuclear vision of the shah as an example of Iran's penchant for all things Western. More to the point the Ayatollah declared weapons of mass destruction to be antithetical to the teachings of Islam because of the danger to innocent civilians. In any event Khomeini planned to impose a pure Islamic identity on the Iranians, making national identity markers such as nuclear prowess redundant.

Paradoxically, in a case of unintended consequences, it was Khomeini's desire to export the Islamist revolution in the region that rehabilitated the nuclear program of the shah. To achieve this Iran embarked upon a series of terror attacks on neighboring countries that threatened to destabilize the Gulf States and the Ayatollah was especially keen to take on Saddam Hussein because of his long-standing record of abusing the Shi'a majority. In response to a number of terror attacks perpetrated by terror cells traced to Tehran Hussein invaded Iran in 1980, but his initial Iraqi imitative stalled and the war degenerated into a bloody stalemate. The Iraqi army used chemical weapons and this prompted the Revolutionary Guards, by then a large parasternal military force that had suffered the brunt of the fighting, to press Khomeini to lift the ban on nuclear weapons. According to the Guards' commanders, a nuclear bomb would have deterred Iraq from starting the conflict and would have evened the playing field between the large and well-equipped Iraqi army and the Iranian forces. At the very least the threat of a counterattack would have stopped the Iraqis from devastating Iranian cities with long-range Scud missiles. Equally important, in the view of the Guard commanders, was a nuclear umbrella which they considered necessary to deter any possible retaliation from countries targeted for the export of the revolution.[14]

In 1987 the desperate commander of the Guard, Major General Mohsen Rezaei, wrote to Khomeini to inform him that "no victory could be expected in the next five years" and that an offensive operation could be undertaken in four years but that necessary equipment had to be obtained first. Rezaei stated that, "with the grace of God" he could embark on offensive operations if, after 1371 [1992], the Islamic republic would be able to field 350 infantry brigades, 2,500 tanks, 300 fighter planes, and 300 helicopters. He also mentioned the necessity of producing a substantial number of laser and atomic weapons which he predicted would be necessary for fighting any future wars.[15]

While the secret letter did confirm the interest of the Revolutionary Guards in developing nuclear project it did not necessarily dispel the Ayatollah's doubts about such weapons. Ayatollah Ali Akbar Hashemi Rafsanjani, one of architects of the revolution and a founding member of the Revolutionary Guards, convinced the Ayatollah that the only way to defeat Saddam and force him to stop using chemical weapons was the creation of a nuclear deterrence. Under intense pressure from the Guards and the regular army, the *Artesh*, Khomeini, agreed to lift his fatwa against weapons of mass destruction. First, a program for chemical weapons was launched, followed by biological and nuclear weapons, but the decision came too late to change Iran's fortunes in the battlefield. Faced with a dire situation at the front, Khomeini agreed to a ceasefire.[16]

In an open address to the nation Khomeini admitted that his acceptance of the United Nations Security Council's Resolution 585 that ended the war with Iraq on July 18, 1988, was like "drinking poison from a chalice." In a secret letter penned to all of Iran's political and military leaders two days earlier, Ayatollah Khomeini recalled this change of mind. Released by Rafsanjani in September 2006, Khomeini's letter mentioned "a shocking" report by the commander of the Revolutionary Guard, Mohsen Rezaei, who expressed utter despair at the course of the war with Iraq. Khomeini emphasized that Rezaei had been unequivocal: "if Iran were to come out of the war with its head held high, it would need plenty of sophisticated weapons, including nuclear ones."[17]

Well before Khomeini lifted his fatwa, Ayatollah Mohammed Beheshti, another of the architects of the revolution and the head of the Council of the Revolution of Iran, had already taken steps to revive the shah's program. After Behesti's death in 1981 Rafsanjani took over the portfolio dealing with weapons of mass destruction and, speaking before Guards commanders in October 1988, he called for developing nuclear and other unconventional weapons: "The importance of such weapons was made very clear during the war. We should fully equip ourselves both in the offensive and defensive use of chemical, bacteriological, and radiological weapons. From now on you should make use of every opportunity and perform this task."[18]

The eight-year war with Iraq was also instrumental in restoring some of the nationalist aspirations that had predated the revolution. Although Ayatollah Khomeini wanted to replace the traditional Persian national identity with a purely Islamic one, once the fighting started the government adopted national themes in the form of patriotic songs and Persian cultural symbols. For instance, the singer Mohammad Golriz performed the highly patriotic war songs of *"Vatanam"* (My homeland), *"Man Iraani'am, aarmaanam shahaadat"* (I am Iranian; my aim is martyrdom), *"Piruzi khojasteh baad"* (May this victory be auspicious) or *"Ey sarafraazaan"* (You heroes). Another singer, Reza Rooyigari, was also known for his popular song *"Iran . . . Iran,"* whose aim was to cultivate a motivation and readiness for self-sacrifice in the Iranian population. The content of the songs, more patriotic than religious, evoked very strong emotional reactions among the soldiers and civilians alike. Without these shared cultural symbols, which stemmed from the core of the national identity, even the charismatic leader of the revolution, Ayatollah Khomeini, would not have been able to mobilize the nation to sacrifice so much.[19]

Even though it did not please the Supreme Leader, the regime realized that the Islamist identity alone was not enough to motivate people. A telling phenomenon, after the war ended, was the fact that the popular entertainment scene changed in that the content of songs became much more religious. The Nohe music genre, which is used by Shi'a Muslims to express their sorrow for their martyred holy Imams, increasingly replaced other war-time patriotic songs.[20] Poetry, a popular public form in Iran, used religious motifs to equate deaths in battle with religious martyrdom and, in their sermons (notably Friday sermons), this was presented as a model for the youth to emulate. The leaders of the Islamic revolution made many references to Hossein's death, to impress the idea that he had consciously chosen death over life because he wanted to convey to the oppressed nations the message that every individual was responsible for participating in the fight against the tyrannical ruler.[21]

Unlike the national sentiments that had been so popular during the Iran-Iraq war, Khomeini's vision of instilling a pure Islamist identity into the nation proved to be an uphill battle. Not surprisingly, as has been the case in other ideological regimes intent on radical social engineering, the clerics soon discovered that extreme coercion was needed to change norms and behavior. Upon becoming president in 1989 the more pragmatic Ayatollah Rafsanjani and his circle became worried that the amount of violence required to impose a pure Islamist identity and sharia-compliant behavior upon the nation was eroding the legitimacy of the regime.

Retreating to the tried-and-true symbols of nationalism was one way to address this deficit in legitimacy and, starting in the early 1990s, leading clerics took to exalting nuclear achievements and the alleged scientific prowess of Iran in ways reminiscent of the shah. This was so prevalent that some analysts concluded that Iran's nuclear program in the 1990s was "in search of a rationale," meaning that security imperatives were put on a par with nationalism, prestige, and legitimacy.[22] Ayatollah Khamenei, who succeeded Khomeini as Supreme Leader in 1989, suggested that Iran had the potential to become the world leader in science in fifty years and praised the nuclear program as a symbol of scientific and technological prowess. Linking future prominence and achievement to historical Persian greatness was clearly perceived to be a winning strategy for the struggling regime.[23]

On a more contemporary note, the Ayatollahs were able to play another winning card—one that touched upon the foreign policy beliefs of the revolutionary government. As espoused by Khomeini, the international system had been greatly corrupted by secular values and dominated by morally defective Western countries led by the United States and Israel. Leading a crusade against the so-called "Great Satan" and "Little Satan" became a virtual mantra in Khomeini's public speeches. By seizing the American diplomats in 1979 the regime proved its total disregard for international norms and, after their release 444 days later, the episode became a symbol of the Iranian's defiance of the West. Building on this legacy the Ayatollahs could point out that the pursuit of the allegedly peaceful nuclear program was a gesture of defiance towards the global powers, notably the United States. Known as oppositional defiance, it was a win-win strategy for the clerics since, they were not only able to pursue their nuclear program, but could also beef up their legitimacy by accusing the international community of denying Iran's sovereign rights to scientific and economic progress.[24]

That the nuclear project became a core marker in the Islamic-Iranian identity was made clear by Ayatollah Mohammed Khatami who was elected on a reformist agenda in 1997. Khatami captured intentional attention with his Dialogue of Civilizations, a concept borrowed from the philosopher Darius Shayegan, who headed the Center for the Study of Civilizations at Tehran University prior to 1979: Shayegan, who studied with Henry Corbin, an eminent French expert on Islam, was also influenced by Hans Kochler, an Austrian philosopher who developed the field of the hermeneutics of transcultural understanding. In 1972 Kochler called for a dialogue between civilizations based on self-understanding and the pursuit of equality between the West and non-Western civilizations. Fusing the elements of Corbin's Islamic transcendentalism and the neo-Marxism of Kochler, Shayegan was the first to place Iranian identity within the sphere of non-Western cosmopolitanism. To borrow an observation from one analyst, Shayegan operated within the "space of transition"—in which the extant international system was declared inadequate in its ability to accommodate the self-understanding and identity of Iranians. Translated into the language of IR by Khatami, this new cosmopolitanism demanded a level playing field in nuclear matters that acknowledged Iran's sovereign right to a nuclear program.[25]

Behind the scenes there was more evidence of Iran's resolve to become a nuclear player. In 2005 the Expediency Council ratified "Iran's Strategic 20-Year Vision Document" ([1384] 2005) that signaled Iran's ambition to transform itself into a developed country that would rank first in the region economically, scientifically, and technologically by the year 2025. "Iran is a developed country in first place in the region in the realms of economy, knowledge, technology; with an Islamic and revolutionary identity, an inspiration for the world; and with productive and influential interaction in international relations. It is endowed with advanced knowledge, capable in science and technology, and reliant on a greater share of human resources and social capital in national production. It is secure, independent, and powerful with a defense system based on multilateral deterrence and an alliance between the government and the population." To anyone even vaguely familiar with the inner symbolism of the nuclear discourse, the term "defense system based on multilateral deterrence," meant only one thing: nuclear weapons. Equally important is the reference to the alliance between the "government and the population" in the same sentence which suggests that a nuclear-based national identity was part of the Vision Document.[26]

While Khatami's Dialogue of Civilizations helped the regime to generate goodwill abroad his fortunes at home became precarious. Elected on a platform of liberalizing the Islamic identity project dubbed the Islamic Reformation, Khatami posed a serious challenge to the clerical order. Alarmed by the popularity of Khatami's Reformation, the Supreme Leader and the Revolutionary Guards ordered the president to be marginalized and his supporters persecuted in a wave of violence not seen since the early years of the revolution. Adding to the crisis of legitimacy was the widespread corruption of the clerical class and their children which was subject to frequent public scandals and endless, salacious rumors. With the regime's legitimacy in tatters a younger generation of activists known as the Principalists emerged to salvage the credentials of the revolution.

THE PRINCIPALISTS AND THE REVIVAL OF THE NUCLEAR CIVIL RELIGION

Unlike the clerics who founded the Islamic Republic the Principalists were mostly secular middle-level officials who had forged ties with one another while serving in the Guards during the Iran-Iraqi war. Mahmoud Ahmadinejad, one of the cofounders of *Isargaran,* and the then-mayor of Tehran, targeted the clerics and their children—known by the derogatory nickname, *Aghazadeh.* He accused them of insatiable materialism that, in his view, betrayed the egalitarian ethos of the revolution and the legacy of Ayatollah Khomeini. Conveniently for Ahmadinejad the sons of Rafsanjani, his main rival in the presidential race, were mired in highly publicized corruption scandals that made them literally perfect poster children of the *Aghazadeh* phenomenon. Again, to those adept at reading between the lines, the Principalists' message was clear: the purely Islamist identity had been so compromised that it needed a robust helping of nationalism.[27]

On entering office in 2005 Ahmadinejad adopted a high-profile, defiance-based foreign policy to make this point. After complaining about alleged Western interference in Iran's affairs during the nineteenth and twentieth centuries, the president pledged to pursue an activist foreign policy whose goal was to gain regional hegemony and a global standing. In his words, "the active foreign policy is not one in which we accept those roles that other powers have determined for us; *Heyhat Mena Zela*! The Iranian nation never accepted such shame in the past and will never accept it in the future." Ahmadinejad stated that "one of the necessities of active diplomacy is embarking on an offensive approach towards the superpowers based on the Shi'a culture. We should have an offensive mood in politics, economy, and in culture. My dears! Shi'ite culture means invasion into the main centers of global corruption." Indeed: "For the realization of the Islamic Revolution's objectives, alteration of the current international order is required."[28]

Clearly, such global ambitions could not be realized without Iran gaining mastery of a nuclear stratagem. Unsurprisingly Ahmadinejad's complaints about the nuclear hegemony of the West sounded especially rancorous. He framed the attack against the NPT in terms of national sovereignty, inalienable rights, international justice, and equality. To recall Hymans and the NIC, the nuclear program was, in the eyes of the president, a way in which Iran could affirm "to itself and to the world, that it was an advanced and sovereign nation. It was also a way of defying what it saw as continued Western efforts to control, exploit, or weaken Iran."[29]

To bolster this argument, Ahmadinejad compared himself to the nationalist Prime Minister Mohammed Mossadeq who had struggled against Britain to nationalize Iranian oil production in the 1950s. Mossadeq was removed in a CIA-supported coup in 1953, but the event loomed large in the Iranian national consciousness. In both cases energy resources encapsulate the large themes of modernity, sovereignty, self-sufficiency, and nonsubmission to Western control. In a metaphor understood by most Iranians the president equated giving up enrichment to losing independence[30] and, as he told a rally on June 26, 2005, "It is the right of the Iranian nation to move forward in all fields and acquire modern technology. Nuclear technology is the outcome of the scientific progress of Iranian youth."[31]

Clearly, to Ahmadinejad, the mastering of nuclear technology was not just a means to produce electricity—or even a nuclear weapon—but also a way to advance the industrial, scientific, and economic standing of the country. Quite telling in reference to his NIC-KCO was the fact that the president also compared the mastery of the nuclear project to the scientific feat involved in the Egyptian Aswan Dam and the American moon landing. At the very least he nursed the ambition of becoming a leader in nuclear technology that would benefit the Muslim Ummah, the entire Islamic community. In a speech on September 15, 2005, Ahmadinejad declared his country's willingness to provide nuclear technology to other Muslim states: "Iran is ready to transfer nuclear know-how to the Islamic countries due to their need."[32]

Closer to home the Ahmadinejad administration embarked on a public relations campaign to turn the nuclear project into a civil religion. In April 2006, the government celebrated the enrichment of a small amount of uranium (at a low 3.5 percent level) with a nuclear holiday and an elaborate ceremony transmitted on national television. A triumphant Ahmadinejad announced the news that Iran had joined the nuclear club to an auditorium packed with officials, Guard commanders, and clergymen flown in for the occasion by saying, "At this historic moment, with the blessings of God Almighty and the efforts made by our scientists, I declare here that the laboratory-scale nuclear fuel cycle has been completed and that young scientists have produced uranium enriched to the degree needed for nuclear power plants," He added, "I formally declare that Iran has joined the club of nuclear countries." Two containers said to contain the independently enriched uranium were displayed as "exotically clad dancers whirled around them" and "choirs thundered Allah Akbar." Some in the audience "stood and thrust their fists into the air."[33] Some Western observers described this and subsequent nuclear-themed celebrations as "bizarre," but the symbolism and rituals made sense in the context of a planned civil religion.

For Ahmadinejad this was a winning strategy that would generate legitimacy for the regime as he appealed to the Iranians' pride in their Persian culture and religion. The pursuit of advanced knowledge and technology, such as nuclear energy, become a national and moral imperative. One analyst commented that, under Ahmadinejad, Iran's nuclear policy had become truly driven by a "state identity" anchored in three discursive themes: independence, justice, and resistance.

The third theme became the trademark of his foreign policy rhetoric particularly after the 2005 election:

> These were formed in the course of Iran's modern history, and their particular articulation contributed to the constitution of the identity of the Islamic Revolution and later the Islamic Republic. Nuclear discourse has been articulated with the main elements of these discourses. Thus, Iran's nuclear policy has

become a matter of identity. These discourses can explain how the nuclear issue has gained significance in Iran's foreign relations, how its priority has been justified within this meaning structure, and how it has enjoyed a significant degree of popularity inside Iran. Furthermore, they can explain the variances in Iran's nuclear policy in different periods.

Another observer commented that Ahmadinejad's "negation" was an expression of the "negative aspect of the hyper-independence discourse." In the nuclear realm, "the emphasis is on refusing any form of dependence or submission to foreign countries."[34]

According to Hymans' scale, Ahmadinejad was an extreme example of being the bearer of a national identity based on oppositional nationalism. Oppositional nationalist leaders tend to see their nations as both naturally and simultaneously at odds with an external enemy and naturally its equal—if not its superior. Such conceptualization tends to generate strong emotions of fear and pride which is a fairly potent psychological cocktail. Driven by fear and pride to self-expression, oppositional nationalists develop a desire for nuclear weapons that go beyond rational calculations. For them, unlike the bulk of their peers, the choice of nuclear weapons is neither a close call nor a possible last resort but an absolute necessity. As a rule, a nationalist NIC leader is bolstered by a pride that can elevate his relative potential power perceptions, illusions of control, the need to act autonomously, and the goals of impressing others to reinforce his own ideas.[35]

Though other Iranian leaders might have been less verbally belligerent, in Hymans's view, they all shared the oppositional nationalist concept of "us against them"—a notion embedded in the foundational ethos of the Islamic Republic. A nationalist NIC also meant a sense of entitlement and status equality captured by the KOC measurements. Nationalist NICs mean that a leader's pride can lead to the need to act autonomously, to develop illusions of control and higher relative potential power perceptions and to pursue the goals of impressing others to reinforce his own ideas.[36] Even political opponents who have criticized Ahmadinejad's foreign policy behavior and his confrontational approach to nuclear issues have emphasized Iran's sovereign right to nuclear technology. For them, as for virtually all Iranians, the nuclear right is part of a metadiscourse on national identity. According to this narrative the Iranian people are among the few nations that can claim to be part of an ancient civilization that goes back several millennia. This glorious past is both a source of national pride and self-confidence and a sign that indicates Iran's potential to be a powerful actor in the future.[37]

There is little doubt that to the Principalists, like the Ayatollahs before them, the broad consensus formed around the nuclear issue was a welcome boost to the flagging legitimacy of the regime. Although the "rally-round-the-flag" pheromone was skillfully inserted into endless speeches and rallies the nuclear appeal went even deeper. Kayhan Barzegar, a political scientist at the Islamic Azad University, has pointed out that domestic critics have held the state responsible for the lack of development, the poverty, and the backwardness that go back two centuries. These and other critics have insisted that it has been the disastrous policies of the state that have prevented Iran from attaining the international power and prestige that it deserves. For the domestic audience the nuclear program is, in many ways, a symbol of technological advancement and—in the not-so-distant future—a ticket to a more respectable international status.[38]

Mass mobilization based on national pride, however, can only be sustained if the price of a program is reasonable. International sanctions have raised the cost of the nuclear project and this has led to a painful reevaluation of this cherished symbol of national identity.

NUCLEAR SANCTIONS: WHO IS WILLING TO PAY THE HIGH COST OF THE NATIONAL IDENTITY?

As is clear from the literature review the sanctions imposed upon Iran are designed to dissuade this target country from engaging in controversial behavior by raising its cost. When the illicit weapon program was revealed by the Mojahedin-e Khalq (MeK) in 2002, Hassan Rouhani, then chief nuclear negotiator, employed skillful diplomacy to delay the decision of the United Nations Security Council (UNSC) to impose sanctions on Iran. President Ahmadinejad's open defiance and belligerent proclamations about Iran's nuclear rights, however, changed the international mood. A number of UNSC resolutions: 1,696 on July 31, 2006; 1,737 on December 23, 2006; 1,747 on March 24, 2007; 1,803 on March 3, 2008; 1,835 on September 27, 2008; and 1,929 on June 9, 2010, then began to choke the Iranian economy. For a country whose budget was supported by oil income the sanctions have been particularly painful.

The sanctions have limited foreign investment in Iran, have slowed Iran's industrial and economic growth, and have dramatically shrunk the GDP. The inflation rate has increased to some 47 percent and the value of the currency has dropped dramatically with the purchasing power of the rial in 2014 shrinking to one third of its value in 2012. Unemployment statistics are equally depressing with the official unemployment rate declared to range from 10 to 15 percent but most analysts believe that the actual figures are more than double, particularly among young Iranians. The percentage of families living in poverty has risen from 22 percent to more than 40 percent and the humanitarian crisis is especially acute in sectors of the economy that are dependent on imports such as medicine. The cost of chemotherapy for cancer patients, for instance, has nearly tripled and the price of filters for kidney dialysis is up by 325 percent, just to mention a few examples. Such grim statistics have been widely disseminated in the public discourse along with sorrowful reflections on how many lives have been lost. To make matters worse the suffering has disproportionally affected the lower classes and, whereas in the past only a handful of critics doubted the wisdom of spending untold billions of dollars on what they called "a vanity" project, this growing "index of misery" began to erode the carefully constructed national identification with all things nuclear.[39]

When applied to the individual level the calculus of the rational-choice theory driving sanctions offers an explanation for the waning nuclear enthusiasm. Studies in political psychology indicate how, given certain circumstances, people may change dearly held beliefs including core national markers. Accordingly, all political beliefs receive a periodic reality test in a process involving *eudemonics,* a construct denoting a generalized sense of well-being. Eudemonics is a multivariate concept since it "simultaneously depends on the state of well-being of the self, the well-being of the reference group and some general norm of what well-being should be." Economics are known to have a universal impact on the sense of well-being and, as economic hardship takes a toll, individuals will reevaluate the cost of holding certain beliefs—even cherished ones. In other words, when the price of developing nuclear weapons became very high, as shown by the "misery index," an increased number of Iranians became ready to discard the nuclear nationalism that had been built into their core identity.[40]

Although public discussion on nuclear matters is heavily circumscribed by the government a number of polls bear out the above pattern. According to a 2007 survey sponsored by "Terror Free Tomorrow," a polling organization in Washington, almost 94 percent of Iranian people supported the country's right to develop nuclear energy. This survey claimed that "a majority of Iranians favored the development of nuclear weapons and believed that the people of Iran would live in a safer world if Iran possessed nuclear weapons."[41] Another survey conducted by Christine Fair and Stephen M. Shellman indicated that "more than 90 per cent said that it was very important for Iran's economy to develop the capacity to produce nuclear energy."[42] According to a January 2008 survey by the Program on International Policy Attitudes (PIPA) at the University of Maryland and by World Public Opinion, 87 percent of Iranian respondents strongly supported Iran's having "a full fuel cycle nuclear energy program."[43] A 2010 Rand Survey found that a whopping 87 percent of Iranians questioned strongly favored the "development of nuclear energy for civilian use" and 97 percent believed "the possession of nuclear energy to be a national right."[44]

By 2012, however, this broad consensus showed signs of erosion. Continued pressure and the rising cost of sanctions prompted a reevaluation of the once popular programs. When, in May 2013, the moderate politician Hassan

Rouhani won the presidential election by a large margin, Iran watchers linked the outcome to the decline of the economy. For example, Tom Donilon, former national security adviser to the Obama administration, noted that "there is a direct line here between the sanctions, Rouhani's election, and their coming to the table."[45] Another observer added that "hurt by sanctions and economic mismanagement, the majority of Iranians have chosen a moderate politician to engage with western countries and to reach a diplomatic solution to the problems Iran was encountering with its nuclear program."[46]

Subsequent surveys indicated a continued drop in support. A Gallup poll conducted on October 14, 2013, revealed that most Iranians still approved of a civilian nuclear program but by a significantly narrower margin with only 56 percent of respondents saying they supported the program, a decrease of 35 percent.[47] A survey of Iranian citizens conducted by the Institute for Policy and Strategy (IPS) at the Interdisciplinary Center in Herzliya, Israel, in May and June 2014, found that 54 percent of surveyed people would support dismantling the nuclear program in exchange for lifting international sanctions against Iran. Forty-five percent of respondents said that, in exchange for lifting sanctions, they would support removing Iran's capability to achieve nuclear weapons in the future.[48] Although the reliability of individual surveys carried out on Iran is sometimes questioned, it would seem that the aggregate trend is unmistakable. Overwhelmed by the "misery index" about half of the respondents were ready to trade the weapons project for a more prosperous future. Put in a theoretical way, a compromised sense of eudemonics has driven down the cost-benefit analysis of a degraded nuclear prowess from being a powerful symbol of national identity to being a less attractive choice.

Still, in Iran's authoritarian system, opinion has a limited input into foreign policy in general and nuclear issues in particular. From its very inception, the program has been highly elitist with a closed circle of politicians and Republican Guards making all the decisions. Communications, as noted, have been top to bottom, with various officials using the program to bolster national pride. Publicly there has not been much change in this pattern. For instance Ali Larijani, the speaker of the Majlis, has stated: "Iran has a strategic perspective with respect to its nuclear program. When other nations of the region such as Egypt and Turkey have managed to progress, there is no reason why Iran shouldn't also be able to do so." Like his predecessors, Rouhani has highlighted the national identity fashioned around this indigenous technological progress. In a recent interview with CNN the president stated that, for the Iranian nation, nuclear technology is part of national pride and that the people are very sensitive to this. Rouhani stressed that "it is a part of our national pride, that nuclear technology has become indigenous, and recently we have managed to secure very considerable prowess with regards to the fabrication of centrifuges and not under any circumstances would Iran destroy any of its existing centrifuges."[49]

Public bravado aside, Iran's conduct during negotiations with the international community represented by the so-called P5+1 (a group of six world powers including United States, Great Britain, France, Russia, China, and Germany) indicates interest in curtailing the weapon parts of the program. During the interim state of the negotiations Iran agreed to some concessions in return for a limited lifting of the sanctions. As of this writing, it is not clear whether the regime will agree to give up its vision of a nuclear bomb. What is evident, however, is that the voice of the people speaking through the "misery index" has triggered a rethinking of the project and, with it, the shaping of Iran's national identity.

CONCLUSION

Iran's decades-long quest for a nuclear weapon fits the category of proliferation using a double agenda. Although security considerations, as espoused by Kenneth Waltz and the neorealists, have been paramount in launching the program, there are factors, other than security, that have been conceptualized by Scott Sagan as "secondary drivers" that have played a large role. Indeed national pride, scientific prowess, and Iran's standing in the international order have all been part of an effort to shape a national identity and thus bolster the legitimacy of the regime.

Elevating nuclear weapons to a prominent role in national identity reached a peak under Mahmoud Ahmadinejad. The president's oppositional defiance of the international order became part of a civil religion designed to bolster the sagging Islamist identity project. Rallying around the nuclear flag was considered to be an expedient way to divert attention away from the violence used to impose strict Islamic standards on an unwilling population. By all accounts this strategy was highly successful and produced a virtual public consensus for the continuation of the program.

Nuclear proliferation, however, is susceptible to international sanctions, and these have forced a painful cost-benefit analysis on decision makers. The turning of the nuclear project into a part of national identity has made it even harder for the Iranian regime to relinquish it without losing its own credibility. The misery index caused by the sanctions has, however, succeeded in undermining the sense of well-being of the population and has triggered a potentially larger threat of delegitimization to the regime. Faced with possible economic unrest the regime has been forced to consider scaling down its nuclear ambitions along with its effort to fashion a nuclear-centered national identity.

NOTES

1. The concept of anarchy is the foundation for realist, neorealist, and neoliberal international relations paradigms.
2. Scott D. Sagan, "Realist Perspectives on Ethical Norms and Weapons of Mass Destruction," in Sohail H. Hashmi and Steven Lee (eds.), *Ethics and Weapons of Mass Destruction: Religious and Secular Perspectives* (Cambridge, MA: Cambridge University Press, 2004), p. 74.
3. Robert J. Art and Kenneth N. Waltz, "Technology, Strategy, and the Uses of Force," in Robert J. Art and Kenneth N. Waltz (eds.), *The Use of Force: International Politics and Foreign Policy* 2nd ed. (Lanham, MD: University Press of America, 1983), pp. 6–7.
4. Robert P. Haffa, Ravi R. Hichkad, and Dana J. Johnson, "Deterrence and Defense in the Second Nuclear Age," *Northrop Grumman Analysis Center* (March 2009), p. 6.
5. Paul Bracken, "The Structure of the Second Nuclear Age," *Orbis, Foreign Policy Research Institute*, Vol 47, No 3, (2003), p. 405. Haffa et al., p. 6.
6. Scott D. Sagan, "Why Do States Build Nuclear Weapons?: Three Models in Search of a Bomb," *International Security*, Vol. 21, No. 3, (1996), p. 63. Gianna Gayle Amul, "Perceptions of the Other: Iran's National Identity and Nuclear Policy," *E-International Relations*, http://www.e-ir.info/2012/06/14/perceptions-of-the-other-irans-national-identity-and-nuclear-policy/, retrieved: June 14, 2012.
7. Victor D. Cha, "The Second Nuclear Age: Proliferation Pessimism versus Sober Optimism in South Asia and East Asia," *The Journal of Strategic Studies*, Vol. 24, No. 4 (2001), p. 85.
8. Jacques E. C. Hymans, *The Psychology of Nuclear Proliferation: Identity, Emotions and Foreign Policy*, (Cambridge: Cambridge University Press, 2006), pp. 22–23.
9. William H. Kaempfer, Anton D. Lowenberg, and William Mertens, "International Economic Sanctions against a Dictator," *Economics & Politics*, Vol. 16, No. 1 (2004), p. 40. Abel Escribà-Folch, "Authoritarian Responses to Foreign Pressure Spending, Repression, and Sanctions," *Comparative Political Studies*, Vol. 45, No. 6 (2012), p. 690. Elizabeth S. Rogers, "Using Economic Sanctions to Control Regional Conflicts," *Security Studies*, Vol. 5, No. 4 (1996), p. 53. Gary Clyde Hufbauer, Jeffrey J. Schott and Kimberly Ann Elliott, *Economic Sanctions Reconsidered: History and Current Policy*, (Washington DC: Peterson Institute, 1990), pp. 87–93. Daniel W. Drezner, "Five Myths about Sanctions," *The Washington Post*, http://www.washingtonpost.com/opinions/five-myths-about-sanctions/2014/05/02/a4f607b6-d0b4-11e3-9e25-188ebe1fa93b_story.html, retrieved: May 2, 2014.
10. Robert N. Bellah, "Civil Religion in America," *Daedalus*, Vol. 134, No. 4 (2005), pp. 40–55. Charles S. Liebman and Eliezer Don-Yihya, *Civil Religion in Israel: Traditional Judaism and Political Culture in the Jewish State*, (Berkeley, CA: University of California Press, 1983), p. 206. Marcela Cristi, *From Civil to Political Religion: The Intersection of Culture, Religion and Politics*, (Waterloo, ON: Wilfrid Laurier University Press, 2001), p. 35.
11. George W. Braswell, "Civil religion in Contemporary Iran," *Journal of Church and State*, Vol. 21, No. 2 (1979), p. 228. Robert E. Looney, *Iran at the End of the Century: A Hegelian Forecast*, (Lexington, MA: Lexington Books, 1977), p. 89.
12. Etel Solingen, *Nuclear Logics: Contrasting Paths in East Asia and the Middle East*, (Princeton, NJ: Princeton University Press, 2009), p. 165. Julian Dawson, *A Constructivist Approach to the US-Iranian Nuclear Problem*, (Alberta: University of Calgary, The Centre for Military and Strategic Studies, 2011), pp. 70–71.
13. Saideh Lotfian, "Nuclear Policy and International Relations," in Homa Katouzian and Mohamad Tavakoli (eds.), *Iran in the 21st Century: Politics, Economics, and Conflict* (London: Routledge, 2008), p. 159.
14. Ray Takeyh, *Guardians of the Revolution: Iran and the World in the Age of the Ayatollahs*, (London: Oxford University Press, 2009), pp. 18–20. Gordon Corera, *Shopping for Bombs: Nuclear Proliferation, Global Insecurity, and the Rise and Fall of the AQ Khan Network* (New York: Oxford University Press, 2006), pp. 60–62.
15. Fars News Agency, "Imam Khomeini's Reasons for Cease Fire," http://www.farsnews.com/newstext.php?nn=8507060230, retrieved: September 29, 2006. The origi-

nal letter was first published by ILNA, "Ayatollah Khomeini Confidential Letter, published by Hashemi Rafsanjani," *Iranian Labour News Agency*, September 29, 2006.

16. Charles C. Mayer, *National Security to Nationalist Myth: Why Iran Wants Nuclear Weapons*, (Los Angeles: Storming Media, 2004), p. 16; Shahram Chubin, "The Politics of Iran's Nuclear Program: Power, Politics, and US Policy," *The Iran Primer* (2010), http://iranprimer.usip.org/resource/politics-irans-nuclear-program, retrieved: September 15, 2014. Kasra Naji, *Ahmadinejad: The Secret History of Iran's Radical Leader* (Los Angeles: University of California Press, 2008), p. 118.

17. ILNA, "Ayatollah Khomeini Confidential Letter."

18. Akbar Hashemi Rafsanjani, *Payan-e Defa, Aghaz-e Bazsazi; Khaterate Ayatollah Hashemi Rafsanjani Dar Sal-e 1367* (The End of Defense, Start of Reconstruction; Memoir of 1988) (Tehran: Maaref-e Enghelab, 2011). Quoted by Leonard S. Spector, "Nuclear Proliferation in the Middle East: The Next Chapter Begins," in Efraim Karsh, Martin S. Navias, and Philip Sabin (eds.), *Non-Conventional-Weapons Proliferation in the Middle East* (New York: Oxford University Press, 1993), p. 143.

19. Behrouz Alikhani, "Popular War Songs and Slogans in the Persian Language during the Iran-Iraq War," *Cambio*, Vol. 3, No. 6 (December 2013), p. 212. Mahnia A. Nematollahi Mahani, "'Do Not Say They Are Dead': The Political Use of Mystical and Religious Concepts in the Persian Poetry of the Iran-Iraq War (1980–88)," PhD diss. (Leiden University, 2014), pp. 233–34.

20. Alikhani, p. 212.

21. Nematollahi Mahani, pp. 237–38.

22. Alon Ben-Meir, "Iran Will Become A Nuclear Power, Unless . . . ," *The Huffington Post*, http://www.huffingtonpost.com/alon-benmeir/iran-will-become-a-nuclea_b_4419902.html, retrieved: December 10, 2013.

23. Solingen, p. 165.

24. Ben-Meir, "Iran Will Become A Nuclear Power, Unless . . ."

25. Darius Shayegan, *Cultural Schizophrenia: Islamic Societies Confronting the West* (Syracuse, NY: Syracuse University Press, 1997), pp. 22–32. Lucian Stone, *Iranian Identity and Cosmopolitanism: Spheres of Belonging* (New York: Bloomsbury Academic, 2014), pp. 28–30. Arshin Adib-Moghaddam, *On the Arab Revolts and the Iranian Revolution: Power and Resistance Today* (New York: Bloomsbury Academic, 2013), pp. 151–55.

26. Seyyed Ali Khamenei, "20 Year National Vision," website of the Ministry of Economy and Financial Affairs, December 4, 2003, http://asl44.mefa.gov.ir/Portal/Home/Default.aspx?CategoryID=c08d0272-f684-4d5b-9836-bc13a45d04bb, retrieved: June 11, 2014.

27. Ofira Seliktar, *Navigating Iran: From Carter to Obama* (New York: Palgrave Macmillan, 2012), pp. 109–10.

28. Mahmoud Ahmadinejad, "In meeting with IRGC commanders" (September 11, 2007); Mahmoud Ahmadinejad, "In meeting with supreme council of Islamic propagation organization at Qom Seminary" (August 29, 2008), http://www.president.ir/fa/1949, retrieved: May 12, 2013. Hamid Molana, *Syasat Khareji Jomhory-e Islami-e Iran Dar Dawlat-e Ahmadinejad* (Iran's Foreign Policy during Ahmadinejad) (Tehran: Dadgostar, 2009), pp. 138–39.

29. Max Fisher, "9 Questions About Iran's Nuclear Program You Were Too Embarrassed to Ask," *The Washington Post*, November 25, 2013.

30. Farhad Rezaei, "Nuclear Proliferation and Nuclear Rollback: The Case of Iran," PhD thesis (University of Malaysia, KL), 2014, p. 250.

31. IRNA, "Ahmadinejad: Iran Will Continue Nuclear Program, Says Does Not Need US Help," *Islamic Republic News Agency*, June 26, 2005, http://www.nti.org/media/pdfs/iran_nuclear.pdf?_=1316542527, retrieved: May 12, 2013.

32. Mahmoud Ahmadinejad, "Masaaley-e Hastehee Iran Sahneye Taghabole Zibaeeha va Zeshtiha Bode Hast," September 9, 2007, http://www.president.ir/fa/6569, retrieved: June 11, 2014.

33. Seliktar, *Navigating Iran*, p. 148. Ali Akbar Dareini, "Iran Hits Milestone in Nuclear Technology," *Associated Press*, April 11, 2006.

34. Homeira Moshirzadeh, "Discursive Foundations of Iran's Nuclear Policy," *Security Dialogue*, Vol. 38, No. 4 (2007), p. 523. Kayhan Barzegar, "The Paradox of Iran's Nuclear Consensus," *World Policy Journal*, Vol. 26, No. 3 (Fall 2009), p. 22.

35. Hymans, pp. 33–34; Amul, *Perceptions of the Other*.

36. Hymans, pp. 25, 33–34.

37. Moshirzadeh, p. 538.

38. Kayhan Barzegar, "Iran's Nuclear Program: An Opportunity for Dialogue," *Center for Strategic Research*, May 2009, http://www.csr.ir/departments.aspx?lng=en&abtid=06&&depid=74&semid=1797, retrieved: July 14, 2014.

39. Seyed Hossein Mousavian, "Twelve Consequences of Sanctions on Iran," *Al-Monitor*, May 3, 2013, http://www.al-monitor.com/pulse/originals/2013/04/iran-sanctions-consequences-list.html#, retrieved: July 7, 2014. Uri Berliner, "Crippled By Sanctions, Iran's Economy Key In Nuclear Deal," *NPR.org*, November 25, 2013, http://www.npr.org/2013/11/25/247077050/crippled-by-sanctions-irans-economy-key-in-nuclear-deal, retrieved: July 7, 2014. Aljazeera, "Iran: The Real Cost of Sanctions," *Aljazeera.com*, June 5, 2013, http://www.aljazeera.com/programmes/insidestory/2013/06/201365928843270.html, retrieved: July 7, 2014. Rich Rubino, "The Counterproductive Effects of Leveling Sanctions on Iran," *Huffington Post*, June 2, 2013, http://www.huffingtonpost.com/rich-rubino/the-counterproductive-eff_b_2578434.html, retrieved: July 7, 2014. Beheshteh Farshneshani, "In Iran, the Wrong People Are Suffering," *New York Times*, January 22, 2014, http://www.nytimes.com/roomfordebate/2013/11/19/sanctions-successes-and-failures/in-iran-sanctions-hurt-the-wrong-people, retrieved: July 7, 2014. PBS, "Economic sanctions have tangible consequences for average Iranians," *PBS Newshour*, February 10, 2014. http://www.pbs.org/newshour/bb/economic-sanctions-have-tangible-consequences-average-iranians/, retrieved: May 25, 2014. IIPJHR, "The Impact of Sanctions on the Iranian People's Healthcare System," *Global Research*, October 18, 2013, http://www.globalresearch.ca/the-impact-of-sanctions-on-the-iranian-peoples-healthcare-system/5354773, retrieved: May 25, 2014.

40. Ofira Seliktar, *Failing the Crystal Ball Test: The Carter Aadministration and the Fundamentalist Revolution in Iran* (Westport, CT: Praeger, 2000), p. 11.

41. Terror Free Tomorrow, "Polling Iranian Public Opinion: An Unprecedented Nationwide Survey of Iran," Washington, DC, June 5–18, 2007, http://www.angusreidglobal.com/wp-content/uploads/archived-pdf/Iran_TFT.pdf, retrieved: June 11, 2014.

42. Christine Fair and Stephen M. Shellman, "Determinants of Popular Support for Iran's Nuclear Program: Insights from a Nationally Representative Survey," *Contemporary Security Policy*, Vol. 29, No. 3 (2008), p. 544.

43. World Public Opinion, "Poll of Iranians and Americans," *Worldpublicopinion.org*, February 9, 2008, http://www.worldpublicopinion.org/pipa/pdf/apr08/Iran_Apr08_quaire.pdf, retrieved: June 11, 2014.

44. Alireza Nader and Sara Beth Elson, "What Do Iranians Think? A Survey of Attitudes on the United States, the Nuclear Program, and the Economy," *Rand*, http://www.rand.org/content/dam/rand/pubs/technical_reports/2011/RAND_TR910.pdf, retrieved: June, 11, 2014.

45. Jason Seher, "Ex-national Security Adviser: 'Direct line' between Iran Sanctions and Rouhani's Election," *CNN*, December 1, 2013, http://politicalticker.blogs.cnn.com/2013/12/01/ex-national-security-adviser-direct-line-between-iran-sanctions-and-rouhanis-election/, retrieved: May 12, 2014.

46. Hashem Pesaran, "Iran Sanctions: Now Is the Time to Negotiate," *The Guardian*, September 17, 2013, http://www.theguardian.com/world/2013/sep/17/world-powers-negotiate-nuclear-iran, retrieved: June 25, 2014. Mousavian, "Twelve Consequences of Sanctions on Iran."

47. Jay Loschky and Anita Pugliese, "Iranians Split, 40% to 35%, on Nuclear Military Power, Gallup," February 15, 2012, http://www.gallup.com/poll/152633/Iranians-Split-Nuclear-Military-Power.aspx, retrieved: July 9, 2014.

48. "Survey finds majority of Iranians would give up nuclear program," *The Global Jewish News Source*, June 8, 2014, http://www.jta.org/2014/06/08/news-opinion/israel-middle-east/survey-finds-majority-of-iranians-would-give-up-nuclear-program, retrieved: July 19, 2014.

49. Ariane Tabatabai, "Iran's Evolving Nuclear Narrative," *Iran Matters*, Harvard's Belfer Center, February 7, 2014, http://iranmatters.belfercenter.org/blog/irans-evolving-nuclear-narra-

tive, retrieved: June 18, 2014. TheTower.org Staff, "CNN Host Describes Diplomatic 'Train Wreck' as Iran President Rules Out Dismantling Nuclear Centrifuges," *The Tower*, January 24, 2014, http://www.thetower.org/cnn-host-describes-diplomatic-train-wreck-iran-president-rules-dismantling-nuclear-centrifuges/&strip=1, retrieved: July 7, 2014.

Chapter Five

Overcoming "the –isms"

The Iranian's Role in the Modern World, from the Perspective of Mahmūd Ahmadi-nezhād

Moshe-hay S. Hagigat

PROLOGUE

Bism-i-llah `Ar-Rahman `Ar-Rahim,
`Al-Khamd-ol-i-llaah-I Rab `Al-Alemin Wa `As-salat Wo `As-salam Ala Seyied-o-na Wa Nabi-o-na Mohammad, Wa Ahl `At-taherin Wa Sahb `Al-montajebin,
`Allah-o-ma Ajal Le-Valiak-o `Al-faraja Wa `Al-aafia-ta Wa `An-nasr, Wa Jaalna Min Kheir-o Ansari-hi Wa Aawaneh Wa `Al-mostashhadina Bein-a Yadai-h

In the name of God, the Most Gracious, the Most Merciful,
With thanksgiving and with praise to God [with] the prayers and the peace [that they should be] upon our Master and Prophet Muhammad and upon His pure family and His chosen friends.
[May] Allah quicken the arrival of the "Vali," the redeemer, and give health and triumph to those reliant upon him and that we shall be [among] his best supporters and helpers and "Shaheeds."

Mahmūd Ahmadi-nezhād begins all his utterances with these words and, while he served as the president of Iran, every TV interview and every conversation with the Iranian or other people in the world opened with the Iranian president mentioning the Seal of the Prophets, his family members, and his successors—the Shi'ite Imams. His words also refer to that which is to come, the "Vali" of God—the Mehdi, he who will bring good into the world and success to his believers.

83

INTRODUCTION

The chapter ahead will deal with Mahmūd Ahmadi-nezhād's Islamic identity
from his own point of view, and the relevance of that identity to our times—a
period of time in history that he believes is critical for every single Muslim
and the Muslims as an Ummah. Religious matters concern him as an Islamic
monotheist, a member of the Shi'a denomination, someone with Iranian heritage, and one who has played a senior political role in his country. Here it
should be noted that, for the most part, when Ahmadi-nezhād talks about the
term "Islam" he especially means its Shi'a denomination.

Ahmadi-nezhād's religious doctrine is the cornerstone of all his doctrines,
including the political and the economic as well as all the other various and
different views he holds. In his speeches he treats the subject of religion as a
sort of invisible "Archimedean point" on which he relies for his other viewpoints. With each idea he adheres to and with each position he expresses,
from the smallest and lightest to the most serious, Ahmadi-nezhād always
turns to the religious ideas of Khomeinistic-Shi'ite-Islam from which to draw
his solutions. At the same time Ahmadi-nezhād also makes mention of the
various ideas and theories originating from the West and dismisses them
derisively. He calls the ruling contemporary conceptions or paradigms "the
–isms" (*ism-ha*, meaning Western colonialism, militarism, paternalism, capitalism, humanism, liberalism, etc.) and considers them to be outdated concepts that most people should abandon. [1]

Ahmadi-nezhād's religious doctrine centers upon messianic doctrine that
sees the Mehdi as a messianic figure who, according to Ahmadi-nezhād, and
Shi'ia Islam as a whole, may not yet have revealed himself to humanity but is
certainly wandering among us and waiting for the right time to declare his
presence. The believers must anticipate his appearance and take actions that,
on the one hand, will hasten his arrival and, on the other hand, upon his
revelation, will endow his conduct on earth with meaning. [2] Ahmadi-nezhād
also combines belief in the Mehdi as a criterion that is an advantage for the
Shi'ite Iranian nation over the nations of Islam in particular and the rest of
humanity in general. Because of this the Iranian people's task is to lead the
entire world into the right monotheistic faith of Islam and bring salvation to
all the world's inhabitants. This salvation will be expressed by the existence
of peace between the nations and be the chosen approach by the government's clerics. [3] Ahmadi-nezhād tried to implement his doctrine while he was
president and in charge of the governmental hierarchy but he believed that,
until the Mehdi comes, it is the duty of the believers to anticipate him, to
obey his instructions, [4] and to do this with active anticipation. [5]

Ahmadi-nezhād's religious doctrine includes and encompasses many various topics from the specific to the general including ideas that deal with
morality, personal and familial justice, social justice, national justice, policy,

and society. The Iran which Ahmadi-nezhād tried to present during his time in office does not oppose other monotheistic faiths but sees the Islamic Republic as a country guided by the perfect religion which holds perfect solutions to every problem and, more than that, is a country which can, and should, take upon itself the moral leadership of the world. Since Iran, according to this, does not oppose Christianity or Judaism, there is no country more suitable to lead such a global development. For Ahmadi-nezhād all those who talk about a collision between Iran and Christianity or Judaism represent "the stance of the enemies of Iran." This, he believes, is a stance that has been forced upon the rest of the world, a stance that maintains that there is a conflict between the views held by Shi'ite Islamic Iran and Christianity or Judaism, which is not at all true.[6]

MAN'S ROLE IN THE WORLD

Ahmadi-nezhād's guiding principle is belief in God and in God's dominion over the world, but he also believes that man stands at the center of the world and provides the justification for its existence. It is man who conducts his affairs and his life on the ground of the earth in the sense that "the heaven, even the heavens, are the LORD's: but the earth hath he given to the children of men."[7] Just as the whole of Ahmadi-nezhād's thinking is, for him, driven by religious elements, so do the existence of man in the world, his qualities, and his role all stem from religious thought. His central claim, which for him serves as a religious starting point, is that man is the crown and center of divine creation. "All that God has created, has been created for the children of men,"[8] says Ahmadi-nezhād.

His claim is that the nature of all humans is essentially divine. All people seek to worship God even if they are not among those who practice monotheism. "It matters not whether you are American, German, French, Iranian, Jordanian, Iraqi, or Palestinian, or from any other place in the world," he says. In any place in the world where there are people, the wills and inclinations are similar and aim at reaching divine perfection and exaltation.[9] Ahmadi-nezhād also measures the world according to the importance of those created by God when he says:

> God created the entirety of this creation for man, and he placed man in the most honored position from amongst all the creatures created, and he set it so that man will live upon this planet in a dignified and happy way.

According to this, man, that marvelous "divine creation" (*khalaqiat*), holds the highest place, and all creatures have a sense of honor towards him. This respect is the first and foremost thing that exists and is what God's creations must apply to themselves. Mutual honor is a divine creation which embodies God's caliphate, his character, his might, and the rest of his good qualities. This means that disrespecting them and disrespecting man is also a direct affront to God. [10]

Ahmadi-nezhād, in fact, says that "this is the time for the revelation of that same divine thinking, for this thinking means man's honor," which means that the basic human rights given to man by God at the time of creation are a divine externalization of the practical respect for the rights of all people, in addition to the acceptance and actualization of true freedom. He adds that there is also a need for external expressions of compassion, love, brotherhood, and friendship between all of God's creations, [11] and emphasizes this by saying:

> Man is the most valuable thing and if man were not to exist, the whole of worldwide creation (*khelqat-e alam*) would have been left without reason or any understanding . . . man should exist to produce benefit from the beauty of the world, to discover the magnitudes and the abilities (of the world) and use them for his needs. [12]

From Ahmadi-nezhād's words it is thus possible to see that his approach can be divided into two. The first part is cosmic and, according to it, God is the whole of the universe. He created mankind and his presence exists and constitutes the powers that fill the world. The second part is earthly and his approach here is anthropocentric. Ahmadi-nezhād places man at the center of creation to such a degree that he sees man as the only justification for the existence of the world and without him there would have been no reason for God's act of creating the world. The very existence of religious, political, or social doctrines depends on the existence of man.

According to Ahmadi-nezhād the roots of the religious Islamic belief as a theory is related to the conception of religious faith within Iran itself. He believes that in Iran, from the religious-ideological perspective, there is no difference or "contradiction" (*taqaboli*) between the conscience and faith of people, and receiving individual rights and freedom. In other words, the religious faith prevailing in Iran, based on the principles of the Islamic Revolution, is also the theory—the "–ism"—in which it believes. He promises that whoever follows the ideas this conception presents, and the different points of view it raises, will be able to see that "the circle of [those] going" (*dayere hamrah*) hand in hand with the ideas of the Iranian nation is large. [13]

Let us return to the matter of human honor. Ahmadi-nezhād claims that Iran opposes "perversion, exploitation, ransacking, and the crushing of human honor and the honor of God, no matter who does it." [14] Accordingly he places the honor of man, any man, together with the honor of God, and, if one places importance on the word order of the sentence, he even places the honor of man before that of his God. It is also possible to see his recurring attempts to make the Iranian approach, which is opposite to the Western approach and has been in existence for decades, distinct. This is the same Western approach which he claims belittles and disrespects both the honor of God and the honor of man. The disrespect for God's honor is evident in the way the Western approach questions God's existence.[15] On the other hand, the disrespect for humans is evident in the West's approach towards all people. Ahmadi-nezhād's consistent claim is that the colonial West has disrespected many people over hundreds, and even thousands, of years.[16]

Ahmadi-nezhād also mentions human rights in the national domain, which often coincides with the international dimension, in which Iran is in a state of conflict with the Western powers. His approach maintains that, if the country is deprived, then it is not merely a problem for its leaders but a problem of each and every one of the citizens. Each citizen might suffer a loss of security or might be hurt economically, socially, and ecologically. Because of this, when Ahmadi-nezhād binds together the honor of man with international relations, his intention is the ultimate end—the individual human being hurt by what is done against the country or the authority or even God.

At the time that Ahmadi-nezhād founded his first government he placed the following four core principles at the center of its activity to constitute guidelines for action that would lead the government.[17]

1. The Expansion of Justice. Ahmadi-nezhād claims that the worth of man, as a product of divine creation, is realized from the establishment of personal as well as social justice. He says that personal and social justice cannot be seen only in the relations between people inside Iran. Rather, they go beyond Iran and into the global environment. In other words, as long as there is one country being deprived, compared to others, not just the country as an institutional object is being deprived. It is also all the individual citizens of that country who are being deprived and whose human rights are being affected negatively. Because of this, Ahmadi-nezhād feels it is right to expand the concept of human justice into the international sphere. Personal justice is therefore seen as being realized in the human rights of every person since the divine creation. In the meantime social justice is expressed by observing the honor of every individual, based on the basic rights given to him as a human and as a creation of God.[18] In this way he binds the honor of man together with both his social rights and the basic rights of the Iranian nation, both as a national collective and as individuals belonging to the same collective.

2. Grace. The idea of justice, an idea whose ramifications are wide and include love, grace, compassion, and service to others, is found in the spirit of the four principles of actions which will later lead to the advancement and prosperity of the society. Ahmadi-nezhād claims that doing grace is the ideal found in the five commandments a Muslim must perform in his life. This spirit also includes mutual aid, and its integration with the four principles is what will enable the idea to become an action in the service of others. He sees the action of doing grace as an ancient ideal which has been part of Islam since the days of the Qur'an and which he claims that stems from the culture of anticipating the Mehdi; and, while the principle of mutual aid was abandoned along with the entire culture of anticipation, he sees the duty of his government to offer restoration on this matter—as well as others.

3. *Service to Others*. Mutual aid, something the Ahmadi-nezhād government places great emphasis upon, is an important injunction from which the matter of giving service to others also derives. According to Ahmadi-nezhād both of the above are derived from the Islamic injunction mentioned in the Qur'an which commands people to be "merciful among themselves."[19] His perception is that the majority of the problems faced by the Iranian people today and the majority of the struggles against the implementation of the Iranian revolutionary message stem from this and derive mainly from the abandonment of the principle of the culture of anticipation for the Mehdi, whose essential message is the creation of a world of good, in which compassion and love rule together with justice.[20]

4. *The Advancement and Elevation of Society*. The advancement of society, according to Ahmadi-nezhād, can only be realized through Islam, which will not only advance man and society but will raise them to new heights. Ahmadi-nezhād explains that it has always been those who have tied their fate to the Prophet Muhammad, from the time he was alive to the present days, who are the ones who have enjoyed all the goods of the world. Because of this any society or any man in search of what is good for the self will choose the path of Islam and take the high road that elevates humans and guides them to the good. Eventually that person will bring good to the world and other positive things for the society in which he lives.[21]

THE CENTRALITY OF JUSTICE

With the establishment of his government, Ahmadi-nezhād asked its members to embrace these principles, to "make them dominant" (*gholbe bedahad*) and part of the internal life of Iran. In this way the citizens of Iran, followed by the rest of humanity, will really look at society from the point of view of justice and then all people will be able to place the world's ruling regimes "under doubt" (*zir-e soal bordan*).[22] We have seen his claim that God created all men equal, but he explains that the reason for wars and killings in the world is that there are people who feel that they are entitled to privileges and treatment superior to than others. This lack of equality, he claims, derives mainly from disrespecting basic social conditions and lacks many of the motifs that derive from the justice that should prevail in the world. In addition he writes, "In our time there are people and groups demanding for themselves above and beyond, and they themselves do not obey the law and are not directed by justice [*adalat-ra nemi taband*]."[23]

The repetition of the term "justice" in Ahmadi-nezhād's utterances emphasizes that nations which do not adhere to justice and do not follow the path of religion, faith, and divine reflection are bound to be destroyed, since only the path of religion is the path of freedom and justice. In regard to this matter he presents the example of the threats of the nations of the West which he says take strong measures against countries they view as weaker. This testifies to "the arrival to an end" (*be payan-e khat residan*) of the capitalistic regimes and liberalistic darkness and, as he claims, to the fact that their disappearance from the world is a "done deal." He says:

> Those that came and spoke of "the end of history," and announced the end of the religions and beliefs, and the divine cogitation, all of these should know that they are the ones whose time has run out. . . . Today is the time for the revelation of divine thinking, because this thinking means the honor of man. . . . Its meaning is the crushing (*leh kardan*) of occupation, aggression and egotism. Its meaning is the raising of the flag (*parcham bardari*) of brotherhood between all nations . . . and the end of the ruling thinking of occupation, aggression, killing and terror.

In other words those who have announced that there is no more place for drawing closer to God and wanting him are the ones who no longer have a place. The importance of God is personified in all the good that he has given man.[24]

These things strengthen man's deep notions concerning divine thought whose function in the creation of man is to elevate him and his place upon earth. Yet the opposite causativeness also exists in his perception, which is to say that man himself was created to implement the honor and glorification of God. Man's earthly position cannot, therefore, remain static but is rather destined to progress and advance divine creation throughout the years and generations. All of this man will do by appropriating the use of the mind given to him by God.[25] This belief in the reciprocal relations found between man and his God is what guides Ahmadi-nezhād who claims that the development of man is part of the godly commandment. Because of this commandment, there are also obligations towards God that parallel the rights given to man[26]; and man must use all of the tools that God gave him to conduct his life on earth, because the world was created for him. In the Jewish perspective we could have said that Ahmadi-nezhād's words are in the spirit of "to dress it and to keep it."[27] For him "justice and the maintaining of the honor of man, these are the two pillars (*rokn-e asasi*) in the keeping of sustainable peace, security and serenity in the world."[28]

Ahmadi-nezhād claims that man is not born as a clean slate but only begins to choose the path he will take for the rest of his life. Man, according to him, is born with a certain path which he develops and which becomes stronger from the day of his birth in order to make it possible for him to reach that desired perfection.[29] That is also why God gave man a mission which is found in the effort of each human being to know his talents and bring them into perfection—both on the personal level and on the communal-social level. This is the goal of bringing a happier life to all humankind and perfection to all the other living creatures on earth.[30]

So, what are the obligations of man towards God? Ahmadi-nezhād says that the Muslims, especially the modern Shi'ites, whose identity has been shaped over the centuries, have been tasked with the greatest responsibility the world has ever seen. "The hearts are thirsty and humanity seeks an enlightened path (*rah-e nourani*)." Yet "this path is currently held only by the monotheists, the God-fearing persons, those dedicating God's name as one, and those submissive to the commandments of God (*movahedan, khoda-parastan va yegane-parastan va kasani ast ke taslim-e amr-e khoda has-tand*)."[31] Another thing expected, is the constant desire and aspiration of each Muslim to reach "the peak of human perfection" (*qole kamal-e ensani*), that which is "based on the enlightened existence of the precious prophet of Islam" (*vojud-e nazanin-e payambar-e gerami-e eslam*).[32] In other words one must always ask to reach the same divine-spiritual perfection attained by Muhammad.

THE ROLE OF THE IRANIANS IN STRENGTHENING THE SPIRIT OF ISLAM

According to Ahmadi-nezhād, the way to lead and manage the world is through the cultural activity of the Iranian people. From the very beginning Islam arose in order to manage the world and the Iranians, as Muslims, are not ashamed to declare this aloud. He even wonders why there are those in the world who declare that they are committed to none of the world's acceptable rules of morality when, in contrast, the Iranians need to hesitate about declaring aloud that they oppose such declarations? Why are there people who combine morality with comprehensive political and economic matters, who try to spread a new religion which in fact believes in nothing but stands in opposition to the monotheistic idea? Ahmadi-nezhād wonders how they can attack the Iranian people, whose culture goes back in time for thousands of years, for wishing to replace them in leading the world.[33]

Irrespective of Ahmadi-nezhād's praise for the Iranian nationality and identity he still claims that the cornerstone upon which Iran was built is Islam—from before the Islamic Revolution and in a clearer and more pronounced way after it. All the efforts and activities of the Iranian people should, he believes, eventually lead to that human perfection. This kind of perfection is a clear Islamic worldview and, after all, Iran's culture and identity are based on this religion. "If the religious faith will weaken, the Iranian culture and the important motifs inside it, like literature and poetry (*adabiyat va shoar*), art and wisdom (*honar va erfan*), self-sacrifice and effort (*isar va jehad*), love and compassion (*eshq va mohabat*), shall all weaken too," he claims.[34]

Islam, as has clearly been seen in Ahmadi-nezhād's words many times, is a religion whose laws, if implemented, spread its light throughout the entire world. If the believers of Islam do not obey and practice the laws of the religion then Islam will collapse. The absence of the worship of God in the life of a Muslim will turn him into dust at the feet of those who blaspheme against God as well as into a plaything in schemes planned against Muslims, as has happened before.[35] Ahmadi-nezhād puts it in his own words like this:

> This is the essence of our words for all those in dialogue with us. There is a need to return to God, to the rule of Islam and the light spreading implementation of Islam (*bayad be khoda, hakemiyat-e eslam va ahkam-e nourani-e eslam bargardim*), or else—all will crash. This is a natural thing, for if the worship of God does not exist, we Muslims will not agree to be dust at the feet of the infidels while life will be Godless, [we will not agree] also to their propaganda, their conspiracy and their plans.[36]

Ahmadi-nezhād asserts that he who wishes to lead an Islamic life that aims at ruling the world one day should return to God and spread the light of Islam.

THE RESOURCES OF ISLAM

As noted earlier Ahmadi-nezhād calls for the replacement of failing Western ideologies with the "light spreading" ideas of Islam and claims that this call actually derives from the demands of enlightened people—the free people of science. Islam, he believes, provides the answer for all of God's creatures whether they be part of the nation of Islam or people of the western world who are seeking solutions to their dilemmas, ways to quench their thirst for new and progressive ideas and the satisfaction of man's basic needs. "The free school" (*maktab-e rahayi*) of the world of Islam can, he claims, satisfy such high demands in a proper way since the Islamic world of today has a variety of spiritual and material solutions to satisfy all the needs of the human race,[37] all of which will come from the same source—the Qur'an.

According to Ahmadi-nezhād man was created by God to develop and improve the initial divine creation so that "man will reach the peak of perfection, meaning the level of divine caliphate (*khalife elahi*)" when he walks upon the earth which God created.[38] Ahmadi-nezhād who will draw upon the Qur'an for the solutions to his problems will quench his religious thirst during his life on the earth created by God so that he may reach the highest peaks. He asserts that humans are in fact God's messengers and representatives on earth and that the prophets are those whose task is to guide them throughout the generations. As he puts it:

> God has placed men to serve as his substitutes (*janeshin-e khod*) upon earth, so that those sons of him will discover the divine qualities and names with the help of intelligence, the guidance of the prophets, the effort and the diligence.[39]

This means that the prophets and leaders have been and are the prophets of Islam from Adam to Muhammad and then to their successors—the Imams, from 'Ali 'ibn-'Abi Talib to the Mehdi. By virtue of the guidance of those sent by God, who lead the world, knowledge, wisdom, beauty, power, and the rest of the divine qualities will be able to blossom among those who substitute for God's presence upon earth, and glorify God's name.

Thus God has imprinted in men the will and motivation to reach and demand the truth, to seek God and perfection. This is also why humanity is always in search of truth, justice, knowledge, and the rest of the good qualities. He says "man is a seeker of perfection (*kamal jou*) who demands truth and justice, and the entirety of humanity seeks purity and honesty . . . lasting peace and security will not exist unless founded upon justice, honesty and purity. Otherwise all of humanity will suffer from oppression, discrimination, ignorance, and poverty which will endanger their honor, their personalities, and in fact, their existence."[40] Without perfection not only is the existence of Islam uncertain but also the continuing existence of man (practically and morally), and even worse, the existence of God for man, being the crown of creation, is the proof of God's existence. Man's perfection is the evidence that God's way is just.

Ahmadi-nezhād maintains that, among other things given to man by God, he has been given the desire to investigate the truth[41] so that he can utilize the potential inherent in the entire creation and use his God-given abilities in ways that make him superior to every other thing created. Ahmadi-nezhād explains this in the following words: "I believe that this entire creation (*afarinesh*) has a meaning when inside it exists assertive intelligence, searching, the abundance of talent and an atmosphere of perfection in a similar way for all of humanity, or else, all the potential that is in the water, the earth, the trees and the rest of the beautiful things, is meaningless."[42] Carrying all of this is man's burden on his way to improve the world as a messenger of God whose intention is to spread God's word.

THE ROLE OF THE MUSLIM

We can find five central points in Ahmadi-nezhād's speeches which, basically, are demands made of Muslims and a description of the goals to which the members of the nation of Islam should aspire. In the first point Ahmadi-nezhād refers to the subject of the place of Islam and the role of the Muslim:

"*1. The belief in God, the Precious Prophet and the Holy Qur'an*: The Islamic faith has always been a safe and motivational pillar of support (*noqte etekayi-e motmaen va angize anande*), as well as an endless source of unity, hope and happiness (*manba-e bi payan-e vahdat, omid va neshat*) for the Muslims."[43]

Accordingly, since Islam descended into the world, faith in this religion has been the only way for all people to solve all the problems of the past, the present, and those that will appear in the future. A belief in Islam is the only safe thing a person can lean on, to feel secure and even from which one can draw encouragement for the continuation of one's life upon the creator's earth. The good that descended into the world together with Islam attached itself to the believers of this religion and, by spreading it throughout the other nations, this good will also bring inexhaustible joy and happiness to humanity.

The need to awaken men and make them march in the direction of Islam is one of today's clear interests for the believers of Islam. The spreading of Islam and the revolution are part of Khomeini's vision which spoke of the Islamic Revolution as "an explosion of light" (*enfejar-e nour*)[44] —the light of Islam. The Iranian people have been given the task of shining this light forward into all possible realms whether they be political, social (inside Iran or globally), or economic. It is the achievement of success in the implementation of the two first stages of accepting and spreading Islam, together with an intermediate stage involving the victory of the Iranian school whose core is knowledge and wisdom, which will unite the world and repair it.

"*2. The growth of the Islamic awakening and the participation of the people in different spheres*: Thanks to the Almighty God, the growth of Islam today, together with the participation and sensitivity—which are growing every day—of the nation of Islam in the political and social spheres are a gain that cannot be estimated or divided."[45] That's it: the growth of Islam is a gain.

The growth of Islam already exists among us and is taking place before the bewildered eyes of those who adhere to Western schools of thought: "the –isms."[46] The stories Ahmadi-nezhād tells about his travels to different parts of the world, and his attitude to this growth as part of "the second wave of the revolution (*mouj-e dovom-e enqelab*),"[47] also serve, for him, as proof that the light of the revolution has indeed burst forth and scattered in all directions. The perceptions which he recounts concerning the attitudes he has encountered towards the spiritual teacher of the entire revolution, Khomeini, testify that the ideas behind the Islamic Revolution still exist. He refers to ideas concerning the superiority of Islam, the need to spread it and let it expand, and the objections he has to the Western conventions that contrast with the Islamic or revolutionary spirit. All these ideas and others, he argues, can and should lead to a revolution of thought when they are confronted with any other dominant perception.

"*3. The scientific progress and advancement*: The growth of science in the Islamic world is growing and the existence of educators, lecturers and the creative youth who have passion and joy in studying scientific subjects gives [The *Ummah*] great hope and is one of the strong pillars of the nation of Islam."[48]

Ahmadi-nezhād emphasizes the subject of education and knowledge over and over again. An improvement in the state of education and science of the members of the nation of Islam is what will constitute the starting point towards succeeding in the spread of Islam to other people, in a nonviolent way. The desired unity between the nations of Islam and the under-developed and deprived countries of the world is what will help create a critical mass in other spheres as well, especially in the political sphere. This mass will sweep with it the enlightened people who seek a change from the failing methods employed by the West and will also be the main and massive counterbalance to the ruling power, and the ideologies they represent. He believes that "Capitalism and Marxism," which once constituted "a pair of blades from the same scissors" (*beyin-e do tigh-e gheyichi-e marksism va sarmayie-dari*),[49] are no longer what they used to be and that men are thirsty for new political, and especially scientific, conceptions.

To him, the fact that the power centers in the world are in the hands of aggressive and cultureless nations that have no true religious belief and deny the religion of Islam or question the unified oneness of God is a negative and even destructive thing. This is also true of all the different "–isms" which, he claims, are actually the same, with colonialism and Western paternalism are the most negative of them all. He says:

> The best condition for the entirety of humanity are that those people who love culture, and knowledge and believe in thinking will control the human power centers . . . from here also stem the problems of humanity, when the central decision making centers of the world fall into the hands of people who have no understanding in culture in its many forms, whatsoever.[50]

He criticizes those who use their power and property solely to accomplish superiority over others and, in contrast to the West, his approach to the Iranian nation also manifests itself in the following statement: "At the time that the Iranian nation was the banner-carrier of science, and thousands of academics were educated under its patronage, you (the West) have lived at the Stone Age. While the Iranians excelled in physics, architecture, engineering, art and craft, you did not yet know what the act of taking a shower is" (*shoma hanouz nemi danestid hamam chist*).[51] Iran to him is the cradle of civilization, the one that brought culture and proper behavior codes to both the old and modern world. Those countries of the West that have existed for a short while should have no monopoly regarding cultural matters at all. Religion is defined by Ahmadi-nezhād as culture and because of that he who is not a monotheist is by definition also without culture and his behavior is aggressive.

"*4. The vast resources*: In addition to the existence of vast resources personified by the believing, intelligent men and the men of thought, we have in our possession also lands in which accumulated varied resources including forests, seas, minerals and energy, this in comparison to scarce political and geographical conditions."[52]

At this point Ahmadi-nezhād's sets out his broad conception of the unity of Islam based on the understanding that the nation of Islam possesses different resources from different disciplines. In a certain way this understanding is Ahmadi-nezhād's call to the children of the nation of Islam to unite and combine forces and this arises out of the basic goal of the entire Islamic Revolution—to ultimately bring Islam to the more remote corners of the world.

In his words, however, there is also an indirect reference to messianic-religious matters as well as to political matters as Ahmadi-nezhād clarifies his approach concerning the revelation of the Mehdi. He says that this revelation should occur after the development of all those undeveloped resources by the sons of the nation of Islam and that all the above is a preparation for that future messianic revelation. For centuries many Shi'ites have sat and waited as a silenced and exploited minority sect for the revelation of the Mehdi. This order of things, in which the Shi'ites were under the rule of others is, he claims, no longer valid due to the model of the Islamic Revolution and the Shi'ite awakening brought forth by Khomeini.[53] As for Ahmadi-nezhād, himself, he thinks there is a need to become more active in all the different matters required by Islam whose goal is to awaken the hearts and bring forth the arrival of the Mehdi into a reformed world in which Islam already rules and all its resources are being utilized.

"*5. [Islam's] culture and cultural past:*" Ahmadi-nezhād believes that Islam is a perfect religion and that the Qur'an is the cure for the suffering of humanity since it provides solutions for comprehensively coping with economic, social, political, and cultural matters. This is consistent with Islamic thought which is filled with principles and values such as monotheism, love, honoring human rights, charity and sacrifice, helping the weak, the treatment of children, honoring women, preserving honor and the honor of man, creating work and effort, production and the dissemination of knowledge and science, the search for justice, and the fight against exploitation and injustice.[54]

Again, Ahmadi-nezhād emphasizes that should all the Muslims in the world unite they will have the power to achieve a higher status than the one they have today and, perhaps, even have the possibility to gain control over the world. Such a unity would give the Muslims the place that they deserve, especially at this time in history when Islam is growing and there is a great awakening among the religion's believers.[55] Apart from the human and material resources that the Islamic countries are blessed with, and which have been mentioned above, all the rest is "pure Islam" (*eslam-e nab*). Ahmadi-nezhād believes that returning to "pure Islam," as he sometimes refers to it, or "the pure Islam of Muhammad" (*eslam-e nab-e mohamadi*), as he refers to it at other times, is the only way to save humankind and solve the problems of the world. What combines all of these ideas about what the right treatment is for the maladies of the whole world and what is needed for the comprehensive coping with mankind's various challenges, is the faith that Islam is what can solve all of these problems.

Since the Islamic Revolution, according to Ahmadi-nezhād, Iran has become the focus of the West's criticism which has prevented it from spreading its ideas concerning matters of repairing the maladies of the world. The reason that Iran has been chosen to be the focus of the West's enmity is, he claims, obvious, for Iran represents "a clear cultural burning point."[56] That is, this is the cradle of civilization and culture. The desire to replace the paradigm that rules the world so that it can be fixed for the sons of humanity is unacceptable to the imposing culture of the West. Ahmadi-nezhād claims that this culture not only supports exploitation and injustice but also does terrible things to the different nations. The West is trying, with this culture, to destroy what Iran and Khomeini have brought to the world. In the eyes of Ahmadi-nezhād, the most important and greatest message that Khomeini has brought to the world is a third way to lead society, a way that is based upon Islam but not on the other two ways of capitalism and/or Marxism.

The place of the Islamic Revolution and Khomeini's doctrine constitute Ahmadi-nezhād's guideline for the consolidation of his doctrine and his conception of different subjects. The five basic points he presents integrate with his perception of Islam which combines man, religion, and those "spiritual guides" that have existed throughout the generations. Together all these ingredients unite Islam into one whole whose value concerns not only Muslims but the entire world. This all begins with the value and role of man in the implementation and application of Islam and its values and, as for the future, it will rule the world after the revelation of the Mehdi, the savior of the world.

Ahmadi-nezhād thinks that, in the current state of affairs in which evil and the evil inclinations (*zāt-e bad*) of different leaders (hinting at the US president, George W. Bush) rule the world, there is a need to rise up against the evil and reorganize. In other words if everybody does what is good in their and God's eyes and acts in a positive way, then God will be on their side. On the other hand the rejection of the continuation of the rule of the divine caliphs (*hakemiyat-e khalife elahi*), the successors of Muhammad, and the Mehdi among them, will ultimately bring about thoughts of heresy and the rejection of God's dominion, which all are things that should be avoided.[57]

Since the word "Islam" means submission to the commandments of God so people should submit in the same way that all the prophets (who were Muslims) sent to men by God also submitted themselves.[58] Chronologically and comprehensively, according to Ahmadi-nezhād, Islam is the peak of divine perfection because it came into being after the two religions that preceded it. It is the peak to which humanity has risen, and the most perfect of the religions that God has given to man since it contains all of the other religions that God has given. Inside the Qur'an, given to humanity also by God, mankind can find the right path for living in this world. The Qur'an contains all of God's commandments together with the Law of Moses (the Jewish Torah) and the Gospels of Jesus.[59] Those who believe in the Qur'an have the right to mend the world that is overflowing with problems in all areas of life.[60]

The Qur'an was given to man to be used as a guidebook that will instruct him in his attempts to achieve accomplishments and fulfil the divine commandments.[61] For the believers of Islam and for those thirsty for a different view of the current conceptions, Ahmadi-nezhād tries to define the place of God, Islam, and the Qur'an in the ideas offered for changing the world order for the better. This is done by giving legitimacy or approval to those conceptions that are concerned with mending the world. Repairing the world, making it better, making it a world ready for the revelation of the Mehdi and "the perfect ending" (*nehayiat-e kamal*),[62] will only be accomplished if it is founded upon the values of Islam and the submission to God's commandments—just as was done by the pioneers of Islam and its spiritual leaders. This is also the reason for his call for the return to pure Islam and unity between the Muslims.[63]

The aforementioned five points[64] were addressed by Ahmadi-nezhād at a convention attended by heads of Islamic states held in Saudi Arabia and, even though the location was not the usual place for these words to be spoken and the audience was not the target audience for this presentation of the Shi'ite-Khomeinistic conceptions presented by him, Ahmadi-nezhād was specifically interested in speaking about what unites the countries and peoples of the *Ummah* in Saudi Arabia which is one of the leading Sunni Arab countries. He felt that this was an opportunity that had fallen into the hands of the sons of the Nation of Islam in order to achieve that which was always their aspiration and that this could be achieved without relating to Shi'ite or Sunni internal differences. His words regarding the vision of Islamic unity which he presented contained three stages: unification, eradication, and salvation, and he addresses all of these using a sort of upside-down funnel as a model that is, at first, in favor of the Iranian people, then in favor of the entire nation of Islam and, at last, in favor of the whole world. Ultimately this process would lead the world into being prepared for the revelation of the Mehdi.

The first stage Ahmadi-nezhād addressed, the unification of the oppressed or exploited nations, was to be solved by the weak and exploited nations joining hands against those countries that discriminated against them, that is, those countries that are imperialist-colonialist-capitalist. He presented several examples of such exploitation such as the slaves that had been taken from the African continent to the North American continent,[65] the suffering of the Palestinians under the State of Israel and the West,[66] and the suffering of the Iraqis and Afghans under the domination of the United States and the coalition countries.[67]

The second stage he addressed was the eradication of wickedness, or evil, from the world, and he demanded that the negative acts committed by the Western countries against the exploited countries must cease. The aspiration to utilize goodness in order to hasten the revelation of the Mehdi by repairing the world accordingly had to pass through the abolition of the evil existing in the world today. The unity referred to in the previous stage would be able to develop only after the elimination of that negative capitalistic authority. The desired unity can, he claimed, be then achieved by the power of intelligence, science, and wisdom, which are all offshoots of education, culture, and other acts that spread goodness and do not involve the use of force. All of these will cause wickedness to be defeated, whether by removing it or fully destroying it.[68]

The third stage dealt with by Ahmadi-nezhād was the salvation of the world through Islam without members of other religions necessarily being committed to the religion of Islam. He argued that what leads to the salvation of the world is the Islamic culture with its perfect religion in which there is a solution to the suffering of every man and any problem. Islam, he claimed, is the religion which can successfully quench the large thirst that exists today,[69] which is able to unite everybody in the face of all the evil and exploitation that exist in our days and which is the one religion that has been successful in dealing with that evil in all the different countries around the world whether they are Islamic or not. The religion of Islam is, therefore, the solution to all the world's ailments and can bring relief to the suffering that is found in it.[70]

The divine truth as expressed by Islam is, according to Ahmadi-nezhād, the most comprehensive religion ever given to men and is augmented by obedience to God's orders as handed down by his messengers from Adam to Muhammad and his successors the Imams all the way to the Mehdi. All of these bring Ahmadi-nezhād to claim that the responsibility for quenching the thirst and filling the void that has plagued the world belongs to those who worship the one and only God in this way—the Islamic monotheists.[71]

EPILOGUE AND CONCLUSION:
IRAN AFTER AHMADI-NEZHĀD AND UNDER ROUHANI

One year after the Ahmadi-nezhād's era ended in Iran, it seems like Ahmadi-nezhād's doctrine has been deliberately abandoned by the new president Hassan Rouhani. It was, however, obvious that President Rouhani's new government would be built upon different basic cornerstones than those of Ahmadi-nezhād's. These differences are wide-ranging starting with a different character, using a different ideology and different doctrine, and having different ideas about how to lead the country. All in all this makes the eleventh government of the Islamic Republic of Iran act almost oppositely to the two governments that preceded it; yet, with all the personal differences that exist between these politicians, it is important to note that they argue about "the way" not "the destination" of the Islamic state since they are both committed to the Iranian revolution and to Khomeini's doctrine.

The difference between these two presidents is so deep that it merits a separate study and a comprehensive discussion; yet, it is worth mentioning two short examples regarding the differences and the personal hostility that exist between the two. The first example appears in Rouhani's famous memoir "National Security and Nuclear Diplomacy" where, although Rouhani does mention president Ahmadi-nezhād, it is, alas, not in a positive way. Under the heading "The first and the last working session with the new president" (*avalin va-akharin molaqat-e kari ba rais jomhur-e jadid*), Rouhani describes the meeting held between him, as the Iranian top negotiator over the nuclear program, and Ahmadi-nezhād right after the latter's inauguration. From Rouhani's description there is no doubt that the hostility between these two figures is mutual and deep:

> I told him that this is not my way of doing things, and that I won't do such thing. "If you insist on doing it (*agar esrar darid*), you should speak with al-Baradai yourself . . . if you want to give instructions that way, without consulting . . . it is for the best if you quickly find a new secretary and give him those instructions," and then I told him goodbye.[72]

Aside from the fascinating vitality of the Iranian politics seen in that text, we can also see the great divide that exists between the acting president and the president-to-be.

The second example is their understanding of the Mehdi's role in the Shi'a belief, where the distinction between these two is much more basic and relates to the perception of the Mehdi. Although, of the two, Rouhani is the cleric, it is Ahmadi-nezhād who mentions the utopian vision and a longing for the future under the ruling of the Mehdi. The statement mentioned at the beginning of this chapter, is attributed to both of them but, unlike Ahmadi-nezhād, Rouhani skips over the ending sentence, mentioning the "Vali" of God. The religious interpretation of this act is not as important here as the political interpretation but it seems that the new president is more down to earth than his predecessor who yearns, philosophically and actively, for the revelation of the Mehdi and the things that will take place after that.[73]

This approach of acting with both feet on the ground is what has been guiding President Rouhani in his first year. Instead of preparing Iran and the world for what is about to come and striving to fulfil the utopian dream of creating a fixed and exemplary model of a world led by the Iranian society, as Ahmadi-nezhād did for eight years, Rouhani's cabinet immediately began to implement what they believed will lead to the rehabilitation of Iranian society. It started by showing smiley faces in the international arena and "Westernizing" Iran's foreign policy agenda, a step that reached its peak at the 68th General Assembly of the UN[74] and continues in the socioeconomic field where the new government is trying to execute an Islamic, yet Western, model of economy, which is already arousing a market that was "sleepy" during Ahmadi-nezhād's term (e.g., tourism).[75] The clearest difference is, however, in what we have already discussed regarding the change in the theological school of thought of the head of the executive branch.

Instead of refurbishing a mosque in Qom which houses the Well of Jamkaran (the location where some believe the Mehdi will reappear) with 17 million dollars in government funds, or having the government sign a "pact" with the Mehdi and throwing it down that same well, or paving a wide highway from *Shahr-e Ray* to Tehran so that the Mehdi's path will be wide open when he comes,[76] is acting in a moderate way. Rouhani avoided doing all these things that Ahmadi-nezhād did the second he became president.[77]

The new president is investing the government's money to encourage growth and increase incomes by providing Iran with a recovering economy instead of adopting Ahmadi-nezhād's utopian aspirations. Ahmadi-nezhād may have been the one with the socialistic vision but, unfortunately for the people, he forgot (most of the time not on purpose) the ordinary working-class citizens who make up the vast majority of the Iranian people. President Rouhani on the other hand, was elected because of his promise to remember these people. President Rouhani (with the massive support of the supreme leader) is acutely aware of the fact that, under Ahmadi-nezhād, the Islamic Revolution experienced one of its biggest crises. Ahmadi-nezhād's attempts to heal the world at a time in which the Iranian economy was experiencing a crisis and other negative developments will not be repeated under Rouhani's watch. He values the message of the expression *Nan-e Shab* ("a bread for the night"), and understands the priority of bread over utopia and, in this way, he is providing Ahmadi-nezhād's expression of an Iranian-Islamic identity with a different outlook. By placing the needs of the people before utopian visions, Rouhani wishes to deal with, and even solve, the crisis that exists in the Iranian-Islamic identity rather than feeding Ahmadi-nezhād's formula for a utopian and unrealistic identity. This clash of ideas, however, inevitably raises the question of which kind of identity Rouhani wishes to present. Assuming this is still a matter for debate, will it be more Iranian, more Westernized, or more Islamic?

NOTES

This chapter is taken from the author's PhD dissertation: *Mahmud Ahmadi-nezhād's Theological-Political-Socioeconomic Doctrine and its Implementation in the Islamic Republic of Iran* (Israel: Bar-Ilan University, 2013), under the supervision of Prof. Ze'ev Maghen.

1. Mahmūd-e Ahmadi-nezhād, "Zorurat-e nazrie pardazi-e masa'el bar asas-e farhang-e entezar" ("The importance of expressing an opinion regarding questions relating to the culture of anticipation"), Visiting religious leaders and their pupils (Qom: January 5, 2006) [speech], http://www.president.ir/fa/president/outlooks, retrieved: September/October 2009.

2. Mahmūd-e Ahmadi-nezhād, "Zorurat-e nazrie pardazi-e mojadad-e vazaef-e montazer dar doran-e gheibat" ("The important need for a reassessment of the mission of the man expecting the Mehdi during the time of occultation"), *Daftar-e Tablighat-e Eslami* (Qom: Islamic Propagation Office, September 28, 2005) [speech], http://www.president.ir/fa/president/outlooks, retrieved: September/October 2009. The word "Revelation" matches the Shi'a and Ahmadi-nezhād's perception of the Mehdi as the savior who is wandering among the Shi'i people, waiting for the right time to reveal himself.

3. Mahmūd-e Ahmadi-nezhād, "Bardashthai-e nadorost az sokhanaon-e rais jomhour darbare emdadhai-e emam-e asr (aj) nesbat be melat-e iran" ("The erroneous impressions from the speech of the president concerning the Mehdi's help to the Iranian people"), Iranian and foreign reporters (Iran: May 13, 2008) [interview], http://www.president.ir/fa/president/outlooks, retrieved: September/October 2009.

4. Mahmūd-e Ahmadi-nezhād, "Da'vat be emam-e asr, mohemtarin kar-e dar donia" ("The invitation of the Mehdi is the most important action in the world"), Exhibition "The Messianic Doctrine" (Iran: August 24, 2007) [speech], http://www.president.ir/fa/president/outlooks, retrieved: September/October 2009.

5. Mahmūd-e Ahmadi-nezhād, "Chahar shoar-e doulat, bargerefte az farhang-e entezar" ("The four slogans of the government were taken from the culture of anticipating the Mehdi"), *Daftar-e Tablighat-e Eslami* (Qom: Islamic Propagation Office, September 28, 2005) [speech], http://www.president.ir/fa/president/outlooks, retrieved: September/October 2009.

6. Mahmūd-e Ahmadi-nezhād, "Mavaze osuli-e jomouri-e eslami-e iran dar ersehai-e bein olmelali" ("The Central Stances of the Islamic Republic of Iran in International Matters"), Meeting with ambassadors and delegates from the various embassies of the Islamic Republic of Iran (Iran: August 11, 2008) [speech], http://www.president.ir/fa/president/outlooks, retrieved: September/October 2009.

7. Psalms 115:16.

8. Mahmūd-e Ahmadi-nezhād, "Jaigah-e ensan dar didgah-e eslam" ("The place of man in the point of view of Islam"), Meeting with political researchers and media people (New York: September 25, 2007) [speech], http://www.president.ir/fa/president/outlooks, retrieved: September/October 2009.

9. Mahmūd-e Ahmadi-nezhād, "Tabdil-e holocast be boti brai-e qodrathai-e solte" ("The turning of the Holocaust into a statue to which all Great Powers bow"), (Qa'em Shahr: December 7, 2006) [speech], http://www.president.ir/fa/president/outlooks, retrieved: September/October 2009.

10. Mahmūd-e Ahmadi-nezhād, "Enqelab-e eslami va daheh fajr, bozorgtarin havades ba'ad az sadr-e eslam" ("The Islamic revolution and the ten days of the Fajr are the greatest events following the establishment of Islam"), Members of the group organizing the "ten days of the Fajr" plan (Iran: January 29, 2008) [speech], http://www.president.ir/fa/president/outlooks, retrieved: September/October 2009.

11. Mahmūd-e Ahmadi-nezhād, "Felestin sahne-ye azmayesh-e andishe liberalism va nezam-e sarmaie dari" ("Palestine is a trial arena for liberalism and the capitalistic regimes"), Cabinet meeting (Tehran: January 2, 2008) [interview], http://www.president.ir/fa/president/outlooks, retrieved: September/October 2009.

12. "Jaigah-e ensan . . ." ("The place of man . . ."), [September 25, 2007].

13. "Mavaze osuli-e jomouri-e eslami . . ." ("The central stances . . ."), [August 11, 2008].

14. Ibid.

15. "Tabdil-e holocast be boti . . ." ("The turning of the Holocaust . . ."), [December 7, 2006].

16. Mahmūd-e Ahmadi-nezhād, "Bozorg kardan-e mas'ale-ye holocast az sui-e qodratha-ye solte dar moqayese ba setamhaye rafte bar sayer-e melatha" ("The inflating of the Holocaust question on the part of the great powers compared to the great exploitation amongst the rest of the nations"), Convention of heads of African states (July 1, 2006) [speech], http://www.president.ir/fa/president/outlooks, retrieved: September/October 2009.

17. "Chahar shoar-e doulat . . ." ("The four slogans . . ."), [September 28, 2005].

18. "Jaigah-e ensan . . ." ("The place of man..."), [September 25, 2007].

19. Surat Al-Fath, 48:29: *Muhammad-u rasoul-u elahi wa-aladhin-a ma'ahu ashidau ala alkufar-i rohama-u bainahum.*

20. "Chahar shoar-e doulat . . ." ("The four slogans . . ."), [September 28, 2005].

21. Mahmūd-e Ahmadi-nezhād, "Kemal-e jame'e bashari dar barpayi-e jame'e mahdavi" ("The place of all men in the bringing forth and creation of the messianic community"), (Ardabil: November 21, 2007) [speech], http://www.president.ir/fa/president/outlooks, retrieved: September/October 2009.

22. "Chahar shoar-e doulat . . ." ("The four slogans . . ."), [September 28, 2005].

23. Mahmūd-e Ahmadi-nezhād, "Elat-e asli-e mas'ale-ye felestin" ("The main reason for the Palestinian problem"), Meeting with spiritual leaders, (Iran: Convention on the subject of the Holocaust, December 12, 2006) [speech], http://www.president.ir/fa/president/outlooks, retrieved: September/October 2009.

24. "Felestin sahne-ye azmayesh-e . . ." ("Palestine is a trial arena . . ."), [January 2, 2008].

25. As seen later, man develops the most dominant quality given to him by God and with it he reaches divine perfection.

26. Mahmūd-e Ahmadi-nezhād, "Mouzo-e haste'i va muz'e iran" ("The nuclear matter and the stances of Iran"), (Tajikistan: Iranian residence, April 20, 2008) [speech], http://www.president.ir/fa/president/outlooks, retrieved: September/October 2009.

27. Genesis 2:15.

28. Mahmūd-e Ahmadi-nezhād, "Sharayet-e ijad-e solh-e paidar dar jahan" ("The conditions for the creation of sustainable peace in the world"), (New York: The 61st General Assembly of the United Nations, September 20, 2006) [speech], http://www.president.ir/fa/president/outlooks, retrieved: September/October 2009.

29. Mahmūd-e Ahmadi-nezhād, "Emam-e zaman vasete feiz-e elahi braai-e hamegan" ("The Mehdi is the divine channel of abundance for all"), Members of "pezhoheshkade mahdaviat" (Iran: The Messianic Research Institute, August 26, 2006) [speech], http://www.president.ir/fa/president/outlooks, retrieved: September/October 2009.

30. "Jaigah-e ensan . . ." ("The place of man . . ."), [September 25, 2007]. And also: Mahmūd-e Ahmadi-nezhād, "Eslam, bonyan-e farhang va tafakor-e melat-e iran va talash bra'ai-e por'rang kardan-e naqsh-e din dar zendegi-e fardi va jam'ei" ("Islam, the cornerstone of Iranian culture and thinking, and the effort to create a diversity in the individual and general spheres with the help of religion"), The ceremony of replacing the president of the state (Tehran: August 6, 2005) [speech], http://www.president.ir/fa/president/outlooks, retrieved: September/October 2009.

31. Mahmūd-e Ahmadi-nezhād, "Eslam, din-e hame Payambaran-e elahi va noqte ta'ali-e adyian" ("Islam, the religion of the prophets, and the high point of all other religions"), Visiting religious leaders and Muslim religious leaders from across the United States (New York: September 24, 2007) [speech], http://www.president.ir/fa/president/outlooks, retrieved: September/October 2009.

32. "Kemal-e jame'e bashari . . ." ("The place of all men . . ."), [November 21, 2007].

33. Mahmūd-e Ahmadi-nezhād, "Eslam dini jahani va jahan shomul" ("Islam, a global and universal religion"), Visiting religious leaders (Qom: January 5, 2006) [speech], http://www.president.ir/fa/president/outlooks, retrieved: September/October 2009.

34. "Eslam, bonyan-e farhang . . ." ("Islam, the cornerstone . . ."), [August 6, 2005].

35. Mahmūd-e Ahmadi-nezhād, "Masa'le holocast va sahionism" ("The subject of the Holocaust and Zionism"), The sixth exhibition of the celebration of the world mosques day (July 28, 2008) [speech], http://www.president.ir/fa/president/outlooks, retrieved: September/October 2009.

36. Mahmūd-e Ahmadi-nezhād, "Rah'kar-e asli-e ensejam-e eslami" ("The main road to Islamic solidarity"), The experts' council of the leadership (Iran: February 24, 2008) [speech], http://www.president.ir/fa/president/outlooks, retrieved: September/October 2009.

37. Mahmūd-e Ahmadi-nezhād, "Eslam, maktab-e rehai-e bakhsh-e donia-ye sarkhorde az maka'teb elhadi va liberal" ("Islam, the school freed from the frustration existing in the atheistic and liberal part of the world"), The convention of the heads of Islamic states (Saudi Arabia: December 7, 2005) [speech], http://www.president.ir/fa/president/outlooks, retrieved: September/October 2009.

38. Mahmūd-e Ahmadi-nezhād, "Qur'an, ketab-e rahnamai-e zendegi-e ensan" ("The Qur'an, a guidebook for life"), Awards-giving ceremony to those diligent in the study of the Qur'an (Iran: October 9, 2006) [speech], http://www.president.ir/fa/president/outlooks, retrieved: September/October 2009.

39. "Jaigah-e ensan . . ." ("The place of man . . ."), [September 25, 2007].

40. Ibid.

41. Ahmadi-nezhād even provides examples of those writing him letters claiming that in their enlightened Western countries they are incapable of investigating and reaching the truth. For one such example see: Mahmūd-e Ahmadi-nezhād, "Mouj-e dovom-e enqelab" ("The second wave of the revolution"), The senior circle of the members of Jihad and Shahada (Iran: September 27, 2006) [speech], http://www.president.ir/fa/president/outlooks, retrieved: September/October 2009.

42. "Jaigah-e ensan . . ." ("The place of man . . ."), [September 25, 2007].

43. Mahmūd-e Ahmadi-nezhād, "Omid'ha va forsat'ha-ye omat-e eslam dar doniaye konuni" ("The hopes and opportunities of the nation of Islam in today's world"), A convention of heads of Islamic states (Saudi Arabia: December 7, 2005) [speech], http://www.president.ir/fa/president/outlooks, retrieved: September/October 2009.

44. "Enqelab-e eslami va daheh fajr . . ." ("The Islamic revolution and the ten days of . . ."), [January 29, 2008].

45. "Omid'ha va forsat'ha-ye omat-e . . ." ("The hopes and opportunities . . .") [December 7, 2005].

46. "Zorurat-e nazrie pardazi-e . . ." ("The importance of expressing an opinion . . ."), [January 5, 2006].

47. Mahmūd-e Ahmadi-nezhād, "Mouj-e dovom-e enqelab, gostarde'tar va amiq'tar az mouj-e aval" ("The second wave of the revolution is wider and deeper than the first one"), (Iran: October 14, 2006) [speech], http://www.president.ir/fa/president/outlooks, retrieved: September/October 2009.

48. "Omid'ha va forsat'ha-ye omat-e . . ." ("The hopes and opportunities . . .") [December 7, 2005].

49. Mahmūd-e Ahmadi-nezhād, "Enqelab-e eslami tablor-e khoast va-erade-e mardom-e iran" ("The Islamic Revolution is the consolidation of the wills and demands of the Iranian nation"), Visiting ambassadors from different countries who are present in Iran, in preparation for Revolution Day (Iran: February 10, 2008) [speech], http://www.president.ir/fa/president/ outlooks, retrieved: September/October 2009; and also: "Enqelab-e eslami va daheh fajr . . ." ("The Islamic revolution and the ten days of . . ."), [January 29, 2008].

50. Mahmūd-e Ahmadi-nezhād, "Rishe-haye moshkelat-e bashar-e emruz" ("The roots of the problems of humanity today"), Meeting with representatives of states that are members of UNESCO (November 15, 2007) [speech], http://www.president.ir/fa/president/outlooks, retrieved: September/October 2009.

51. "Mouzo-e haste'i va muz'e iran" ("The nuclear matter and the stances . . ."), [April 20, 2008].

52. "Omid'ha va forsat'ha-ye omat-e . . ." ("The hopes and opportunities . . .") [December 7, 2005].

53. "Kemal-e jame'e bashari . . ." ("The place of all men . . ."), [November 21, 2007].

54. "Omid'ha va forsat'ha-ye omat-e . . ." ("The hopes and opportunities . . .") [December 7, 2005].

55. Just as he also mentions in his words at: Mahmūd-e Ahmadi-nezhād, "Bazgasht be eslam, tanha rah-e hal-e moshkelat-e alam" ("The return to Islam is the only way to solve all the world's problems"), Friday prayer (Gambia: June 30, 2006) [speech], http:// www.president.ir/fa/president/outlooks, retrieved: September/October 2009.

56. Mahmūd-e Ahmadi-nezhād, "Talash-e estekbar-e jahani barai-e takhrib-e bonianhaye akhlaqi dar iran" ("The arrogant global efforts for the destruction of the foundation of morals in Iran"), Visiting religious leaders (Ilam: December 6, 2007) [speech], http://www.president.ir/ fa/president/outlooks, retrieved: September/October 2009.

57. "Bardashthai-e nadorost az sokhanaon-e . . ." ("The erroneous impressions from the speech . . ."), [May 13, 2008].

58. "Eslam, din-e hame Payambaran-e . . ." ("Islam, the religion of the prophets . . ."), [September 24, 2007].

59. Ibid.

60. The justification for Islam being superior to all other religions, or as Ahmadi-nezhād claims, "a perfect religion" he explains in his speech (Ibid.), by saying: "Islam is the religion of the divine prophets (*payambaran-e elahi*). All of the prophets were Muslims, from Abraham to Muhammad. The meaning of the term Muslim is that they were submissive (*taslim*) to the divine commandments. Abraham said that God named us Muslims. Abraham was a Muslim. The prophet Moses was a Muslim. Jesus was a Muslim and all the other prophets were Muslims. Islam is the religion of the divine prophets and constitutes the peak and the height of perfection of the divine religions. Meaning, this is the place to which humanity arrived and for (humanity) God bestowed his religion in its perfect and final form. So when we say Islam, we mean the truth of God's religion."

61. "Qur'an, ketab-e rahnamai-e . . ." ("The Qur'an, a guidebook . . ."), [October 9, 2006].

62. With the meaning of the best possible ending for humanity.

63. Mahmūd-e Ahmadi-nezhād, "Sahionistha a'omel-e ijad-e tefreqe bein-e shi'e va-soni" ("The activity of the Zionists to drive a wedge between the Shi'ites and the Sunnis"), Foreign correspondents (Senegal: February 12, 2008) [interview], http://www.president.ir/fa/president/ outlooks, retrieved: September/October 2009.

64. "Omid'ha va forsat'ha-ye omat-e . . ." ("The hopes and opportunities . . .") [December 7, 2005].

65. "Mavaze osuli-e jomouri-e eslami . . ." ("The central stances . . ."), [August 11, 2008].

66. Mahmūd-e Ahmadi-nezhād, "Edeai-e vahi-e qodratha-ye solte mabna bar hemayat az hoquq-e bashar va demokrasi" ("The false claims of the great powers that are based on the support for human rights and democracy"), Meeting with residents (Pakdasht: October 30, 2006) [speech]. http://www.president.ir/fa/president/outlooks, retrieved: September/October 2009.

67. Mahmūd-e Ahmadi-nezhād, "Doulat-e amrika, bozorg'tarin tahdid-e khavar-e miane va jahan" ("The American government, the greatest threat to the Middle East and the world"), At the D-8 summit (Kuala Lumpur, Malaysia: June 27, 2008) [interview], http://www.president.ir/fa/president/outlooks, retrieved: September/October 2009.

68. "Felestin sahne-ye azmayesh-e . . ." ("Palestine is a trial arena . . ."), [January 2, 2008].

69. "Mouj-e dovom-e enqelab" ("The second wave of the revolution"), [September 27, 2006].

70. Mahmūd-e Ahmadi-nezhād, "Emam (aj), ramz-e vahdat-e bein-e hame adian" ("The Mehdi is a symbol of unity amongst the religions"), Visiting religious leaders and the "Friday Imams" (Bushehr province: January 31, 2008). [Speech], http://www.president.ir/fa/president/outlooks, retrieved: September/October 2009.

71. "Eslam, din-e hame Payambaran-e . . ." ("Islam, the religion of the prophets . . ."), [September 24, 2007].

72. Hassan Rouhani, *Amniat-e meli va-diplomaci-e haste-i* (Tehran: Majma-e tashkhis-e maslahat-e nezam, Markaz-e tahqiqat-e estratezhik, 2012), pp. 594–96 (In Persian).

73. Mohammad Said-e Najafi Moqadam, "Matn-e kamel-e sokhanan-e doktor rouhani dar shast-o-hashtomin majma-e omumi-e sazeman-e melal-e motahad," September 25, 2013, http://www.president.ir/fa/71572, retrieved: August 27, 2014. Mohammad said-e Najafi Moqadam, "Matn-e kamel-e sokhanan-e doktor rouhani dar marasem-e tanfiz-e hokm-e riasat jomhouri az sui-e rahbar-e moazam-e enqelab," August 4, 2013, http://www.president.ir/fa/70471, retrieved: August 27, 2014.

74. Al-Arabiya in English from AFP Washington, "Iran FM accuses Netanyahu of 'lie attack' on nukes," September 29, 2013, http://english.alarabiya.net/en/News/middle-east/2013/09/30/Iran-FM-accuses-Netanyahu-of-lie-attack-on-nukes.html, retrieved: January 09, 2014.

75. Zvi Bar'el, "A year after his election, Rohani is changing Iran without shaking it up," June 14, 2014, http://www.haaretz.com/news/middle-east/.premium-1.598619, retrieved: August 27, 2014.

76. Ze'ev Maghen, "Occultation in Perpetuum: Shi'ite Messianism and the Policies of the Islamic Republic," *The Middle East Journal*, Vol. 62, No. 2 (Spring 2008), p. 234.

77. BBC Persian, Business Reporter, "Vazir-e eqtesad-e iran: Ahmadi-nezhad eshtebah-e shah ra tekrar kard," August 17, 2013, http://www.bbc.co.uk/persian/business/2013/08/130817_l01_tayebnia_economy_iran.shtml, retrieved: September 1, 2014.

Part III

Sexuality, Beauty, and Social Networking: Between the Private, Self, and the Public Sphere

Chapter Six

The Identity Designers of the Self in Sexuality, Beauty, and Plastic Surgery in Iran

Ronen A. Cohen

Iran is a theocratic state that combines the fundamental implementation of Shi'a Islam and an adoration of the history and language of Persia; but when these two basic elements, Shi'a fundamentalism and Persian roots, are taken into account together, one can sometimes find contradictory and even aliened identities. Ever since the Persians adopted first Sunni Islam and later, during the Safavid era (sixteenth century), Shi'a Islam, there has been a struggle over the basic identities of the native population. While Islam (Sunni at first and then Shi'a) vigorously imposed its creed and religious regulations upon Iranian society, the society's ethnocultural and linguistic anchors were powerful enough to preserve Iran's Persian uniqueness and identity.

Although this chapter does not intend to deal with all the elements of the Persian identity it will deal with the elements of self-image that, in general, belong to the worldwide outlook of the self in regard to beauty, sexuality, and gender and will relate to these elements according to their Persian interpretation. This will especially be the case when these elements are being questioned, and even denied, in the religious society that Iran is. This means that these elements will be treated as external parameters that help, or prevent, the self to identify itself in its relations with both its immediate and global societies.

The main goal of this chapter is to expose any current symbiosis that may exist between elements of religion and culture, the past and the present, and what is forbidden and allowed in the new Iranian society, and will present the ways the Iranians deal with the phenomena of concealed beauty and revealed sexuality that are both still being used as ways of self-identification and self-creation. The cultural anchors that will be examined in this article are gender, sexuality, and beauty while the uses of plastic surgery will be examined as a presenter of cultural change and design within Iranian society. All of these together are components that represent a view of the self-images of both the general public of Iranian society and of the private, all of which, when combined, are the result of the interactions and clashes between religion and culture that have taken place in Iranian society.

ONCE WE WERE YOUNG AND BEAUTIFUL

Sociologists have concluded that, in a modern world that is becoming more modern and supertechnological, people are becoming more and more individual and egocentric. The contribution of the facilities provided by the social media has only made this faster, stronger, and absolute. The appearance and distribution of this phenomenon is better known, and even welcomed, within Western societies more than in Eastern ones, including the Middle Eastern states. Modernity and technology have not skipped over the latter, but the forms and ways in which this phenomenon appears have become more and more controlled by Middle Eastern regimes in order to exert traditional control over their society rather than allowing them to become modernist and progressive.

In traditional societies, such as those in the Middle East and especially Iran, the questions of self-esteem and identity have become important questions since, as a result of the spread of the social media and technology, the Iranian people can now compare and make distinctions between themselves and the modern westerners. More than that, the Iranian people are now also able to borrow and adopt modern trends in clothes, technology, literature, social media facilities, and plastic surgery to assist them to become much closer to what is fashionable in the Western world.

Modernity and technology did not come to Iran only in the last few decades but actually began to appear during the late nineteenth century. Afsaneh Najmabadi, in her outstanding article about "Gendered Transformations: Beauty, Love, and Sexuality in Qajar Iran," actually makes the point that the adoption of Western beauty and sexuality models probably arose from copying European art which led to "[the Iranian artists] placing themselves on equal footing with the Europeans."[1] In addition, women, especially at the beginning of the twentieth century and especially members of the royal family, entered "into the domain of visibility."[2] Their entrance into society brought these standards of beauty into society producing a side effect which empowered women to make themselves more and more attractive and beautiful—but this was also true of the princesses of the Qajari monarchy.

"The importance of beauty is enhanced in modern society and culture, the ideal of beauty being defined by the media through magazines, television, and music. Both men and women are becoming increasingly concerned about their physical appearance and are seeking cosmetic interventions."[3] Carla Gramaglia and Enrica Marzola chose to start their article: "Self-Esteem and Personality in Patients with Body Dysmorphic Disorder Undergoing Cosmetic Rhinoplasty" with this statement to describe self-esteem: "Self-esteem is an abstract concept with a composite and controversial nature, which is an important component of psychological health."[4] We can see this statement as a very general and vague definition. Yet, it does not deal with any aspect of self-esteem, only the psychological basis for it. Still, the building of one's self-esteem, image, and personality is more welcome and acceptable in the context of modern society than within traditional societies. Nevertheless Iran, as a traditional country, has many modern aspects and, as in any other modern-traditional country, its people are busy with building up their self-esteem but, perhaps more than in any other Middle Eastern country, there are many contradictory factors that influence self-esteem. Some of these are body dysmorphic disorder (BDD) and the influence of education and culture that, all in all, form a platform for decision-making regarding whether one should, for example, "undergo cosmetic surgery interventions."[5]

BEAUTY AND SEXUALITY UNDER THE VEIL

The history of the Iranian veiled women is too ancient to be presented in this short chapter but our working premise is that, in the current situation, Iranian women must be veiled whether it be because of Iranian and Islamic laws or the influence of historical and cultural traditions. While the Islamic context was canonized during the Islamic conquests, the regulations set down were not that contradictory of what was already prevalent as local practice that the Persians had adopted much before the Islamic arrival. In the *Mishna* (the Jewish oral law literature) which was written during the first and second centuries CE, in the tractate Shabbat chapter 6 article 6 we are informed about the clothes that women were allowed to wear once they walked out of their homes on Shabbat (Sabbath) within places that had no *Eiruv*:[6] "Women may go out with a coin fastened to a swelling on their feet; little girls may go out with laces on and even with screws in their ears; Arabians may go out in their long veils and Medians in their mantillas."[7] Either way, women were not allowed to go out of their houses without any head coverings—be they veils or mantillas or whatever they might be called. Still, the *Mishna* acts as an extraordinary witness to the costumes the Arabian and Median women used to wear. In the original Hebrew text the mantillas were called *Parufot* (plural of *Paruf*) which in Hebrew means to tighten with a button or stitching, but the translator chose to call them mantilla(s) as if they were shawls or kerchiefs. They were certainly not like veils which in the Iranian context were called *Chador* (*tent* in Persian), which covered all the head, shoulders, and upper level of the body—like a tent. It is important, however, to note that, during this period, the Median Empire was part of Persia so we can surely assume that not only the Jewish women in this diaspora wore these clothes, since they had probably adopted the native practice.

Shireen Mahdavi in her article, "Shawhar Ahu Khanum: Passion, Polygamy and Tragedy," tries to present the struggle taking place between obedience to the sharia laws and the traditional Persian women's virtues through referring to episodes in the book *Shawhar Ahu Khanum* that, although published in 1961, deals with the 1920s–1930s. The story not only reflects upon the protagonist's daily struggle to make a living but also upon the human inclinations regarding temptations such as the reaction to forbidden beauty, unfaithfulness, and the price a man is willing to pay in order to fulfill the sexual passions stirred by his imagination. Mahdavi, however, argues that the *Shawhar Ahu Khanum*'s author, as might be expected, does not deny the readers the detailed descriptions of the outward form of the characters. For example, he describes one of the women as "a woman in her thirties with thick, flowing black hair, black, tender eyes, beautiful skin and a happy smiling face, all denoting a contented, fortunate woman."[8] The act of describing the woman's beauty is to emphasize the uniqueness of the standards of beauty of the area and especially the fact that this beauty has to be concealed as something forbidden not only to strangers but also to family members. The central hero, Seyyid Miran, is aware of the feminine beauty that is all around him and because of this awareness he arrives at several crucial decisions that ignite the whole story and allow it to evolve. Although, as one would expect, the women are religious and modest in their wearing of *the white Chador*, the ability of the women to play with it and expose parts of their faces and hair, finally arouses the curiosity and passion that Seyyid Miran feels towards one of these women, and he is overwhelmed by her beauty. Ironically the same religious prohibitions that are imposed on women in order to prevent temptation and consequent seduction are exploited by the women in order to manipulate the men and attract their attention. Mahdavi, however, goes on to say that, in the name of the sharia, the Islamic law, the men are led to abuse the women's rights through suggestive behavior, *Mut'a*, the practice of polygamy, and imposed veiling[9] and that this is done in order to satisfy their passions while nodding in the direction of religious acknowledgment.

Despite the above, the traditional and religious society that Iran was and still is sees women's sexuality "as essentially passive and responsive and in other contexts as a vital and active force in its own right." In other words women have power over men through using their sexuality and beauty and, therefore, this power needs to be controlled and "channeled toward positive social ends."[10] Who, however, is to be responsible for channeling and navigating this power towards positive ends and what constitutes the authority and legitimacy for these actions? Is the above process to be driven by tradition or by religious creed? Who conducts the process? Is it politics, economic realities, or Islam?

These questions might be answered in different ways depending on when we ask the questions and provide answers. This also depends on political periods, international influences, cultural and social developments, and levels of religious moderation or stricture. Up until modern times the unspoken "game" played out by Iranian society was one in which neither politics nor the society wished to break or stop what was going on, and, ironically, this game could also be considered to be a form of revolutionary thought, although its purpose was not necessarily to revolutionize the Islamic Republic. Anyway, each side played the game gently and fairly without any desire to abuse its power to bring about any fundamental shift in the way the game was played. Despite this conception, this balance was finally broken when Mohammad Reza Pahlavi, the last monarch of the Pahlavi Dynasty, tried to forcibly secularize Iranian society despite the fact that the major population was and still is fundamentally religious and traditional. His actions, however, were only a continuation of the process his father had begun during the 1930s.

The emergence of the Islamic revolution and the formation of the Islamic Republic left the impression that Islam, at least as represented by the Ayatollah Khomeini, was "the antithesis of modernity and surely incompatible with any form of feminism."[11] This conception has its truth and reality as once the religious revolutionaries achieved political power, "women's status appeared to deteriorate due to the reversal of earlier reforms [of the Pahlavis]."[12] Ever since then, however, reality has shaped a different picture, one of symbiosis between economic and political realities. These realities are mainly concerned with general and public issues like population, policy-making, family planning, women's socioeconomic status, birth control, and so forth, rather than just with matters of sexuality and beauty. Apparently these latter issues are more likely to represent private matters rather than public or general issues even though they do have an immediate influence on public life.

The part played by women in leading these issues is apparently significant even though women Islamist activists have ambivalent, and sometimes contradictory, positions regarding these issues and, of course, others. In order to achieve their goal of improving the status of women within the country, the women activists have played the "game" and have "encouraged the government to introduce reforms in the areas of marriage, divorce and education."[13] The Iranian government from its side is aware of the fact that any change that needs to be introduced into Iranian society, especially regarding the status of women, must include broad legal and social changes. The leading conception has been that the integration of women into all the social and public fields is a necessary move that needs to be made in order to improve the quality of public life.[14]

As a result of the greater tolerance and the softening of severe attitudes towards the status of women and their rights, as one of general issues that finally influenced the general public, Iranian women were now able to utilize new interpretations of a mixed Persian and Islamic approach to beauty and sexuality. By allowing Iranian women to be an essential part of Iranian society, by giving women social and legal rights, and by allowing them to achieve social positions and take up the options of higher education—whether by learning or teaching or by gaining civil positions within the work frameworks—Iranian society made it possible for Iranian women to now express a new interpretation of their sexuality and beauty. This formative reality of women's new role in Iranian society and the new outlook on gender had to take into consideration the necessity to frame it all "within the Islamic vision of society."[15] In regard to the issue of the veil, for instance, we can see that "the veil, once a mark of backwardness, has been resurrected as a sign of empowerment."[16]

THE MODERN APPEARANCE OF BEAUTY AND SEXUALITY IN THE ISLAMIC REPUBLIC

The reappearance of the modern Iranian woman's beauty and sexuality could be seen everywhere in the social life of Iran. What had been accepted in the past as the standard religious dress code regarding the attitude towards beauty and sexuality during the first years of the Islamic Republic was now undergoing an undeclared evolutionary process. It is hard to say that this process has been warmly welcomed by the regime that is still trying to maintain the formal and declared expectations they have from clothes designers and outfitters, but the changes are especially welcome to women who feel that they now have some kind of formal and informal religious authorization for their actions.

The political change that the Islamic revolution has brought to Iran has also been a cultural change which, in this case, was based upon religious conceptions. The prerevolution situation regarding veiled women divided them into two main groups, each of which had its own reasons for adopting its practices: the policies of the Pahlavis and the traditional model. The Pahlavis' model of the unveiled women came from the middle class which included the white-collar workers, the students who had studied abroad (especially in Europe and North America), and some who were connected to left guerrilla organizations such as the *Mojahedin-e Khalq* and *Fadā'iyān-e*

Khalq and other Marxist movements. These were joined by liberal women who wished to promote women's rights through changing Iran's organizational structures and facilities.

In contrast there were veiled women who generally came from the lower classes and from the rural areas and provinces. These women who were basically traditional, if not fundamentally religious, were also less socially integrated and were associated with bazaar merchants and traditional producers. They lived a life of seclusion at home and suffered from social segregation in the public spheres; thus they found it hard to find their place within the modern and developed Iranian society that the Pahlavi monarchy wanted to offer its citizens. It seems clear that they were in real conflict about what to do if a job or any social opportunity were at hand. Should they take off the veil in order to integrate into society or should they maintain their religious obligations?[17]

The way Reza Shah Pahlavi related to the enforced unveiling of the Iranian women came mainly from his intention "to promote a nation-building" agenda.[18] While the promotion of a European dress code for men was accepted more easily and logically (except in religious circles), the issue of unveiling women created serious political and, especially, social-religious debate. The dress-code policy that Reza Shah wanted to promote for Iranian society was done in order to advance the westernization of the state through westernizing their clothing.[19]

On the other hand clothing adaptations made for Iranian women was met with mixed feelings and great ambivalence and, as a result, Iranian women were, in general, divided into two groups: the Western-oriented and the traditional. The latter had real difficulty in adapting to the rapid change and therefore found themselves secluded not only from social life but, and this is important to say, from independent choice, a state which was also enforced by law. For the Crown, the veil meant backwardness and primitivism and the regime thought that the key to showing the world that Iran was becoming modern and sophisticated was by presenting the Iranian people—especially the women—as modern and educated as their sisters in Europe.[20]

The question of beauty, not to mention sexuality, never arose in this context but it was immediately associated with the aesthetic that Reza Shah wanted to show as something Persian but with the flavor and taste of Europe, modernity, and progress. Forcing the women to go about unveiled and, not only that, but to appear in public as European ladies, was permeated with the idea that Iran needed to show its beauty and aesthetics to the world (as his son, Mohammad Reza Shah, would do by way of displaying Persian archeology and glory). The Iranian women, however, who had never been used to walking around unveiled in public, were embarrassed and desperate and, while this move was seen by the modernists "as a liberation of women," the Ulama "saw it as an attempt to turn the symbol of virtue into a symbol of

vice,"[21] and "as an 'imported' or 'West-toxicated' model of women's emancipation."[22]

All in all this crucial period ended once the shah was exiled to South
Africa and Iranian women, especially the traditional ones (i.e., those who
never crossed the unveiling lines), again returned to the wearing of medieval
clothing. Reza Shah's initiative did, however, reveal another unspoken issue
within Iranian society. The modern women, first from the Shah's circles but,
later, also from the Iranian elites, discovered the aesthetic of the beauty
rather than the beauty itself and this, perhaps unintentionally, also made it
possible for the traditional and religious women to explore more modern
aesthetics albeit with their religious interpretation.

Situations had worsened during the Mohammad Reza Shah period
(1941–1979). In his first years, especially up to the overthrowing of Dr.
Mohammad Mossadeq's government in August 1953, the shah was not able
to advance his father's ambitions and plans to modernize and secularize Iran.
In fact, the opposite was true as the religious factions only grew to be more
radical and fundamentalist due to their belief that the weak Shahs, Reza
Shah, and especially his son—Mohammad Reza Shah—had lost credibility
and any political power they had had to promote their cultural war against
religion and the Ulama.

The tables, however, were turned. The young shah had only ten years
(from 1953 to 1963) to strengthen his power and declare the White Revolution—a set of modern reforms that were as much about fighting the clerics
and their economic power as about embarking on an economic revolution to
improve the people's wealth and lives. In this respect secularizing the state
and providing it with a Western outlook and prestige was what the shah saw
as the torch that would allow him to recapture Iran's ancient glory which
would light the way to renewal and a better life for the Iranians.

By taking these ambitions and motivations into account and extrapolating
them into expressions of social life we will be able to render a picture of the
social framework in Iran which will help us to understand how deeply and
fundamentally the shah understood that Iran needed to be a modern, Westernized, and secular state. To achieve this the shah had to promote the Iranian's image of beauty, whether this was the image of Iran as a modern state
or the image of its people, and promote modern, Western dress codes and
intellectual visions in order to force the people to believe that Iran could be
the welcome model of a pleasant, beautiful, gentle state that valued intelligence and progress.

The importation of these ideas and wishes into Iran could only be
achieved by repressing the religious factors in the state, and he might have
been able to achieve his conceptual goals for the first few years but not for
the far future. These imported ideas came face-to-face with reality when the
shah made it possible for Western states, such as the United States, to feel

free enough within the country, at least in what was related to the cultural life of the Iranian people, to introduce such things as theatres, cinemas, pubs/ bars, and Western dress codes that would allow Iranians to feel and look like Western, advanced people.

In this climate questioning the veil and other religious practices was only a matter of time. The shah who, at least in this respect, saw himself as the one who needed to implement his father's vision, chose to challenge the Iranian women (and men of course) with old-new dress-code demands. As the relevant model the royal family presented a Western appearance especially with their uncovered heads and the absence of veils. The "modern Iranian woman" that the royal family chose to present was an Iranian woman who presents her natural beauty and appearance without any shame or fear. Presenting the royal women without a Chador or scarf was aimed at providing a modern cultural example for Iranian women to copy so that they could be seen to be modern and so display their belief in and support for the monarchy.

In regard to this Khomeini had only one thing to say: the women must wear the veil, especially outdoors. The women's rights movements opposed him and made it clear that "they had no intention of handing over to the Shi'ite clergy what they felt they had achieved with the Shah's overthrow."[23] However, and in contradiction to the previous years, the revolutionary atmosphere of the late 1970s led these women's rights organizations to fight against the shah and actually, unintentionally, invited Khomeini to impose religious regulations in place of the rights the shah had allowed regarding women.

The Ayatollah Khomeini, like other theoreticians such as Ali Shariati and Murtaza Motahhari, only strengthened the stand taken by religious women against removing the veil. These pro-veil women had three main arguments for why should they wear the veil at a time when their sisters from the left were fighting to discard it. The first was the need to resist the influences of the outside world, which led to the second argument about the need to maintain their identity as Muslim women; and the last was because it supported women's emancipation "as opposed to other images projected by the secular political tendencies."[24] The religious women rejected the idea of a "modern consumer woman" by again wearing their veil since, according to them, this action "encouraged the traditional puritanical image advocated by Islam, as against the rising 'modern' woman, which was seen as yet another sign of the corruption of Islamic culture and values by the Shah and the West."[25]

These ideas led Iranian Muslim women to seek their "emancipation through Islam." At one time they were not able to influence the new Islamic government but now the Ayatollah Khomeini was there to embed it within the new Iranian Constitution by saying that the primary task of the Islamic woman was motherhood, especially from a national outlook. From this time on there was a snowball effect regarding women's rights and this grew bigger and bigger until the veiled women become a constitutional fact. The left and other women organizations, on the other hand, lost any chance they had had to sustain the prerevolutionary situation, at least in all that was related to the veil.[26]

This is not the place to deal with the way Khomeini saw the question of women's rights within the Islamic Republic, but it is worth mentioning that the figure of Fatima, the Prophet's beloved daughter, played a role in the writings and sayings penned by both Khomeini's and Ali Shariati. Fatima is presented as the model for all Shi'i Muslim women who are expected to imitate her religious devotion, modesty, and contribution to the strength of the Ummah—and all this succeeded in diminishing any debate regarding the role of women within Iranian society.

ATTITUDES TOWARDS BEAUTY AND SEXUALITY IN MODERN IRANIAN LITERATURE

Although we cannot carry out a total review on modern Iranian literature and the way it relates to beauty and sexuality in the current Iranian society, we can discuss a few examples that can shed light upon this issue from a few different perspectives. Most of the literature selected is from books written by exiled Iranian women some of whom are Jewish and now live in Israel and who describe their past lives in Iran and their yearnings for the Iran they knew as children. In their books they sometimes unintentionally describe the manifestation of beauty and sexuality in Iranian society.

The first example *The Saffron Kitchen* by Yasmin Crowther describes the author's anxiety about the past and the present, being caught between her roots and exile, between a deep yearning for the "other Iran" she knew and her dream to once again see Iran as she knew it. The author deals with many issues that reflect the cultural structure of Iranian society including tradition and society's attitude towards it, the dress code, modesty, the adoption of modern Western fashion, and the demand made by religious leaders to conceal the sexuality and beauty of women. The two main figures, both women, represent two sides of the dualism regarding women's rights in Iran, with Maryam representing the religious and conservative side and Parvin the modern and Western side. Both, however, are actually on the same side even though they still both represent opposite sides of the cultural and religious battle and debate that was carried on between the Pahlavi monarchy and the Islamic Republic.

While Crowther, reflects upon the days in Iran when a Western dress code was considered to be something desirable and a sign of prosperity, she still emphasizes the ambivalence that was felt when she, on the one hand, says how much those days reflected modernity and a welcome Westernization but, on the other hand, describes the contradictions as one character, after reminiscing about the once-fashionable Western coats, says to her friend Maryam: "We had great times then, didn't we? . . . But I think that you were in shock as someone who had come from Mashhad . . . you never agreed to show your ankles to anyone." The reply from Maryam, the conservative woman, was "I grew up in a religious town and my family was very orthodox . . . it's not easy to run away from it."[27]

Even though Crowther criticizes tradition and religion and shows her preference for Persian culture she still presents it as something that fundamentally combines with traditional-religious elements. The fundamental need of the main figure Maryam to show off her femininity and beauty despite the prevailing social and religious norms are always under question and wrought with contradictions.[28] There is, however, an often contradictory need to exercise the option of displaying beauty in a world where women have to cover up their bodies and heads while allowing them a small space, or option, to express their sexuality and beauty to the world, whether by revealing their faces and hair or allowing their forehands to be seen, but all of this is still done with religious restrictions.

Maryam, the main figure, experiences internal conflict with her desires and the religious norms. She brushes her hair and arranges it aesthetically, but then covers it up with a pink *Chador*; she uses English Lavender perfume and she moisturizes her facial skin with English moisturizing cream as a reminder of the attractions of Western beauty or of the option that the above elements could provide.[29] However, for Maryam, the Islamic Revolution has destroyed her basic womanly desire to be feminine like the women during the Shah's time who could go out of their homes wearing high-heeled shoes and scarves around their necks (not their heads) since, after the revolution, women were forced to wear un-knocked shoes and hejabs that covered up their heads and hair.[30]

The author of *Prisoner of Tehran,* Marina Nemat, also deals with the contradictions between religion and the daring culture that first appeared during the Pahlavi period and the first years of the Islamic Republic. The author, who is a Christian woman who was born and raised in Iran, had to adopt cultural and religious traditions that had never been a part of her religious life and practice before the Islamic revolution, makes many references to the situation and status of Iranian women before the revolution, and presents this as the preferred model for Iranian feminism. Her descriptions of beauty and sexuality are very bold as if to favorably emphasize the variegated past as a contrast to the dark present. For example, she describes her grandmother's friend as "a Russian old lady who had short and curly blond hair, red lipstick on her lips, bluish shading on her eyelids and smelled like a field of flowers."[31] She also describes her mother's beauty as something special that could not be looked at in the current Iran: "My mother was a nervous and beautiful lady. She had brown eyes, a perfect nose, thick lips and long legs; and she loved to wear dresses with décolletage that emphasized her smooth, white skin."[32]

The outbreak of the revolution and the institutionalization of Islamic law also brought with them antibeauty and antisexuality winds to Iran which declared that "the *Hejab* is a must, and women are forced to wear long and dark cloaks and cover their hair with long scarves or, alternatively, are allowed to wear a chador" and that the use of "ties, perfume, cosmetics or nail polish were 'satanic' deeds that deserved heavy punitive actions."[33] In fact "many women were attacked and beaten as a result of putting lipstick on or allowing a few hairs to emerge from the covering of their scarves."[34]

The author tries to describe aspects of beauty and its appearances as something that strengthens self-image and provides confidence and social acknowledgment: "I loved the gentle click clack my new and fashionable shoes made when once I crossed the Church aisle went to sit where the choir sits. I loved even more the whisperings of the choir members that told me how gorgeous I looked."[35] Another time she was described as a thin woman by her mother's friend who told her mother that she needed to feed "this pretty girl" up as she would "look much better with some curves."[36] The regime's attitude towards such manifestations of beauty, however, depended a lot on who the supreme leader was, whether it was Khomeini when the IRGC were more radical and aggressive or Khamene'i when the IRGC were more "blind" and ignored minor violations of the dress codes such as women using some lipstick or showing a little hair.[37]

PLASTIC SURGERY IN MODERN IRAN

One of the main ways of affecting aesthetic presentation and beauty all over the world, but especially in Iran (and most Muslim states) is the use of cosmetic plastic surgery, and this practice has exposed the debate over the importance of beauty in issues involving self-image, the relations between what one can do in the private sphere as opposed to the public sphere, and the cultural-religious acceptance of embarking upon such a radical move. It appears that the psychological and sociological elements that stand behind the decision to go through with plastic surgery are both more emphatic and hidden in Iran than in any western country.

The debate over self-image and the right to have a private identity in a theocratic Shi'i Iran which is fostering an Islamic identity rather than a national or self-identity has led to people having to live in a dualistic and ambivalent atmosphere. This enables people to adopt Western cultural models of beauty and aesthetics without fighting the religious institutions but also without their blessing. These practices adopted actually function as the sum of the social and public forms of behavior that have been navigated between the ancient Persian culture and the Shi'a religion with some additions from modern Western fashion.

The social changes that have taken place within Iranian society come mainly from internal needs, evolutionary political developments, Western influences, and the acknowledgment of religious traditions—which is a significant factor for the process and inevitably necessary since, without such acknowledgment, the changes could not have taken place. More than that, the symbiosis between the immediate history of the Pahlavi monarchy and its promotion of women's rights, especially the unveiling and the revival of Persian aesthetics, together with the Islamic Republic's encouragement of the social-religious tradition of the *Mut'a* (Temporary Marriage), has opened the gate for men and women to be socially integrated and has, therefore, enabled women to practice new kinds of external appearances that could not be offered in the past.

The history of plastic surgery in general and in Iran in particular is quite ancient. Abdoljalil Kalantar-Hormozi in his article "A Brief History of Plastic Surgery in Iran" says that "archeological discoveries have proven that plastic surgery in its primitive forms dates back to sometime between 3000 BC and 2500 BC in Iran while modern plastic surgery was founded just about 60 years ago."[38] Abdoljalil describes the development of plastic surgery in the Persian-Iranian context from ancient times till the early twentieth century. The most significant developments in plastic surgery were made during the 1950s and the 1970s during the Mohammad Reza Shah era, and mainly involved reconstructive rhinoplasty, modern facial plastic surgery, and craniofacial surgery[39] not particularly in the context of beauty and sexuality.

Kalantar-Hormozi notes that "after the Islamic Revolution in 1979, the approach of many fields of research changed from globalization into localizing fields of knowledge"[40] but this does not explain how the Islamic Revolution brought about the change from globalization to localization. Up until then Iranian plastic surgery only concentrated on craniofacial and reconstructive microsurgery and hand surgeries, rather than on other forms of plastic surgery that already existed in other parts of the world, especially cosmetic surgery for the improvement of beauty and sexuality.

The outbreak of the Iran-Iraq war, however, "was another opportunity for the now capable plastic surgeons of Iran to demonstrate their capabilities in reconstructing many wounded soldiers' craniofacial, trunk, and extremity problems."[41] Because of the acquisition of this experience the plastic surgeons became better known, first and foremost, for their abilities to resolve problems of health and handicap and for making it more possible for the wounded to live more comfortably. The Academic Plastic Surgery Department at Shahid Beheshti University was established "as a training center" and soon become a focal point for other centers around the country (Shiraz, Isfahan, Mashhad, and Ahwaz). Kalantar-Hormozi goes on to tell us that "this field [plastic surgery] of medicine is now one of the most dynamic fields of medical research in Iran and has a promising future."[42]

Although plastic surgery in the theocratic state of Iran now has this "promising future," one must ask the obvious question of whether the Islamic religion allows such surgeries, especially if it is used for cosmetic/beauty improvement and not just as a corrective health and injury problems. More importantly how has Shi'a Islam, which developed separately from Sunni Islam and was developed to become more actively and rationally accepted the reality of plastic and cosmetic surgery?

Like any established and developed religion Islam has its own approach towards plastic and cosmetic surgery, and it is based on philosophical debate over the need for such surgery and bioethical problems that arise from an agenda that believes that the fate of people should come before any desire to change God's creation. The Islamic law (the *Shari'a* or sharia), regarding the issue of the treatment of the sick "is principally concerned with five objectives: protecting life, safeguarding the freedom to believe, maintaining the intellect, preserving human honor and dignity and protecting property."[43] The need for plastic surgery does not fall within any of these five principles.

In this respect Islam is divided over two major issues that both involve the believer's religious fundamental beliefs. The first is "the concept of predestination and the concept of testing." The struggle between the free will and the notion that the believer must believe in his/her predestination is acute since it comes from Quranic verses and interpretations that allow or forbid the believers to make or not make any changes to their bodies, except when it is necessary to cure disease or improve health.[44]

The Sunni and Shi'a Islam approaches are apparently not too different from each other regarding their interpretations of bioethics since, for both, "Islamic bioethics is based on a combination of Islamic principles, duties, obligations, and rights as well as on virtue to a certain extent." On the whole the Shi'a position on "bioethical rulings do not differ fundamentally from the Sunni positions."[45] The question still remains despite these assessments. How is it that plastic and cosmetic surgery, or just "aesthetic surgery" that is not defined as necessary for health reasons "is spreading fast in Muslim countries"[46] and especially in Iran?

In order to answer this question the Muslim scholars had to ask themselves what the motives were that led to the desire of these Moslems to have aesthetic surgery performed on them. "Is it to be condemned as a futile luxury, or does it answer a real physical and psychological need?" In response to this question and assessment they divided the issue into two basic categories the first of which deals with "essential surgery genuinely needed to correct congenital or acquired defects." In such cases they decided that the surgery was permissible since "it is not meant to change the creation of God." The second category was "surgery performed for beautification" and, in this case, they decided that "the surgery is unnecessary and is therefore unlawful (haram) and not permissible."[47]

The general conclusion that can be reached from this debate is that, Islam, like any other civilized philosophy, has its own interpretations and guidelines. Islam does not completely reject plastic surgery and even welcomes it as long as it benefits the patient's health. The real question that needs to be asked here is whether the surgery is done to bring about physical benefits—and so is permissible—or psychological benefits—whose necessity is more difficult to prove. The religious approach towards those who choose to have aesthetic surgery for the purposes of luxurious self-indulgence is certainly negative as this is not a case of "sound legitimate reasons." There is, however, a wide area of ambiguity about this issue that leaves space for interpretation and the need to make decisions, since "the technological, economic, political, and spiritual issues surrounding the life science controversies"[48] differ from one cultural tradition to another. In the case of Islam any decision-making about religious issues gives the Ulama the responsibility to calculate what the nature of a patient's surrounding culture is in order to arrive at an optimal decision regarding the patient's physical and psychological needs.

In surveys that were carried out in both Tehran, Iran (88 participants), and Tel Aviv, Israel (97 participants), during 2013–2014 regarding the readiness of people to have plastic surgery, questions were asked in order to identify social streams, religious dependence and independence, and attitudes towards religion as a factor in making decisions about the surgery. The survey also inquired into the participants' social strata, their marital status, religious identity, and the reasons people had for deciding to have the surgery and so on.

The results are quite interesting and might be seen as predictors of social shifts in Iranian more than Israeli society. In Iran 100 percent of the participants in the survey came from cities and 20 percent of them were aged 18, 50 percent of them were between the ages of 18 and 29, while another 20 percent were between 30 and 39. This parameter signifies that it is the younger generation that is having plastic surgery and indicates that 90 percent of the participants were born after the Islamic revolution.

The marital status says that 59.1 percent of the participants are single, 30.7 percent married, and 10.2 percent divorced. In regard to religious identity 47.7 percent claim that they are traditional, 28.4 percent are religious, and 23.9 percent declare that they are secular. It is interesting to note that those who declared that they are "traditional" added that, despite this, they cannot see themselves as either religious or secular. Although 76.1 percent came from the traditional-religious sector, only 10.2 percent consulted any religious authority (such as a *Mullah* or *Mujtahed*) before having the surgery, and 89.8 percent declared that they did not consult any religious authority. Nevertheless, 80.7 percent said that they themselves paid for the surgery while the rest—19.3 percent—were granted a governmental subsidy. It is important to note that the Iranian government does not subsidize plastic surgery to improve one's cosmetic appearance.

Another interesting parameter that can tell us something about the Iranian-Persian nose is that 59.1 percent of the participants chose to have rhinoplasty surgery while only 9.1 percent had breast surgery (enlargement, reduction, and cancer), 5.7 percent virginity fusion, and the remaining 26.1 percent had other procedures such as Botox injections and facelifts. The reasons given for why these participants chose to have these procedures were to improve their self-image (55.7 percent), social pressure (9.1 percent), and health reasons (18.2 percent). Another interesting parameter is how the immediate environment reacted to the surgical procedures with 67 percent of people being supportive, 22.7 percent being passive, and only 10.2 percent objecting to them. These results are a welcome sign that Iranian society is becoming more and more open and modern than we might have thought. Moreover, 75 percent of the participants said that the surgical procedures had improved their lives while the rest (25 percent) said they had not, but not one claimed that they had made his/her life worse. With regard to self-image and confidence, 71.6 percent reported that the surgery had improved them, 18.2 percent said it had neither changed nor worsened their self-confidence, and only 11.4 percent said that it had not improved their self-image and confidence. The correlation between education and Western influence is significant since only 8 percent of the participants were uneducated while 67 percent were undergraduate students and 25 percent had master's degrees or higher.

When one compares these findings to the Israeli society's attitudes towards plastic surgery, one finds that 78 percent of the participants were under the age of 45 and the remaining 22 percent were older. Four percent consulted a religious authority regarding the procedure while 96 percent did not consider this option (in Iran 10.2 percent consulted a religious authority). Seventy-six percent claimed that the surgery had improved their self-confidence and only 2 percent said it had not while the rest said that it had neither improved it nor made it worse. However, 90.7 percent were happy with the results of the surgery, 2.1 percent claimed they were not, and 7.2 percent said they were ambivalent about it.

In regard to why the participants had chosen to have plastic surgery, 64.9 percent claimed they had had it to improve their self-confidence, 2.1 percent because of social pressure, 11.3 percent because of health problems, 3.1 percent for religious reasons, and the rest for a variety of different reasons.

Regarding the type of surgery they had undergone, 23.7 percent had rhino-plasty surgery, 28.9 percent had breast enlargement, 3.1 percent had virginity fusion, 2.1 percent had facelifts, and the remaining 28.9 percent had other procedures such as Botox injections and body-skin lifts, with another 4.1 percent undergoing surgery for sex-reassignment (SRS).[49]

The reaction of Israeli society to these surgical procedures is a little different from the Iranian as only 48.5 percent reacted in a positive way, while 1 percent objected and 8.2 percent was passive; 23.7 percent were curious about the surgery and 15.5 percent reacted in different ways. Single participants amounted to 55.7 while 37.1 percent were married, 3.1 percent were divorced, and another 3.1 percent were widowed. As for religious iden-tity 66 percent claimed to be secular, 15.6 percent were traditional, and 17.7 percent were orthodox-religious. In regard to the educational status of the participants, in Israel the figures were totally different from Iran's with 39.2 percent of the participants being high-school students, 23.7 percent under-graduate students, 19.6 percent BA graduates and 16.5 percent MA and PhD students. Only 1 percent was uneducated.

When we delve deeper into the statistics and percentages we find very interesting correlations and significance (Sig.). For example if we take the correlation in Iran between the age of the participants and whether they consulted a religious authority before having the plastic surgery or not, we see that all of the participants who consulted a religious authority were under the age of eighteen (P<0.000).

When we examine the results of the religious and nonreligious groups in Iran separately and look for correlation and significance to see whether they are happy with their choice of surgery we find that, for the religious, there is really no change, the secular are very happy with their choice, and the tradi-tional are divided between those who are happy and those who do not really care about it. In Israel, the situation is quite different with 85 percent of the religious happy and 88 percent of the secular people happy with their sur-gery. The question that needs to be asked is: Why do religious Iranians who choose to undergo plastic surgery do it? It seems that the answer is probably much simpler than one would expect.

In Iran, the type of surgery chosen is apparently related to religious iden-tity. For example, in the case of rhinoplasty surgery 42 percent who did this were religious and 58 percent were traditional (compared to Israel where 27.2 percent were religious, 50 percent secular, and the rest traditional). In the case of breast plastic surgery 100 percent of the clients were traditional, and for "other" surgeries, such as liposuction, facelifts or virginity fusion, 95.7 percent were religious and 4.3 percent were traditional.

The reasons for having plastic surgeries in this respect and from what strata the clients come are more important factors to us than what kind of surgery the Iranian government subsidizes. Ninety percent of the religious

Iranian that took part in this survey said that the plastic surgery did not improve their self-confidence, but all the secular and traditional clients said it did improve their lives. In general 75.3 percent said it did improve their self-confidence while the rest felt it did not.

The last set of figures that will help us to construct an Iranian prototype that will help us know the reasons for why Iranian people have plastic surgery and what motivates them, relates to the type of surgery versus the reasons. Sixteen percent of the rhinoplasty surgery participants said they had it because of social pressure and 84 percent said it was to improve their self-confidence. One hundred percent of the breast-enlargement or reduction and cancer participants said it was due to health reasons. As for "other" types of surgeries (liposuction, facelifts, virginity fusion, and sex reassignment surgeries), 34.8 percent claim they had it for health reasons and 65.2 percent for religious reason, and, again, this could also include sex-reassignment surgeries or virginity fusion.

CONCLUSION

As declared in the introduction the main goal of this chapter has been to show the current symbiosis between religion and culture, past and present, and what is forbidden and allowed in the new Iranian society, and to present the way the Iranians deal with concealed beauty, and uncovered sexuality to identify and create self-esteem. In our limited research we have only been able to scratch the surface of the issues involved but have tried, through examining attitudes towards sexuality, beauty and gender in Iran, to arrive at a better understanding of the general issue which is the functioning of the factors that fashion self-identity.

Shahla Haeri, in her brilliant chapter entitled "Temporary Marriage: an Islamic Discourse on Female Sexuality in Iran," says, regarding Iranian/Shi'i women's sexuality, that "[A]lthough Shii legal texts devote extensive attention to such matters as marriage, divorce, custody of children, and the reciprocal obligations of husband and wife, they have remained virtually silent on issues of female sexuality."[50] Abandoning sexual matters in the context of *Mut'a* (temporary marriage) has led Iranian women to finding other ways to discover their sexuality and beauty. The vacuum left by the Shi'i religious leadership has given these women the ability to re-create and reinterpret their understanding of beautification and sexuality.

The few options that exist within the Iranian climate and the little publicity that exists are insufficient for the needs of Iranian women compared to her comrades in the West. Nevertheless Iranian women have managed to reach undeclared *modus vivendi* with the religious leadership, which has enabled them to use the current dress-code obligations and the religious options regarding cosmetic and aesthetic surgery for their benefit. Making these efforts in the religious atmosphere that exists in Iran has helped Iranian women to rebuild and to renew their sense of self and identity as modern women, who, although they live under religious restrictions, do not give up their desire to shape their feminine characteristics.

Putting aside the psychological pressures and influences that Iranian women surely feel, whether they be social, cultural, or religious pressures, we can surely say that, through an examination of the culture of plastic surgery in Iran, we have been able to identify a significant trend that emphasizes the need of the self in women to feel sexual and beautiful and so improve the quality of their lives by utilizing the possibilities offered by plastic surgery. Moreover, the surprising, significant, and correlated finding that Iranian people who have plastic surgery do so without consulting or seeking religious advice indicates a level of social independence and probably indicates a certain level of disconnection and disassociation with the religious system. This lack of consultation, especially concerning deeds associated with Western lifestyles, may indicate that there are social changes taking place that even the Iranian government has no power to fight or change, especially since plastic-surgery clinics are now spread all over the country and since some of the procedures are being subsidized by the regime.

Those who did consult the clerics before having the surgery are under the age of eighteen, which indicates that they are basically under their family's supervision and influence. We obviously cannot say whether they have done this willingly or have been forced to but, either way, the numbers are too small to indicate any public trend of consulting the clerics. The other conclusion that can be drawn is that people feel more responsible for their own fate when it, of course, does not lead to any confrontation with religious public life but is concentrated within the private worlds of people.

We can also conclude that Iranian men and women are taking advantage of the availability of these surgical procedures which, aside from improving self-esteem and personality, can also be a way to increase the options available to people within society, whether these involve the workplace or connubial bliss. Beauty and sexuality also contribute to a sense of power and security and, in countries in which the ability to utilize these advantages is severely limited by religious restrictions, people need to accept these limitations and turn them into advantages. Even though some of the results of plastic surgery are hardly displayed publicly, such as breast surgery for enlargement/reduction and cancer, liposuction, and virginity fusion, they do enhance a feeling of self-esteem and personality improvement and, of course, solve religious and health problems.

NOTES

1. Afsaneh Najmabadi, "Gendered Transformations: Beauty, Love, and Sexuality in Qajar Iran," *Iranian Studies*, Vol. 34, No. 1/4 (2001), p. 91.

2. Ibid., p. 92.

3. Carla Gramaglia and Enrica Marzola, "Self-Esteem and Personality in Patients with Body Dysmorphic Disorder Undergoing Cosmetic Rhinoplasty," in Melvin A. Shiffman and Alberto Di Giuseppe (eds.), *Advanced Aesthetic Rhinoplasty—Art, Science, and New Clinical Techniques* (Springer: Verlag Berlin Heidelberg, 2013), p. 77.

4. Ibid., p. 82.

5. Ibid., p. 83.

6. Or *Eruv* which is a kind of virtual border or enclosure that was placed around the city and that allowed the settlers to take in or out stuff or things from their houses to other houses.

7. Mishna, *Shabbat*, chapter 6, article 6.

8. Shireen Mahdavi, "Shawhar Ahu Khanum: Passion, Polygamy and Tragedy," *Middle Eastern Studies*, Vol. 24, No. 1 (Jan. 1988), p. 113.

9. Ibid., pp. 116–17.

10. Patricia J. Higgins, "Women in the Islamic Republic of Iran: Legal, Social, and Ideological Changes," *Signs*, Vol. 10, No. 3 (Spring 1985), p. 492.

11. Homa Hoodfar, "Devices and Desires: Population Policy and Gender Roles in the Islamic Republic," *Middle East Report*, No. 190, Gender, Population, Environment (Sep.–Oct. 1994), p. 11.

12. Ibid., p. 15.

13. Ibid., p. 11.

14. Ibid., pp. 13–14. The Bahais elaborated this conception into ideology. For further information about it, see my *The Hojjatiyeh Society in Iran: Ideology and Practice from the 1950s to the Present* (New York: Macmillan Palgrave, 2013), pp. 49–64.

15. Hoodfar, p. 15.

16. Firoozeh Kashani-Sabet, "Who Is Fatima?—Gender, Culture, and Representation in Islam," *Journal of Middle East Women's Studies*, Vol. 1, No. 2 (Spring 2005), p. 20.

17. Azar Tabari, "The Enigma of Veiled Iranian Women," *Feminist* Review, No. 5 (1980), pp. 23–24.

18. Houchang E. Chehabi, "Staging the Emperor's New Clothes: Dress Codes and Nation-Building under Reza Shah," *Iranian Studies*, Vol. 26, No. 3–4 (Summer/Fall 1993), p. 209.

19. Shahla Haeri, "Temporary Marriage: An Islamic Discourse on Female Sexuality in Iran," in Mahnaz Afkhami and Erika Friedl (eds.), *In the Eye of the Storm—Women in Post-Revolutionary Iran* (New York: Syracuse University Press, 1994), pp. 107–8.

20. Chehabi, pp. 210–12.

21. Ibid., p. 219.

22. Haeri, p. 110.

23. Tabari, p. 20.

24. Ibid., p. 26.

25. Ibid., pp. 26–27.

26. Ibid., pp. 27–29.

27. Yasmin Crowther, *Saffron Kitchen* (Penguin Books, 2007), pp. 33–34.

28. Ibid., p. 73.

29. Ibid., p. 160.

30. Ibid., p. 163.

31. Marina Nemat, *Prisoner of Tehran: One Woman's Story of Survival Inside an Iranian Prison* (Free Press, 2008), p. 37.

32. Ibid., p. 53.

33. Ibid., p. 135.

34. Ibid., p. 138. For more information and a fascinating brief history on the cosmetic in the Iranian world see Fatema Soudavar Farmanfarmaian, "Haft Qalam Arayish: Cosmetics in the Iranian World," *Iranian Studies*, Vol. 33, No. 3/4 (Summer–Autumn, 2000), pp. 285–326. It is important to note the limitation of this research regarding the *hejab* advantages and disadvan-

tages among Muslim women. For further discussion and details, see Viren Swami, Jusnara Miah, Nazerine Noorani, and Donna Tylor, "Is the hijab protective? An investigation of body image and related constructs among British Muslim women," *British Journal of Psychology*, 105 (2014), pp. 352–63.

35. Nemat, p. 164.

36. Ibid., p. 199.

37. Ibid., p. 288.

38. Abdoljalil Kalantar-Hormozi, "A Brief History of Plastic Surgery in Iran," *Archives of Iranian Medicine*, Vol. 16, No. 3 (Mar., 2013), p. 201.

39. Ibid., p. 203–5.

40. Ibid., p. 206.

41. Ibid., p. 206.

42. Ibid., p. 206.

43. Bishara S. Atiyeh, Mohamad Kadry, Shady N. Hayek, and Ramzi S. Musharafieh, "Aesthetic Surgery and Religion: Islamic Law Perspective," *Aesthetic Plastic Surgery* 32 (2008), p. 3.

44. Ibid., p. 4.

45. Ibid., p. 5.

46. Ibid., p. 6.

47. Ibid., p. 6.

48. Ibid., p. 8.

49. For more information about the legality of SRS in Iran see Afsaneh Najmabadi, "Transing and Transpassing across Sex-Gender Walls in Iran," *Women's Studies Quarterly*, Vol. 36, No. 3/4, (Fall–Winter, 2008), pp. 23–42.

50. Haeri, p. 104.

Chapter Seven

Iranians against the "Other"

Iranian Identity in the Social Media Era

Raz Zimmt

In December 2013 Iran was drawn to play against Argentina in Group F of the 2014 World Cup football games in Brazil. After the draw ended Iranian "netizens" flocked to the official Facebook page of the Argentinean soccer star, Lionel Messi, to curse and insult him. One of the Iranian fans used the fact that the star's name in Persian means "made of bronze" to mock Messi and wrote the following on his Facebook page: "Messi, you are made of bronze but even if you were made of gold, you wouldn't be able to do a thing against Iran." At some point, the soccer player felt compelled to respond to the aspersions and wrote: "I'm sorry for these people because it's so unfriendly to use such words."[1] The reactions of these Iranian soccer fans were criticized by their fellow countrymen who argued that the aspersions cast upon Messi showed a lack of civility. "These are not Iranians. Real Iranians wouldn't have acted like that," read a comment on the news site *Tabnak*. Another comment stated: "I opposed the blocking of Facebook [by the Iranian regime], but now I think Facebook should be blocked because we're not culturally developed enough to use it."[2]

The late English historian Eric Hobsbawm argued that:

> What has made sport so uniquely effective a medium for inculcating national feelings . . . is the ease with which even the least political or public individuals can identify with the nation as symbolized by young persons excelling at what practically every man wants, or at one time in his life has wanted, to be good at. The imagined community of millions seems more real as a team of eleven named people.[3]

Whether the reactions of Iranian soccer fans were expressions of patriotism and national pride or of vulgarity and a lack of civility, they do provide evidence of the potential social networking sites (SNS) have to express a collective identity against "the Other."

The growing usage of the social media and the persistent control exercised by the Iranian regime over the traditional media outlets have turned these social networking sites into a central arena for social and political battles in the Islamic Republic. The Internet has evolved into a channel that allows Iranian citizens to hold relatively free discussions, convey messages, and form contacts with fellow netizens in Iran and abroad. Research done on social media in Iran in the past decade, especially since the riots that erupted after the 2009 presidential elections, has tended to emphasize the potential of social networks to initiate political protests and promote democratization. Although this potential cannot be ignored, focusing on the political aspects of SNS usage tends to overlook additional, central issues that are part of the discourse taking place on SNS.

An examination of the public discourse on Iranian SNS shows that they are used as a platform for mass rallying on issues that are perceived by the Iranian public as having significant national value. In cases when Iran faces external threats the discourse on social media tends to express a shared national identity that sometimes succeeds in rising above the political disagreements that normally characterize Iranian society. The reactions of Iranian netizens often reflect a sense of national pride and a willingness to defend national symbols, especially when they find themselves in confrontation with a non-Iranian "Other." Using several case studies this essay intends to demonstrate how social networks have become a channel for a patriotic discourse that conveys a national collective identity.

THE INCREASING USE OF SOCIAL NETWORKING SITES IN IRAN

The penetration rate of the Internet in Iran has been rising since the country was first connected to it in the early 1990s, and by the end of the twentieth century 230 research institutions in Iran were connected to the global network. In addition, there was not only a rise in the number of local Internet providers but the infrastructure was expanded, and access to the Internet was improved, especially in urban centers. A sharp rise was also recorded in the number of private connections and public points of access in libraries and cafés. According to the International Telecommunications Union (ITU), the number of Iranian Internet users rose from about two hundred thousand in 1999 to 25 million by 2009. [4] The penetration rate of the Internet has risen steadily since then and by 2014 reached 49.1 percent of the population. In

Tehran, the penetration rate is even higher and stands at about 68 percent of the residents.[5]

In contrast to the regime's enduring control over traditional media (print, radio, and television) the Internet has developed as a relatively free communication channel for expressing opinions, sharing information, and creating connections. Fairly early on, the leadership of the Iranian regime was concerned about the popularity of the Internet and the free flow of information it facilitated, especially among young urbanites, because of the exchange of information online from Iran and to it and especially because the penetration of Western cultural influences challenged the regime's information management strategy. The policy of the Islamic Republic vis-à-vis the Internet gradually developed into the imposition of a complex set of legal, technical, and social limitations on the one hand, and an openness to information exchange that allowed individuals and civil society to flourish on the other. The regime's ambivalent policy toward the Internet is, in its purest form, manifested in the approach to social networking sites that high-ranking Iranian officials sometimes paradoxically refer to as tools used by Iran's enemies and western intelligence agencies.[6]

Starting in the late 2000s Iranian cyberspace began to undergo significant changes. The Iranian blogosphere, which had grown significantly between 2002 and 2010, saw a decrease in its importance and activity and, at the same time, social networking sites began growing in popularity. A study published in March 2014 by the Iran Media Program at the University of Pennsylvania showed that many Iranian netizens and bloggers have found SNS to be a quicker and more useful platform.[7] Subsequently the spread of the global social networks Facebook and Twitter have led to a phasing out of blogs and have squeezed out smaller SNS, many of which had catered to professional, national, and other groups, thus limiting their potential size. Despite the efforts of Iranian authorities to limit the use of these SNS by blocking the sites and restricting surfing speed, the SNS are creating a growing communication infrastructure that serves Iranian netizens who are using illegal tools to circumvent the various government blocks and filters used since 2009.[8] Although there is no clear data available regarding the number of Iranians who use Facebook and other SNS, their numbers are estimated to be in the millions. In an interview to Al-Jazeera English in January 2014, the Minister of Culture and Islamic Guidance, Ali Jannati, stated that four million Iranians have Facebook profiles.[9]

THE DISCOURSE ON THE POTENTIAL FOR POLITICAL DISSENT ON SOCIAL NETWORKS

The riots that erupted following the Iranian presidential election in the summer of 2009 spotlighted the ability of social networks to promote political protest and democratization in societies where the traditional media are controlled or restricted by the regime. Following the outbreak of the protest movement Western observers and commentators rushed to point out the great influence of Twitter in the struggle, and some even dubbed it the "Twitter Revolution."[10] Others doubted the importance of the role of social networks in leading significant processes of political and social change. Clearly, there is no doubt that the protest movement in Iran used social networks to organize and that SNS gained prominence because all the other media were controlled by the regime. The SNS made the speedy dissemination of information possible and allowed the reformist opposition to bypass the restrictions placed by authorities on the traditional media and so drum up nationwide support. From the moment mass protests erupted, following the announcement of the results of the June 12 elections, the Internet was flooded with photographs, videos, and personal testimonies of protesters from the streets of Tehran. Digital activists used their connections to netizens around the world who cooperated with them throughout the riots.[11]

The importance of SNS in supporting the protest movement in Iran led to the adoption of an optimistic—if not naïve—attitude in the Western media which tended to perceive the social media as a "miracle cure" that would usher democratic reform into the Middle East. This attitude gained further popularity due to the role SNS played in the political change processes that the Arab world underwent in 2011–2012 called "the Arab Spring." The development of the analytical discourse on social networks in Iran and the Middle East in the past few years has contributed to a better understanding of their role in democratization processes and promoting political reforms in the region. The protests demonstrated the fact that the Internet is a wide-reaching and accessible platform for spreading ideas. At the same time, the protests showed that the SNS alone cannot bring about significant social and political change without there being the physical activity of citizens to make such changes real. Vasileios Karagiannopoulos, who discussed the role of the Internet in the political struggles in Iran and Egypt, argued that, "Perceiving the use of these online applications as the epicenter of national political struggles . . . promotes a unilateral and narrow understanding of these events."[12] The Internet was, according to him, useful in organizing and advertising the protest movement as well as in exerting political pressure on the regimes; but the riots did not happen due to the use of SNS and these did not guarantee their failure or success which mostly depended upon "various contextual elements, such as background socio-political conditions, tactical choices, the organizational level of adversaries, and the extent of popular and international support."[13]

Just a year following the eruption of the riots Golnaz Esfandiari, a reporter for *Radio Free Europe*, argued that Iran did not actually experience a "Twitter Revolution" since, according to her, most of the tweets about the protest movement came from outside of Iran and the SNS were not used for rallying the Iranian masses.[14] Polls carried out in the past few years indicate that most Iranian netizens don't use SNS for political purposes. A survey among 188 Iranian netizens conducted in October and November 2012 showed that just 5 percent of those surveyed reported that the main reason they used Facebook was to promote political and social activism, 60 percent reported that they used the site to communicate with friends and relatives, 16 percent to access news and information and 11 percent for entertainment purposes.[15] In addition most Iranian Facebook users tend to be passive rather than active which means they prefer to follow updates on Facebook and not share information themselves, especially content that is political in nature.[16] Another poll conducted among twenty-eight hundred Iranian youths in 2011 showed that most of the content posted by netizens (54 percent) was about their personal lives while 44 percent dealt with news and current events of which 32 percent dealt with foreign policy, 25 percent with community issues, and 21 percent with economics.[17]

Although there is no doubt about the importance of the debate concerning the potential for political dissent in social media, focusing on this issue has diverted attention from other uses of the social networks that are not aimed at challenging the regime or promoting political or social activism. Due to the instantaneous, accessible, and widespread nature of the Internet, it allows the public to make their voices heard on various issues that do not necessarily express opposition to the regime. Although the social media cannot promote immediate political change they can provide a platform for free civil discourse that may reify collective consciousness and allow for public mobilization around common national symbols, and the campaign waged in early 2014 to bring about the release of five Iranian soldiers captured on the Iran-Pakistan border provides a good example for just that.

THE CAMPAIGN TO RELEASE THE CAPTURED SOLDIERS: NATIONAL MOBILIZATION ON THE SOCIAL MEDIA

In early February 2014, the extremist Baloch group, *Jaysh-ul-'Adl* (Army of Justice), announced the capture of five Iranian soldiers on the Iran-Pakistan border. Since its founding in 2012 the group has claimed responsibility for several attacks against Iranian security forces in the Sistan-Balochistan region in southeast Iran. This region is inhabited by the Baloch minority which consists of Sunni Muslims and makes up 2 percent of Iranian society.[18] On March 23, *Jaysh-ul-'Adl* announced the execution of Jamshid Danaeifar, one of the five soldiers. The group threatened that if Iranian authorities refuse to comply with its demand to release Sunni prisoners jailed in Iran, another soldier would be executed in another ten days.[19] On April 4, the organization released the four remaining soldiers alive, following negotiations conducted through the mediation of senior Baloch clerics.

Shortly after the abduction of the soldiers, a mass public campaign was launched on the social media sites calling for their release. Thousands of Iranian netizens opened Facebook pages, shared photos, published supportive messages for the effort to release the captured soldiers, and signed a petition calling for their release. As part of this campaign, the hashtag #FreeIranianSoldiers was used to raise awareness about the fate of the five soldiers and the execution of one of them aroused a great deal of discussion on the SNS. The timing of the execution, in the midst of the Nowruz (New Year) break, a period in which traditional media barely operate, transformed the social networks into the main media arena for the story. The death of the soldier aroused expressions of sorrow and anger and many of the netizens directed their rage at the Baloch group as well as Pakistan and Saudi Arabia, who were accused of supporting the group. The Facebook page titled "Protests in Front of Pakistani Embassies Worldwide" garnered thousands of "likes" and was used to coordinate protests in front of Pakistani embassies in Iran and outside of it.[20]

Most of the criticism was leveled at Iranian authorities for failing to release the soldiers and some of the netizens blamed President Rouhani and his government for not doing enough to bring about the release of the captured soldiers. The Facebook page of the Foreign Minister, Mohammad Javad Zarif, was flooded with thousands of comments from Iranian citizens who argued that he had not made enough of a diplomatic effort to resolve the crisis. Due to this harsh criticism, the foreign minister was forced to issue a statement in which he emphasized the government's commitment to releasing the soldiers. Zarif mentioned that he could understand the criticism of the government but added that slogans alone could not bring about the release of the soldiers and might complicate the situation.[21] In their effort to emphasize the government's ineptness, some of the netizens mentioned the efforts made by the Israeli government to release its captured soldiers, especially Gilad Shalit whose photo was shared hundreds of time on the social media while highlighting the intensive efforts of the Israeli government to bring about his release. "Sometimes I say that Israelis are better than us," stated one of the netizens, "even though they don't spare Palestinians, they are willing to trade hundreds of Palestinians for one of their soldiers."[22]

The social media campaign to release the soldiers demonstrated the netizens' ability to exert public pressure on the regime but importance of the campaign was not just the public pressure that forced the Iranian authorities to act. First and foremost this campaign reflected the willingness of the Iranian public to mobilize themselves around struggles for issues that it deemed to be of utmost national importance. The discourse on the SNS in this affair reflected a shared national consciousness despite the disagreements expressed among netizens about the right policy for resolving the crisis. The struggle to release the soldiers managed to unify citizens with different political outlooks including citizens living both in Iran and Iranian expatriates. The social media's ability to foster a shared national consciousness is especially evident in issues that arouse sensitivities related to matters involving Iranian identity and national honor.

COLLECTIVE AND INDIVIDUAL NATIONAL IDENTITY IN THE SOCIAL MEDIA ERA

With the appearance of modern Iranian nationalism in the late nineteenth century secular Iranian intellectuals began defining Iran as a nation; one way of defining what constituted the Iranian identity was in terms of the Other, be it western, Islamic, or Arab in terms of language, race, history, culture, religion, or ideology. [23]

Academic discourse on Iranian nationalism has been influenced since 1990s by theoretical literature on the development of Nationalism. [24] Influenced by Gellner who ruled that nationalism "invents nations where they do not exist," [25] Mostafa Vaziri claimed that Iranian nationalism was invented and adopted by Iranian intellectuals influenced by European Orientalist research. [26] Other researchers, such as Mohammad Tavakoli-Targhi, referred to the importance of local forces such as territory, history, language, religion, and culture in building national narrative and national identity. [27]

When Iran is compared to modern nations, one sees that Iran has a number of pre-modern characteristics that have contributed to the rise of nationalism. The idea of Iranian territory (*Iranshahr*) has existed since antiquity with one state or empire ruling the territory that is now Iran for several hundreds of years preceding the rise of Islam and again under the Safavid Dynasty (1501–1722) and the Qajars (1796–1925). Iran's identification with the Persian language and literature has also greatly contributed to the development of Iranian nationalism and, although the use of the Persian language does not exactly match Iran's borders, it is considered to be the most important language within its borders. One more unifying national factor is, of course, the fact that about 90 percent of Iranians are Shi'ite Muslims. [28]

The Persian cultural identity is a central component for the definition of the Iranian national identity and its importance has been preserved even after the Islamic Revolution (1979). Despite the hostility of the Islamist regime towards the blatant secularism of the Pahlavi regime and its apprehension about the efforts of this regime to highlight the pre-Islamic past of Iran, the Islamic Republic has adopted the nationalist narrative, although it presents it in an Islamic framework of time. The persistence of pre-Islamic traditions in the Islamic Republic, such as the Persian New Year (*Nowruz*) and the *Chaharshanbe Suri* which is a traditional purification ceremony for removing misfortune on the eve of the new year, are a testament to the powerful nature of the national-cultural component of the Iranian identity. This component exists alongside the religious-Islamic component and sometimes surpasses it. Iranian authorities have failed in their attempts to eliminate these pre-Islamic traditions that originated in the Zoroastrian religion, and have been forced to accept them while trying instead to Islamize them.

The Islamic Republic has also not abandoned the national-cultural narrative in its foreign policy. Ideologically, it would seem clear that nationalism is a foreign concept to the Islamic regime but the postrevolutionary regime had to consider Iranian national interests in shaping its foreign policy. The Islamic Republic's foreign policy placed a high priority on establishing and increasing Iran's influence among Muslim Shi'ites, who were slated to be the standard bearers of the idea of the Islamic Revolution. This was especially apparent in Iran's special relations with Hezbollah in Lebanon and the Shi'ite movements in Iraq. While, in its relations with fellow Shi'ite Muslims it highlighted the religious commonality, in its relations with the Muslim republics in central Asia, Iran highlighted the common national-cultural Iranian aspect.[29] This combination of different components in Iran's national identity to achieve national interests is what has allowed Iran to most effectively realize its historic aspirations for regional dominance and hegemony.

The ability of Internet technologies to cross geographical borders has given rise to the hope that nationalism and other narrow bases for creating communities will be replaced by other, more inclusive, forms of identity. It seems that new media is able to provide the perfect ground for people to establish new social relationships and this possibility seemed to find fertile ground, especially in Iran where the ruling regime identified everything in religious terms.[30] At the end of the 1990s and early 2000s the development of the Internet led scholars to speculate about its potential to affect nationalism, national identity, and national boundaries. Some argued that the contraction of physical distances would make national borders less relevant and would lead individuals to form bonds as members of global, rather than national, communities. The idea that digital communication allows netizens to create "virtual communities" based on choice and is not limited by physical or political conditions continues to be popular among netizens.[31]

It appears that the spread of new media also seems to have the potential to augment trends towards individualism in society as evidenced by the rise of blogs and social media, which has reflected the possible desire for individual expression. Many Persian-language blogs have focused on the authors and expressed the aspirations, thoughts, and feelings of individual bloggers. The importance of the individual taking control over the content and finding his/her own unedited voice has been expressed in the name of the blog entitled "Editor Myself," posted by Hossein Derakhshan, who is considered to be the godfather of blogging in Iran. Many blogs transformed themselves into arenas in which the individual lives of the writers, with family photographs, love songs, and confessions about relationships, could be presented.[32] Surveys that examined the use of Facebook also indicate that users of the global network usually use it to publish private content.[33]

The capability of the SNS to bolster individualistic tendencies at the expense of collective identity in Iran is especially important due to the growing tendency towards individualism in Iranian society, especially among the younger generation. Recent years have witnessed an increase in internal criticism in Iran regarding the weakness of Iranian society and the growing tendency for individualism at the expense of social solidarity. Some of the critics have blamed the growing Western influence especially among middle-class young urbanites, for these weaknesses, while others have attributed them to the deteriorating economic crisis and social hardships. In March 2012 an Iranian journalist published a report about the "double lives" of the middle class in Iran who take advantage of every opportunity to have fun, drink alcohol, and attend parties. One year after the 2009 riots the journalist addressed the argument about the lack of social solidarity among the Iranian public. One Iran-Iraq War veteran shared his impressions with the journalist: "During the war soldiers were proud to lose a limb because they believed they were fighting for something holy. Kids these days don't feel that. They don't know what they're fighting for."[34] Reformist activist Alborz Zahedi mentioned the lack of social solidarity in Iran in an article he published in October 2012 in which he argued that Iranian citizens want all the civil rights of citizens in a modern democratic society but are unwilling to bear social responsibility, express even basic social solidarity, or carry out simple tasks such as cleaning the streets around their homes. They act only for themselves and not for others.[35]

Discussions on the crisis of values in Iranian society have also taken place in the social media as well. On January 30, 2014, thousands of people stormed dozens of movie theaters across Iran in an attempt to gain admission to free movie screenings organized by the Cinema Association of Iranian cinema to mark the thirty-fifth anniversary of the Islamic Revolution. Due to the stampede, some of the cinemas became scenes of physical confrontation among ardent moviegoers. In several cities the crowds broke the glass windows of the movie houses in attempts to get inside and, in the city of Mashhad, the police had to intervene because of the onslaught of the public. A few days later the government began distributing baskets of free basic goods to needy citizens earning the minimum wage ($175 per month) or less. The distribution spots became scenes for mass gatherings, long queues, crowdedness, physical confrontations, and the storming of citizens towards the baskets, which included small amounts of rice, eggs, chicken, oil, butter, and cheese. Both events led to sharp social criticism mostly expressed on the SNS. The mass onslaught on the cinemas and the physical confrontations that erupted in the distribution spots of the food baskets were perceived to be demonstrations of the crisis of values in Iranian society which according to critics, is being expressed in the adoption of Western patterns of behavior and tendencies for individualism and escapism. Some of those who have commented on the events online have found a connection between them and the processions marking Revolution Day which, according to them, have been transformed from being political and revolutionary events into colorful festivals devoid of meaning and mostly an excuse for going out and shopping.

Despite the potential ability of new media to diminish the importance of collective national identities and empower individualistic and pan-national trends it seems their influence is not clear-cut. In her research Niki Akhavan argues that: "While Internet technologies facilitate the gathering of disparately located individuals, it is nationalism that in some sense does the heavy lifting in motivating and maintaining the transnational mobilizations that digital media makes possible."[36] Blogs, which are one of the most individual and private forms of expression in the public space, also have visible trends toward collective efforts not only in producing a web log but also "in creating networks through linkages between friends, professional colleagues, sympathizers, and other relevant bloggers and site operators."[37]

The virtual space has become an important meeting place for Iranian activists and intellectuals and provides them with not only alternative channels of communication, but also, international support and solidarity, including that of expatriate Iranians, for example, by collecting signatures for petitions or raising money through the net in support of national goals.[38] I will examine the way Iranian social networks are used for civilian mobilization based on collective national identity using several case studies in which Iranian netizens express their identity versus the "Other," that is, the Arabs and the West.

IRANIAN IDENTITY ON THE SNS AND THE IRANIAN-ARAB CONFRONTATION

The connections between Arabs and Iranians were first forged during the ancient Persian Empire, which existed between 550 BCE and 331 BCE. Limited cultural and trade relations existed between these two ancient civilizations of the Iranians in Persia and the Arabs living between the Euphrates and Tigris rivers and in the Arab peninsula.[39] The Arab occupation and arrival of Islam in the seventh century led to a significant change in political alignment in the Middle East and closer relations between the Iranians and the Arabs. After they had been defeated by the Arabs the Iranians converted to Islam but did not lose their language and unique identity. Iran preserved its cultural and ethnic distinctiveness, its residents remained Iranian, and their language continued to be Persian, although it was significantly influenced by Arabic. The adoption of Islam by Iranians did not decrease the tensions that existed between them and the Arabs and, it can be said, even intensified the struggle between them and a form of cultural competition about the extent of their contributions to Islamic culture. [40]

Iranian attitudes toward Arabs is directly linked to the complexity of the Iranian identity, and this is one of the main issues intellectuals and political movements in Iran have been dealing with since the late nineteenth century. The complexity of Iranian identity has to do with two main focal points of identification: 1) the tradition of Iranian national culture which developed both before and after the Arab conquest in the seventh century; and 2) the Islamic-Shi'ite culture that ingrained itself in Iran mostly following the institution of Shi'a as the state religion by the Safavids in 1501. Meskoob has pointed out the appearance of a separate Iranian identity apart from the Arab "Other" and argues that, after they had been defeated by the Arabs and converted to Islam the Iranian people returned to their past. Like Arabs the Iranians were now Muslims but spoke a different language. In the tenth century, when they established their first local dynasties and began composing poetry in their own language, Iranians renewed their character as an independent nation. After four hundred years, when it was clear that all other means and attempts to break away from Arab control had failed, they turned to two things to preserve themselves as a distinct nation separate from other Muslims: their history and language.[41]

The emphasis placed upon Iran's pre-Islamic past as a source of national-cultural pride became a central component in the national narrative under the rule of the Pahlavi dynasty. Iran's secular intelligentsia adopted the Aryan hypothesis and began basing its historical arguments on this narrative. Textbooks contained messages about Iranian superiority compared to the inferior invaders who wished to conquer Iran's spirit—which meant the Arabs, Mongols, and Turks. This theory became the basis for a new history, and the separation between the pre-Islamic and Islamic periods, as it was described in textbooks, became emphasized and well preserved.[42] The struggle led by the Pahlavi regime against the clergy and its efforts to glorify pre-Islamic traditions contributed to the rise of anti-Arab feelings connected to the humiliation the Arabs had inflicted upon the Sassanid Empire in the seventh century.[43]

Following the establishment of the Islamic Republic the conflict between the focal points of national and religious identification quickly rose to the surface in the policies of the new regime. Unlike the nationalist attitude that had guided the previous regime, the teachings of the leader of the Islamic Revolution, Ayatollah Rouhullah Khomeini, was based on the unity of the Muslim *ummah*. Iran's policies towards its Arab neighbors were now characterized by ambivalence and were guided by a mixture of ideological considerations and national interests. The question of Iranian identity, the past bitterness between the Iranians and the Arabs, and the definition of Iranian national interests, are clearly evident in the public discourse taking place on the SNS, especially when Iranian netizens believe that the "Others," the Arabs, are threatening their national identity or the territorial integrity of their country.

On February 14, 2013, the hardliner cleric Hojjat-ul-Islam Mehdi Ta'eb, gave a speech at a conference organized by student Basij members in Tehran, in which he argued that Iran should make Syria a priority over the Khuzestan region in southwest Iran. In a discussion on the developments in the Syrian civil war, Ta'eb referred to Syria as "the thirty-fifth and strategic province of Iran" and said that if the enemy attacked Iran and wanted to occupy either Syria or Khuzestan, Iran should decide that safeguarding Syria is a priority since, if Iran continues to hold on to Syria, it would still be able to reclaim Khuzestan while, if Iran lost Syria, it would not be able to even hold on to Tehran.[44]

Ta'eb's comments sparked an angry reaction in the Iranian media and SNS with many saying that the cleric's statement showed preference for giving foreign aid to an Arab country over citizens of his own country. Iranian netizens angrily responded to his statement, attacking him personally and calling him a "motherland sellout" (*vatan foroosh*) and even accusing him of treason. One netizen suggested sending Ta'eb to fight in Syria alongside President Assad. In their criticism many netizens mentioned the great sacrifices Iranian citizens had made during the war against Iraq (1980–1988) which had affected the province of Khuzestan the most. One of the netizens wondered how the cleric could claim that Syria was more important than Khuzestan after eight years of warfare that had resulted in such a large number of casualties, injured, disabled, and POWs. Another netizen argued that if Ta'eb meant to emphasize Syria's importance for Iran he could have used another example and not Khuzestan, which has served as a symbol of heroism and a monument to the blood of the soldiers who fought for it. He then went on to say that Iranians would never agree to give up any of Khuzestan's land not only not for Damascus but not even for all of Syria and that, in a case of war breaking out between Iran and Syria, Iranians would only be willing to defend their own land.[45] Kourosh Zaim, a member of the Central Council of the Iranian National Front, posted a note on his Facebook page in which he addressed Ta'eb directly and condemned his statement, writing, "If we ever give up Khuzestan, we will never be able to reclaim it. . . . We will lose the country's revenues from oil and you will not be able to help Syria." He ended his address with these words: "If you wish to replace my Khuzestan with Syria, I will go to war against you." Zaim received numerous supportive reactions from Iranian netizens who harshly criticized the conservative cleric. In one of the responses, an Iranian Facebook user wrote: "Our fathers fought for Khuzestan, while you, cleric, are going to fight for Syria. This is the difference between us."[46]

Ta'eb's statement was used by regime opponents to lambast the Islamic Republic's policy that prefers, according to its critics, to provide foreign aid to its allies over focusing on solving the hardships of Iranian citizens. An expatriate Iranian blogger published a post on his blog in response to the cleric's statement, entitled, "The Provinces of the Islamic Republic of Iran." In the post, he listed the "provinces" of Iran according to the priorities of the Islamic Republic. The list included Palestine, Lebanon, Venezuela, Karbala, and Najaf in Iraq, North Korea, Syria, and a long list of several countries in Africa.[47]

This wave of patriotic sentiment expressed as a result of Ta'eb's statement was also evident following other incidents that aroused the sensitivity of Iranian citizens to their national-cultural identity and Iran's territorial integrity. Thus, for example, a conference supporting the Arab minority in Khuzestan held in Cairo in January 2013 aroused angry reactions from Iranian netizens on the SNS. The conference was attended by representatives from the separatist Ahwazi justice movement, clerics from all over the Muslim world, representatives of al-Azhar College in Cairo and several representatives of Egyptian political movements associated with the Muslim Brotherhood, headed by 'Emad Abd al-Ghafour, the advisor of former Egyptian President Muhammad Morsi. The conference was held during a visit to Cairo of Iranian Foreign Minister Ali Akbar Salehi. and Iranian netizens quickly took to the SNS to angrily react to ideas of separatism in Iran. They condemned the Egyptian government and President Morsi and demanded a severe Iranian response to Egypt's actions against Iranian interests.[48]

A statement made by Iranian Foreign Minister Mohammad-Javad Zarif sparked a similar firestorm in December 2012. In his statement the Foreign Minister said that Iran was willing to negotiate with the United Arab Emirates about Abu-Musa, one of the three islands that had been occupied by Iran since 1971 and which were at the center of a dispute between the countries.[49] Following this statement, the social media, including the Facebook page of Zarif, were flooded with the angry reactions of Iranian netizens who criticized his statement and the UAE's rejection of Iranian sovereignty over the disputed islands. According to the netizens these islands have always belonged to Iran and Iran would never agree to any compromise over their

territorial integrity. Some of the netizens even mentioned that the Arab emirates themselves once belonged to Iran and that Iranian land could never be a
matter for negotiation.[50]

The great sensitivity that the issue of Iranian identity arouses among
Iranians was clearly evident in the social media reactions of Iranian netizens
on November 2010 to a YouTube video that was a compilation of parts of a
speech given by Hezbollah Secretary General Hassan Nasrallah. In his
speech, Nasrallah referred to Iran's Muslim identity and claimed that its
sources are Arab and not Persian. Nasrallah claimed that there was nothing
"Persian" in Iran nor any "Persian civilization," only an Islamic civilization
and the Arab religion of the Prophet Muhammad. He argued that the leaders
of the Islamic Revolution were also Arab descendants of the grandsons of the
Prophet Muhammad, and that the current Supreme Leader of Iran, Ali Khamenei, is a *seyyed*, indicating that his lineage stretches back to the Prophet
Muhammad and his Arab descendants.[51] The video caused a storm among
netizens and angry reactions from Iranian bloggers. One of the bloggers
wrote in response to Nasrallah's speech that it reflects the reality that the
Iranian nation, the Iranian culture, the Iranian civilization, and Iranian resources are held captive by foreigners.[52] The blogger Azarmehr wrote:

> Thank You Sheikh Nassrallah. . . . Now we know exactly what is going on in
> Iran and who is ruling in Iran. Thank you, Sheikh Nassrallah, for stating the
> obvious. Our country is under occupation by foreign usurpers who are threat-
> ening our identity, heritage and culture. But don't be too happy Sheikh Nass-
> rallah, Iran has dealt with worse usurpers than you and turned them into
> Iranians. You too will not be successful. Iran will never die.[53]

Facebook, too, was flooded with the angry reactions of Iranian netizens who
attacked Nasrallah personally and Arabs in general using derogatory terms
such as "bastards," "moochers," and "lizard eaters."[54]

FROM THE SAMSUNG PROTEST TO THE JEANS PROTEST:
SANCTIONS AND NATIONAL HONOR IN THE SOCIAL MEDIA

While the reactions of Iranian netizens on the SNS towards Arabs often
reflect the tensions whose source is in the past between Arabs and Persians—
and a degree of arrogance—their approach toward Western countries and
their policies towards Iran tend to reflect an Iranian refusal to accept any
arrogant and disrespectful attitude or insult to their national pride. Each time
Iranian citizens have felt humiliated and thought that their country's rights
have been unfairly violated, they have turned their anger toward "the foreigners" whom they accuse of trying to impinge upon their legitimate rights. This

anger reflects the common perception that Iran deserves respect and international recognition of its standing and rights.

In April 2013 the South Korean company Samsung announced its intention to block Iranian users from accessing the company's application store as part of the economic sanctions the international community had placed on Iran due to its nuclear program. This announcement triggered condemnations by Iranian netizens on the SNS and included a sharp attack on the company, a call to boycott its products and opposition to sanctions that harm Iranian citizens. Some of the netizens derided Samsung's decision arguing that the sanctions were meaningless since Iranians have many ways to bypass the new restrictions. Others claimed that the company's products were inferior and that there were better products available manufactured by Nokia as well as local Iranian companies. "Samsung should thank Iranians for purchasing such low-quality phones. . . . If Iranians don't purchase the devices, the company will be bankrupt in a month," responded one of the netizens. The most common reaction to Samsung's decision was a call to boycott its products in response to the disrespect it had demonstrated towards its Iranian customers. The Facebook pages of the BBC and Voice of America were flooded with the reactions of Iranian netizens who called to boycott the company, and expressed their national pride. One of the netizens wrote that if Iranians had any pride they wouldn't be buying the company's products. Another netizen opined that it was impossible to remain silent in the face of Samsung's abusive treatment of the Iranian people. [55]

Some of the Iranian SNS users emphasized that they opposed the decision of the South Korean company even though they did not support the Iranian regime. Only a few of the netizens expressed support for Samsung's decision and blamed the Iranian regime for leading Iran into increasing isolation. The company's decision, which was similar to sanctions placed on Iran by other international companies in recent years, was perceived by the Iranian public as another manifestation of the continuous effort made by Western countries to prevent their nation from realizing its legitimate rights to scientific and technological advancement, and an insult their national pride. The sanctions reinforced the feeling of victimhood among Iranians and led them to blame the West more than they blamed the Iranian regime. The tendency of Iranians to ascribe their financial woes to the West was reflected in a Gallup poll done in December 2012. The poll showed that 47 percent of Iranians blamed the economic situation in Iran on the United States, 9 percent blamed Israel for it, 7 percent blamed European countries for it, 7 percent blamed the UN, and only 10 percent thought their government was responsible for it. [56]

An interview given by Israeli Prime Minister Benjamin Netanyahu, in October 2013 to the BBC Persian Service, provided Iranian netizens with another opportunity to use the SNS to collectively protest against what they perceived as a slight against their national honor. Young Iranians were infuriated mostly by Netanyahu's claim that Iranian citizens had been forbidden from enjoying Western culture. The Israeli Prime Minister claimed in the interview that "if the Iranian people had their way, they'd be wearing blue jeans, they'd have Western music, they'd have free elections."[57]

The hostility towards Israel is the issue on which the Islamic Republic's revolutionary policy has most clearly remained constant and unwavering. Since the Islamic Revolution, Iran adopted a relentless anti-Israeli stance that openly calls for Israel's destruction. The hostility towards Israel is a central component in the regime's worldview and Iran's attitude has stemmed from its refusal to accept Israel as a Jewish state. All the revolutionary goals of the regime are combined in its animosity towards Israel which expresses itself as a basic hostility toward the Jewish state, opposition to Western imperialism and capitalism, and the hatred of the shah who collaborated with Israel. The animosity towards Israel is the most prominent issue on which there is near total agreement among the major political factions in the Iranian establishment.[58]

Although Iran's basic policy towards Israel has remained the same there have been initial signs of a certain change in the attitude of some Iranians towards the Jewish state. Although this change is limited to circles that are devoid of influence on Iran's policies, it does reflect the attitude of some groups in Iran, especially the younger generation. A poll conducted by Israeli researchers from the Interdisciplinary Center in Herzliya published in June 2014 showed that about 40 percent of Iranians support recognizing Israel if a peace agreement is reached between Israel and the Palestinians and Israel withdraws from the occupied territories.[59] Although the methodology used to conduct the poll is questionable, the poll does indicate a trend that can be corroborated by other evidence. For example, Iranian netizens responded enthusiastically to an initiative launched in March 2012 by an Israeli graphic designer to promote friendship between Israelis and Iranians. The campaign entitled "Israel Loves Iran" received many responses from Iranians who expressed their friendship towards Israel and a desire to see good relations established between the two countries.[60]

These positive responses stand in stark contrast to the reactions of Iranians to Netanyahu's statements on the BBC's Persian Service only a year and a half later. Iranian netizens responded to Netanyahu's claims by saying that they indicate the ignorance and arrogance of the Israeli Prime Minister. Some of them criticized his portrayal of liberties in Iran and a few used the opportunity to attack Israel's treatment of Palestinians. Iranians with different political views, including expatriates and those who oppose the regime, criticized Netanyahu's statements. Most of the opposition to the Israeli Prime Minister took place on Twitter, which was flooded with dozens of images of Iranian netizens showing themselves wearing jeans. Among the photos uploaded online was the famous photo of Neda Agha Soltan, who was shot dead in the 2009 riots in Iran while she was wearing jeans and became a symbol of the Green Movement. Another photo showed the son of an Iranian nuclear scientist, Mostafa Ahmadi Rowshan, who had been assassinated in 2012, accompanied by the following message: "Netanyahu, meet Alireza Ahmadi Roshan, son of Iranian nuclear scientist u killed! He wears blue jeans."[61] In this case too, the insult many Iranians felt following what was perceived by them to be arrogance by the Israeli Prime Minister triggered numerous reactions on the SNS and showed a willingness to mobilize to defend their national honor.

CONCLUSION

In 1997 Nicholas Negroponte, the architect of the "One Laptop per Child Project" and then-director of MIT's communications lab argued that "twenty years from now children, who are used to finding out about other countries through the click of a mouse, are not going to know what nationalism is."[62] Judging by the discourse on Iranian social networks his assessment was overly naïve and nationalism continues to play a central role in the rallying of the Iranian public around common national goals.

The growing usage of social media in Iran is taking place on the backdrop of growing alienation between the Iranian public in general and the younger generation in particular from the state institutions and religious establishments. Many young Iranians are gradually growing distant from the values of the revolution and are adopting a Western lifestyle despite the regime's efforts to stem what they see as a cultural offensive perpetrated by the West. In addition, Iranian society is increasingly characterized by individualism which comes at the expense of social cohesion. These trends are clearly evident in Iranian social media, which increasingly represent various and varied sectors in Iranian society. While, in the past, the SNS has mostly been used by young, educated, middle-class urbanites, today they are used as a platform for public discourse by additional sectors of Iranian society. While in the past the SNS were mostly associated with reformists and regime opponents, today regime supporters from the conservative Right and even senior clerics are present in the social media and use them to spread their political and ideological teachings.[63] In a post published on Google+ by Seyyed Akbar Mousavi, an Iranian religious seminary student in Qom, he argues that "expansion of the Internet and the creation of smart phones have made everyone familiar with Facebook. Five or six years ago, the Persian-speaking sphere of Facebook had an intellectual ambiance, but now it reflects the entire society."[64]

As the use of social media increases among additional sectors of Iranian society, so the Iranian collective identity is more and more able to serve as a base for mobilizing citizens around common national goals. This does not necessarily mean that the potential ability of the SNS to encourage political dissent is decreasing. Indeed the social media are providing an opportunity to invigorate the public discourse, enhance civic consciousness, and increase social involvement. These may—even if they take place only in the long term—encourage democratization and the processes that can lead to social change. It thus appears that Iranian national identity not only has not diminished in the era of social media, but has actually found a new channel for its expression.

NOTES

1. Leo Messi's Facebook page, December 4, 2013, https://www.facebook.com/LeoMessi/posts/713193608700236.

2. Tabnak, "Javab-e Messi be Irani-ha dar Facebook," December 7, 2013, http://www.tabnak.ir/fa/news/362982, retrieved: September 3, 2014.

3. Eric Hobsbawm, *Nations and Nationalism Since 1780: Program, Myth, Reality* (Cambridge, 1990), p. 143.

4. Babak Rahimi, "The politics of the Internet in Iran," in M. Semati (ed.), *Media, Culture and Society in Iran: Living with Globalization* (New York, 2008), pp. 38–41. Liora Hendelman-Baavur, "Live Protest: the Islamic Republic and the Green Revolution on the Internet," *Zman Iran*, No. 10 (July 2009), http://humanities.tau.ac.il/iranian/he/pre/9-iran-pulse-he/67-10, retrieved: September 3, 2014. [In Hebrew.]

5. Mehr News Agency, "Fanavary taht-e taathir-e jamjahani / jaded-tarin Amar karbaran-e Internet dar iran ee'lam shod," 26 June, 2014, http://www.mehrnews.com/detail/News/2319958, retrieved: September 1, 2014.

6. Liora Hendelman-Baavur, "'The Mirror Has Two Faces': The Islamic Republic's Dual Policy toward the Internet," *Orient*, 4 (2013), pp. 44–48.

7. L. Giacobino, A. Abadpour, C. Anderson, F. Petrossian, and C. Nellemann, "Whither Blogestan: Evaluating Shifts in Persian Cyberspace," March 2014, http://www.iranmediaresearch.org/en/research/download/1607, pp. 1–49.

8. Iran Media Program Center for Global Communication Studies and Annenberg School for Communication University of Pennsylvania, "Liking Facebook in Tehran: Social Networking in Iran," March 2014, http://www.iranmediaresearch.org/en/blog/227/14/03/14/1610, pp. 1–38.

9. Asr-e Iran, "Vazir-e Ershad: 4 Milion Irani a'dhu Facebook," January 23, 2014, http://bit.ly/1ohpb9u, retrieved: September 1, 2014.

10. "Iran's Twitter Revolution," *Washington Times*, June 16, 2009, http://www.washingtontimes.com/news/2009/jun/16/irans-twitter-revolution/, retrieved: September 2, 2014.

11. Hendelman-Baavur, "Live Protest."

12. Vasileios Karagiannopoulos, "The Role of the Internet in Political Struggles: Some Conclusions from Iran and Egypt," *New Political Science*, Vol. 34, No. 2 (2012), p. 162.

13. Ibid., p. 170.

14. Golnaz Esfandiari, "The Twitter Devolution," *Foreign Policy*, June 7, 2010, http://www.foreignpolicy.com/articles/2010/06/07/the_twitter_revolution_that_wasnt, retrieved: August 26, 2014.

15. "Liking Facebook in Tehran," pp. 14–15.

16. Ibid., p. 18.

17. Magdalena Wojcieszak and Briar Smith, "Will politics be tweeted? New media use by Iranian youth in 2011," *New Media & Society*, 16 (2014), pp. 98–99.

18. For more on the escalating struggle between the Iranian regime and the Baloch organizations, see: Raz Zimmt, "New Government, Old Conflict: Renewed Escalation in Iran's Balochi-

stan Province," *Iran Pulse*, no. 62 (December 5, 2013), http://humanities.tau.ac.il/iranian/en/previous-reviews/10-iran-pulse-en/266-iran-pulse-no-62, retrieved: August 28, 2014.

19. Edalat News' Facebook page, https://www.facebook.com/pages/%D8%B9%D8%AF%D8%A7%D9%84%D8%AA-%D9%86%DB%8C%D9%88%D8%B2/224122577778684, retrieved: September 2, 2014. Jaish al-Adl Twitter Acount, https://twitter.com/jaishaladl_, retrieved: September 3, 2014. Edalat News, March 23, 2014, http://edaalatnews.blogspot.co.il/2014/03/blog-post_8549.html, retrieved: September 3, 2014.

20. https://www.facebook.com/pages/%D8%AA%D8%AC%D9%85%D8%B9-%D8%AF%D8%B1-%D9%85%D9%82%D8%A7%D8%A8%D9%84-%D8%B3%D9%81%D8%A7%D8%B1%D8%AA-%D9%87%D8%A7%DB%8C-%D8%AF%D9%88%D9%84%D8%AA-%D9%BE%D8%A7%DA%A9%D8%B3%D8%AA%D8%A7%D9%86-%D8%AF%D8%B1-%D8%A7%DB%8C%D8%B1%D8%A7%D9%86/1405722353029192, retrieved: September 1, 2014.

21. Javad Zarif's Facebook page, March 28, 2014, https://www.facebook.com/jzarif/posts/776295132381937.

22. https://www.facebook.com/photo.php?fbid=850924438254551&set=a.419359904744342.112700.418014398212226&type=1.

23. Richard Cottam, *Nationalism in Iran* (Pittsburgh, 1964), p. 128.

24. See, for example, Ernest Gellner, *Thought and Change* (London, 1964); Benedict Anderson, *Imagined Communities, Reflections on the Origin and Spread of Nationalism* (London, 2006); Antony Smith, *The Ethnic Origins of Nations* (Oxford, 1996).

25. Gellner, p. 169.

26. Mostafa Vaziri, *Iran as Imagined Nation* (New York, 1994), p. 109.

27. Mohammad Tavakoli-Targhi, "From Patriotism to Matriotism: A Topological Study of Iranian Nationalism, 1870–1909," *International Journal of Middle East Studies*, Vol. 34, No. 2 (May 2002), pp. 217–38.

28. Firoozeh Kashani-Sabet, "Cultures of Iranianness: The Evolving Polemic of Iranian Nationalism," in Nikki R. Keddie and Rudi Matthee, *Iran and the Surrounding World: Interactions in Culture and Cultural Politics* (Seattle and London, 2002), p. 163.

29. Raz Zimmt, "Nationalism, Shi'ite Islam & National Interests in Iran's Foreign Policy," in Daniel Zissenwine (ed.), *Nationalism, Secularism, and Religion in the Middle East* (Tel Aviv, 2012), pp. 87–95. [In Hebrew.]

30. Niki Akhavan, *Electronic Iran: The Cultural Politics of an Online Evolution* (New Brunswick, NJ, and London, 2013), p. 13.

31. Ibid., p. 15.

32. Gholam Khiabani and Annabelle Sreberny, "The Politics of/in Blogging in Iran," *Comparative Studies of South Asia, Africa & the Middle East*, Vol. 27, No. 3 (2007), pp. 572–73.

33. "Liking Facebook in Tehran," pp. 14–15. Wojcieszak & Smith, pp. 98–99.

34. Jafar Farshian, "The Double Lives of Tehran's Middle Class," March 20, 2010, http://iwpr.net/report-news/double-lives-tehrans-middle-class, retrieved: September 3, 2014.

35. Alborz Zahedi, "Criticism of Iranian Middle [Class]," October 16, 2012, originally published in: http://bamdadkhabar.com, available in: https://plus.google.com/115287909263682590925/posts/GGjjCc5DaKg, retrieved: September 1, 2014. [In Persian.]

36. Akhavan, p. 33.

37. Khiabani and Sreberny, p. 573.

38. Ibid., p. 577.

39. Abdul Aziz Ad-Duri, "Arab-Iranian Relations: Historical Background," in Khair el-Din Haseeb (ed.), *Arab-Iranian Relations* (Beirut, 1998), p. 4.

40. Shirin T. Hunter, "Iran and the Arab World," in Miron Rezun (ed.), *Iran at the Crossroads: Global Relations in a Turbulent Decade* (Boulder, San Francisco, and Oxford, 1990), p. 98.

41. Shahrokh Meskoob, *Iranian Nationality and the Persian Language* (Washington, DC, 1992), p. 34.

42. Mostafa Vaziri, *Iran as Imagined Nation* (New York, 1993), p. 196.

43. Ibid., p. 193.

44. *Kalemeh*, "Tae'b: Suriya astan si va panjam iran ast," February 14, 2013, http://www.kaleme.com/1391/11/26/klm-133479/, retrieved: September 3, 2014.

45. Raz Zimmt, "Iran has to prefer Syria to the Khuzestan region: Ammar Headquarters chief's announcement draws angry reactions," *Spotlight on Iran*, February 17, 2013, http://www.terrorism-info.org.il/Data/articles/Art_20477/E_031_13_734144126.pdf, retrieved: August 16, 2014.

46. https://www.facebook.com/notes/kourosh-zaim/
%D9%86%D8%A7%D9%85%D9%87-%D8%B3%D8%B1%DA%AF
%D8%B4%D8%A7%D8%AF%D9%87-%D9%83%D9%88%D8%B1%D8%B4-
%D8%B2%D8%B9%D9%8A%D9%85-%D8%A8%D9%87-%D8%AD%D8%AC%D8%AA-
%D8%A7%D9%84%D8%A7%D8%B3%D9%84%D8%A7%D9%85-
%D9%85%D9%87%D8%AF%D9%8A-%D8%B7%D8%A7%D8%A6%D8%A8/
471699799544947, and see further Iranian users' reactions to Taeb's speech here: https://www.facebook.com/mamlekate/posts/10151419366463711?fref=nf, retrieved: August 16, 2014.

47. Harf-ha-ye Nagofte, "Astan-ha-ye Jomhuri-ye Eslami-ye Iran," http://harfhaye-nagofte-elham.blogspot.co.il/2013/02/blog-post_14.html, retrieved: September 3, 2014.

48. Raz Zimmt, "Conference in support of Khuzestani Arabs convenes in Cairo during Foreign Minister Salehi's visit to Egypt provoking anger from Iran," *Spotlight on Iran*, January 14, 2012, http://www.terrorism-info.org.il/Data/articles/Art_20462/E_009_13_503708825.pdf, retrieved: September 3, 2014.

49. Mehr News Agency, "Zarif: Omadgi baray-e goftegu mowzue' hamishegi-ye iran dar khasus-e jazireh abu-musa ast," December 2, 2013, http://mehrnews.com/detail/news/2187411, retrieved: September 3, 2014.

50. Botian News, "Facebook Zarif va jazire abu-musa," December 4, 2013, http://fa.botianews.com/2013/12/87677/, retrieved: August 23, 2014. https://www.facebook.com/mehdi.parpanchi/posts/452643708191276.

51. BBC Persian, "Sokhtan-e bahth barangiz debirkol hezballah darbara-e tamadan-e irani," November 8, 2010, http://www.bbc.co.uk/persian/world/2010/11/101107_u03_nasrallah_iran.shtml, retrieved: September 2, 2014.

52. Sight, "Hassan Nasrallah ba tamam bi shauriyesh fahmid ke iran be garugan gerefted shode ast," http://bit.ly/1pPXAk3, retrieved: September 3, 2014.

53. Azarmehr, "For a Democracy Secular Iran," http://www.azarmehr.info/2010/11/thank-you-sheikh-nassrollah.html, retrieved: September 3, 2014.

54. See, for example: https://www.facebook.com/note.php?note_id=447544827986&id=83359068840; https://www.facebook.com/note.php?note_id=462745579089&id=950409 33929.

55. https://www.facebook.com/voapersian/photos/a.10150137543321882.329322 .97414266881/10151630714521882/?type=1; https://www.facebook.com/bbcpersian/posts/10151463403752713.

56. "Iranians Feel Bite of Sanctions, Blame U.S., Not Own Leaders," February 3, 2013, http://www.gallup.com/poll/160358/iranians-feel-bite-sanctions-blame-not-own-leaders.aspx, retrieved; September 1, 2014.

57. BBC, "Iranians mock Netanyahu over jeans comment," October 7, 2013, http://www.bbc.com/news/world-middle-east-24435408, retrieved: September 2, 2014.

58. Meir Litvak, "Iran and Israel: The Ideological Enmity and its Roots," *Iyunim be-Tkumat Yisrael*, Vol. 14 (2004), p. 367–69. [In Hebrew.]

59. Isabel Kershner, "Openness on Israeli Issues Seen in Survey of Iranians," *New York Times*, June 6, 2014, http://www.nytimes.com/2014/06/06/world/middleeast/israeli-survey-iranians-found-support-giving-up-nuclear-arms-in-exchange-for-lifting-sanctions.html, retrieved: September 3, 2014.

60. Oded Yaron, "Iranians respond to Israeli Facebook initiative: Israel, we love you too," March 19, 2012, http://www.haaretz.com/news/national/iranians-respond-to-israeli-facebook-initiative-israel-we-love-you-too-1.419505, retrieved: September 3, 2014.

61. Saeed Kamali Dehghan, "Iranians hit back at Israeli PM by tweeting pictures of their jeans," October 7, 2013, http://www.theguardian.com/world/iran-blog/2013/oct/07/iranians-israeli-pm-tweeting-jeans, retrieved: September 3, 2014.

62. Reuters, "Negroponte: Internet is way to world peace," November 25, 1997, http://edition.cnn.com/TECH/9711/25/Internet.peace.reut/, retrieved: September 3, 2014.

63. See, for example, "Small media" reports entitled "Iranian conservative bloggers," http://storify.com/smallmedia/.

64. Ali Mamouri, "Facebook use among the seminary in Qom," *Almonitor*, January 3, 2014, http://www.al-monitor.com/pulse/iw/originals/2014/01/qom-seminary-facebook.html#ixzz361C9zo8l, retrieved: September 2, 2014.

Conclusion

In the multicultural, multireligious, multigender, and multinational world of today, no one can truly stick to one coherent identity. The selves of most of us have been formed from many identities and subidentities be they private or shared identifications or national, religion, ethnic, gender, sexual, and the like. Yet, even as the world becomes multi-whatever-you-call-it, nations are striving and struggling to rebuild and reshape their identities. Nations are, as they have always been, very jealous and avaricious about land and sovereignty and, therefore, they always turn for validation and justification to one thing—the past.

From a general point of view this way of surviving, whether by justification or by real merit, is a challenge for a nation that wishes to preserve its cultural and religious values at the same time that other nations are doing the same thing—and sometimes more successfully. In this world of microcosms we can apply this concept to the inner world of nations, upon which many factors and forces are acting that will maintain, invent, learn, feed, shape, and possibly even destroy their identities. The point is that society is built upon fundamental sources and roots such as human nature, religion, obligations, and cultural basics that mostly look alike all over the world.

Iran as a case study is very interesting since it is a nation that has existed for more than twenty-five hundred years that, for centuries, reigned over an empire that stretched from India to Greece and has a real and solid history that has formed an identity that only few nations can be as proud of. The occupation of Persia by many nations throughout its history, especially from the Euro-Indian area, proved to be less significant than the last occupation by the Muslim nomads which ultimately led to this place being characterized by an eternal clash between Islam and Persianism.

The long and stubborn struggle carried on by the *Khorramiya* movement of the ninth century against the Abbasid Empire, was finally doomed to failure and this only left the Persians eager to find other ways to fight the Muslims and what they perceived to be their unsophisticated religion. Only six centuries passed until this nation, through its monarchy, willingly chose to become Shi'ite instead of Sunnah. This choice, although it looks irrational, was made in total awareness and, as Dr. Rhode argues in his excellent chapter, was made in order to save the Persian culture from the corrosion caused by the practice of the Sunnah Islam and, despite the fundamental contradictions between the two forms of Islam, left a significant impression all over the Middle East.

If we apply these conceptions to the inner world of the Iranian people and its regime, we will find Ms. Zarabadi's conclusions and discussion very interesting. The present regime's willingness to impose its religious doctrine on Iran by denying Iranian history is something that we can compare to the Taliban's destruction of the monumental statues of Buddha in Bamiyan.

The case study of Bam is something which could easily have taken place in similar places in Iran and probably reveals the regime's desire to shape its cultural heritage as more religious and less Persian; and the adaptation of Islamic values, Zarabadi says, is being done in order to more strongly and eternally construct the regime's legitimacy in the eyes of its people.

Changing a nation's narratives and history is not a new matter when carried out under the rule of a theoretical and dictatorial regime and is justified by the political circumstances. Ultimately this changing of the history of Bam is being carried out because of the political needs of the government, but the question remaining is: How does it influence the national identity of the Iranian people throughout the country? Will they accept this passively or, given the idea that the Iranian people are smarter than their government, will they not—and for how long will these changes be tolerated?

The story of Bam brings us to Ofira Seliktar's theoretical description of the building up and engineering of Iran's Islamic identity. Professor Seliktar analyzes the formation of the Islamic identity after the revolution and its reformation and liberalization under President Mohammad Khatami. Seliktar argues that "the complex balancing of all these forces [within Iranian society] has created a pattern of movement between coercion and voluntarism in the process of shaping the Islamic identity," thus, the regime is, "barring a dramatic change either exogenous or endogenous and the Islamic identity project is expected to continue for the foreseeable future." All in all, the Islamic Republic is learning how to handle the other forces within Iranian society which they hope will finally lead to a strengthening of the Islamic identity—but by using different methods and practices from those used during the first years of the revolution.

Seliktar's chapter leads us to Mr. Farhad Rezaei's chapter that deals with the nuclear program as a builder of Iran's national identity. It is really hard, and perhaps impossible, to build an identity which needs to survive among the surrounding Arab nations based upon a national project. For Rezaei, however, the story is much bigger and is not about surviving or being secure in the Middle Eastern boiling pot but about "national pride, scientific prowess and Iran's standing in the international order" all of which "have all been part of an effort to shape a national identity and thus bolster the legitimacy of the regime." By building this project as a national mission to renew and shape the Iranian identity Iran wants to strengthen its legitimacy especially in the eyes of its people and especially when the sanctions are making life hard for the people.

The next chapter by Dr. Moshe-hay S. Hagigat brings us back to Mahmūd Ahmadi-nezhād's era and it is worth focusing on his presidential period as a time when he tried to apply his messianic agenda using the tools of politics. Dr. Hagigat says that "Ahmadi-nezhād also makes mention of the various ideas and theories originating from the West and derisively dismisses them. He calls the ruling contemporary conceptions or paradigms—'the –isms' (*ism-ha*, meaning Western colonialism, militarism, paternalism, capitalism, humanism, liberalism, etc.) and considers them to be outdated and something that most people should abandon." After presenting Ahmadi-nezhād's Islamist ideology and his desire to impose it on Iran, Dr. Hagigat tries to find the similarities, and especially the contradictions, between the presidencies of Ahmadi-nezhād and Hassan Rouhani. He leaves us with the open question of which kind of identity Rouhani wants to present. Assuming this is still a matter for debate we must ask whether it will be more Iranian, more Westernized, or more Islamic since his approach basically contradicts Ahmadi-nezhād's Islamic ideology and this is something which has left Iranians a little puzzled and confused.

The last part of this book opens with my chapter, "The Identity Designers of the Self in Sexuality, Beauty and Plastic Surgery in Iran," in which I have tried to find the old-new elements that have driven the shapers of Iranian identity. From a universal point of view these are no different from those of any other place on earth but if one relates to the contradictions between Shi'a Islam and Persian culture that Dr. Rhode describes we see that they are two different shapers of identity that exist, willingly or forcibly, under one roof. I relate to these elements that involve both the obligations of religion and Persian/global/environmental cultural needs to help us understand the new shapers of the self by examining them through the lens of sexuality, beauty, and plastic surgery in an attempt to find the "symbiosis that may exist between elements of religion and culture."

The attempt to improve self-esteem and build/emend the identity is not, of course, solely developed on the basis of sexuality, beauty, and plastic surgery. There are many factors that have been presented throughout the book that present a wide range of characteristics that affect the identity but in modern Iran, and taking into consideration the clash between Persian values and Shi'a Islam, these elements (sexuality, beauty, and plastic surgery) seem to present a new model that has the potential to accept Shi'a obligation while still being used as a platform to discover anew the cultural elements of "Persianism" and as a way of improving and strengthening the Iranians' sense of self-esteem within the melting pot where culture and religion threaten to boil over.

In the last chapter of this book, "Iranians against the "Other": Iranian Identity in the Social Media Era," Dr. Zimmt deals with the flourishing of social media in Iran and its impact upon the Iranian identity. This time the confrontation is not only between culture and religion but also between the Iranian identity and other identities presented in the wide spectrum displayed by the social media.

Making use of these tools to present a patriotic agenda is quite understandable especially when one's country is under scrutiny and imposed sanctions (nuclear) or when a bad image is projected by its political system. In general this can lead to one or another group reacting with acceptance or denial of the global accusations. Nationalistic and patriotic feelings have, however, only grown as a result of these Internet wars and, in Dr. Zimmt's words, "As the use of social media increases among additional sectors of Iranian society, so the Iranian collective identity is more and more able to serve as a base for mobilizing citizens around common national goals." Finally, this will "encourage democratization and the processes that can lead to social change."

If we try to draw lines through all these chapters regarding the issue of "identities in crisis in Iran" we have to ask ourselves how fundamental, temporal, eternal, imagined, or, more pointedly, soluble these crises are. When we look at the historical record of Iran as a nation whose leader chose to adopt Shi'a Islam in favor of Sunni Islam in 1501, we see that he did this in order to segregate his nation from the loathsome Arab world and its Sunnah Islam—all in order to save the Persian culture from corrosion and diminution.

The Iranian identity, I believe, like every national identity, is developing because of two main factors. The first, as Judith Butler's work shows, is comprised of the natural basics of the Iranian nation; and the second is comprised of the environmental circumstances that influence and impose domestic change and identity adaptations. Just like the snake, which sheds its skin in order to renew itself and grow, shine, and propagate, the Iranian national identity, especially under the very special circumstances of Persian culture versus religion, also undergoes evolution in its ideology and identity.

It is hard to predict what refinements of the identity the Iranian nation will be willing to submit to but it is clear that, in the current situation, in which the theocratic government is under domestic, regional, and global pressure, the factors and forces discussed are the tools that will fashion the national and personal identities of the Iranian people. What these chapters do add up to is the understanding that Iran, as an ancient and respected nation, which has developed its pride not only from its social, military, and bureaucratic innovations but also from its poetry, literature, and other cultural manifestations, wishes to renew its proud and respected place among the nations—not at the cost of abandoning Shi'a Islam, but with its help, and this time with much help also from modernization, liberalization, and democratization.

Bibliography

BOOKS IN ENGLISH

Abdo, Geneive, and Lyons, Jonathan, *Answering Only to God: Faith and Freedom in 21st Century Iran* (New York: Henry Holt, 2003).

Adib-Moghaddam, Arshin, *On the Arab Revolts and the Iranian Revolution: Power and Resistance Today* (New York: Bloomsbury, 2013).

Akhavan, Niki, *Electronic Iran: The Cultural Politics of an Online Evolution* (New Brunswick, NJ and London, 2013).

Anderson, Benedict, *Imagined Communities, Reflections on the Origin and Spread of Nationalism* (London, 2006).

Arjomand, Saïd Amir, *After Khomeini: Iran under His Successors* (New York: Oxford University Press, 2009).

Ayazi, Shahin, "Persian Iranian Versus Islamic Iranians: 1979 Social Movement of Iran," Master's thesis, University of San Francisco, May 2003.

Bayat, Asef, *Making Islam Democratic: Social Movements and the Post-Islamist Turn* (Stanford, CA: Stanford University Press, 2007).

Cohen, Ronen A., *The Hojjatiyeh Society in Iran: Ideology and Practice from the 1950s to the Present* (New York: Macmillan Palgrave, 2013).

Corera, Gordon, *Shopping for Bombs: Nuclear Proliferation, Global Insecurity, and the Rise and Fall of the AQ Khan Network* (New York: Oxford University Press, 2006).

Cottam, Richard, *Nationalism in Iran* (Pittsburgh, 1964).

Cristi, Marcela, *From Civil to Political Religion: The Intersection of Culture, Religion and Politics* (Waterloo, ON: Wilfrid Laurier University Press, 2001).

Crowther, Yasmin, *Saffron Kitchen* (Penguin Books, 2007).

Dawson, Julian, *A Constructivist Approach to the US-Iranian Nuclear Problem* (Alberta: University of Calgary, The Centre for Military and Strategic Studies, 2011).

Fazeli, Nematollah, *Politics of Culture in Iran: Anthropology, Politics and Society in the Twentieth Century* (New York: Routledge, 2006).

Forbis, William H., *Fall of the Peacock Throne* (New York: Harper and Row, 1980).

Frye, Richard Nelson, *Cambridge History of Iran*, Vol. 4 (London, 1975).

Gellner, Ernest, *Thought and Change* (London, 1964).

Halliday, Fred, *100 Myths about the Middle East* (Berkeley, CA: Univ of California Press, 2005).

Hobsbawm, Eric, *Nations and Nationalism since 1780: Program, Myth, Reality* (Cambridge, 1990).

Hufbauer, Gary Clyde, Schott, Jeffrey J., and Elliott, Kimberly Ann, *Economic Sanctions Reconsidered: History and Current Policy* (Washington DC: Peterson Institute, 1990).

Hymans, Jacques E. C., *The Psychology of Nuclear Proliferation: Identity, Emotions and Foreign Policy* (Cambridge: Cambridge University Press, 2006).

Iranian Cultural Heritage, *Bam and Its Cultural Landscape World Heritage: Property, Comprehensive Management Plan* (Tehran: Iranian Cultural Heritage, 2008), http://whc.unesco.org/en/list/1208, retrieved: October 6, 2011.

Liebman Charles S., and Don-Yihya, Eliezer, *Civil Religion in Israel: Traditional Judaism and Political Culture in the Jewish State* (Berkeley, CA: University of California Press, 1983).

Looney, Robert E., *Iran at the End of the Century: A Hegelian Forecast* (Lexington, MA: Lexington Books, 1977).

Majd, Hooman, *The Ayatollah Begs to Differ: The Paradox of Modern Iran* (New York: Doubleday, 2008).

Matthee, Rudi, *The Pursuit of Pleasure: Drugs and Stimulants in Iranian History, 1500–1900* (Princeton, NJ: Princeton University Press, 2005).

Mayer, Charles C., *National Security to Nationalist Myth: Why Iran Wants Nuclear Weapons* (Los Angeles: Storming Media, 2004).

Meskoob, Shahrokh, *Iranian Nationality and the Persian Language* (Washington, DC, 1992).

Mir-Hosseini, Ziba, and Tapper, Richard, *Islam and Democracy in Iran: Eshkevari and the Quest for Reform* (New York: I. B. Tauris, 2006).

Moin, Baqer, *Khomeini: Life of the Ayatollah* (New York: Thomas Dunne Books, 2000).

Molavi, Afshin, *The Soul of Iran: A Nation's Struggle for Freedom* (New York: W. W. Norton & Company Inc., 2010).

Momen, Moojan, *An Introduction to Shi'i Islam* (Yale University Press, 1985).

Naji, Kasra, *Ahmadinejad: The Secret History of Iran's Radical Leader* (Los Angeles: University of California Press, 2008).

Nasr, Vali, and Ghessari, Ali, *Democracy in Iran: History and the Quest for Liberty* (New York: Oxford University Press, 2006).

Nemat, Marina, *Prisoner of Tehran: One Woman's Story of Survival Inside an Iranian Prison* (Free Press, 2008).

Nematollahi Mahani, Mahnia A., "'Do Not Say They Are Dead': The Political Use of Mystical and Religious Concepts in the Persian Poetry of the Iran-Iraq War (1980–88)," PhD diss., Leiden University 2014.

Poulson, Stephen C., *Social Movements in Twentieth-Century Iran: Culture, Ideology, and Mobilizing Frameworks* (London: Lexington Books, 2005).

Rajaee, Farhang, *Islamism and Modernism: The Changing Discourse in Iran* (Austin: University of Texas Press, 2010).

Rezaei, Farhad, "Nuclear Proliferation and Nuclear Rollback: The Case of Iran," PhD thesis, University of Malaysia, KL, 2014.

Roy, Olivier, Sfeir, Antoine, and King, John, *The Columbia World Dictionary of Islamism* (New York: Columbia University Press, 2007).

Seliktar, Ofira, *Failing the Crystal Ball Test: The Carter Administration and the Fundamentalist Revolution in Iran* (Westport, CT: Praeger, 2000).

Seliktar, Ofira, *Navigating Iran: From Carter to Obama* (New York: Palgrave Macmillan, 2012).

Shaery-Eisenlohr, Roschanack, *Shi'ite Lebanon—Transnational Religion and the Making of National Identity* (New York: Columbia University Press, 2011).

Shayegan, Darius, *Cultural Schizophrenia: Islamic Societies Confronting the West* (Syracuse, NY: Syracuse University Press, 1997).

Smith, Antony, *The Ethnic Origins of Nations* (Oxford, 1996).

Solingen, Etel, *Nuclear Logics: Contrasting Paths in East Asia and the Middle East* (Princeton, NJ: Princeton University Press, 2009).

Stone, Lucian, *Iranian Identity and Cosmopolitanism: Spheres of Belonging* (New York: Bloomsbury Academic, 2014).

Takeyh, Ray, *Guardians of the Revolution: Iran and the World in the Age of the Ayatollahs* (London: Oxford University Press, 2009).

Takeyh, Ray, *Hidden Iran: Paradox and Power in the Islamic Republic* (New York: Times Book/Holt, 2006).
Timmerman, Kenneth R., *Countdown to Crisis: The Coming Nuclear Showdown with Iran* (New York: Crown Forum, 2005).
Vale, Lawrence, *Architecture, Power and National Identity* (New Haven, CT: Yale University Press, 1992).
Vaziri, Mostafa, *Iran as Imagined Nation* (New York, 1994).
Wilfried, Buchta, *Who Rules Iran: The Structure of Power in the Islamic Republic* (Washington DC: The Washington Institute for Near East Policy, 2000).
Winter, Stefan, *The Shiites of Lebanon under Ottoman Rule, 1516–1788* (Cambridge: Cambridge University Press, 2010).
Wright, Robin B., *Dreams and Shadows: The Future of the Middle East* (New York: Penguin, 2008).
Wright, Robin, *The Last Great Revolution: Turmoil and Transformation in Iran* (New York: Vintage Books, 2001).

ARTICLES IN ENGLISH

Ad-Duri, Abdul Aziz, "Arab-Iranian Relations: Historical Background," in Khair el-Din Haseeb (ed.), *Arab-Iranian Relations* (Beirut, 1998), pp. 3–17.
Adib-Moghaddam, Arshin, "Iran, Bazargan and the Provisional Government," *The Library of Congress Country Studies*, July 4, 2002, http://workmall.com/wfb2001/iran/iran_history_bazargan_and_the_provisional_government.html, retrieved: August 22, 2014.
"Ahmad Kasravi Azerbaijani Linguist," March 23, 2011, http://ahmadkasravi-iranhistory.blogspot.com/2011/03/ahmad-kasravi-azerbaijani-linguist_3301.html, retrieved: October 5, 2014.
Al-Arabiya in English from AFP Washington, "Iran FM accuses Netanyahu of 'lie attack' on nukes," September 29, 2013, http://english.alarabiya.net/en/News/middle-east/2013/09/30/Iran-FM-accuses-Netanyahu-of-lie-attack-on-nukes.html, retrieved: January 9, 2014.
Alikhani, Behrouz, "Popular War Songs and Slogans in the Persian Language during the Iran-Iraq War," *Cambio*, Vol. 3, No. 6 (December 2013).
Aljazeera, "Iran: The Real Cost of Sanctions," *Aljazeera.com*, June 5, 2013, http://www.aljazeera.com/programmes/insidestory/2013/06/201365928843270.html, retrieved: July 7, 2014.
Amul, Gianna Gayle, "Perceptions of the Other: Iran's National Identity and Nuclear Policy," *E-International Relations*, June 14, 2012, http://www.e-ir.info/2012/06/14/perceptions-of-the-other-irans-national-identity-and-nuclear-policy/, retrieved: June 14, 2012.
Arjomand, Saïd Amir, "The Rise and Fall of President Khātami and the Reform Movement in Iran," *Constellations*, Vol. 12, No. 4 (2005), pp. 502–520.
Art, Robert J., and Waltz, Kenneth N., "Technology, Strategy, and the Uses of Force," in Robert J. Art and Kenneth N. Waltz (eds.), *The Use of Force: International Politics and Foreign Policy*, 2nd ed. (Lanham, MD: University Press of America, 1983), pp. 1–32.
Asgharzadeh, Alireza, "Azerbaijan and the Challenge of Multiple Identities: In Search of a Global Soul," GLORIA Center, IDC Herzliya, December 2, 2007, http://www.gloria-center.org/2007/12/asgharzadeh-2007-12-02/, retrieved: October 6, 2014.
Atiyeh, Bishara S., Kadry, Mohamad, Hayek, Shady N., and Musharafieh, Ramzi S., "Aesthetic Surgery and Religion: Islamic Law Perspective," *Aesthetic Plastic Surgery* (2008), pp. 1–10.
Azarmehr, "For a Democracy Secular Iran," http://www.azarmehr.info/2010/11/thank-you-sheikh-nassrollah.html, retrieved: September 3, 2014.
Bar'el, Zvi, "A year after his election, Rohani is changing Iran without shaking it up," June 14, 2014, http://www.haaretz.com/news/middle-east/.premium-1.598619, retrieved: August 27, 2014.
Barzegar, Kayhan, "Iran's Nuclear Program: An Opportunity for Dialogue," *Center for Strategic Research*, May 2009, http://www.csr.ir/departments.aspx?lng=en&abtid=06&&depid=74&semid=1797, retrieved: July 14, 2014.

Barzegar, Kayhan, "The Paradox of Iran's Nuclear Consensus," *World Policy Journal*, Vol. 26, No. 3 (Fall 2009), pp. 21–30.

BBC, "Iranians mock Netanyahu over jeans comment," October 7, 2013, http://www.bbc.com/news/world-middle-east-24435408, retrieved: September 2, 2014.

Bellah, Robert N., "Civil Religion in America," *Daedalus*, Vol. 134, No. 4 (2005), pp. 40–55.

Ben-Meir, Alon, "Iran Will Become A Nuclear Power, Unless . . . ," *The Algemeiner* (December 10, 2013).

Berliner, Uri, "Crippled By Sanctions, Iran's Economy Key In Nuclear Deal," *NPR.org*, November 25, 2013, http://www.npr.org/2013/11/25/247077050/crippled-by-sanctions-irans-economy-key-in-nuclear-deal, retrieved: July 7, 2014.

Bracken, Paul, "The Structure of the Second Nuclear Age," *Orbis, Foreign Policy Research Institute*, Vol. 47, No. 3 (2003), pp. 399–413.

Braswell, George W., "Civil Religion in Contemporary Iran," *Journal of Church and State*, Vol. 21, No. 2 (1979), pp. 223–46.

Cha, Victor D., "The Second Nuclear Age: Proliferation Pessimism versus Sober Optimism in South Asia and East Asia," *The Journal of Strategic Studies*, Vol. 24, No. 4 (2001), pp. 79–120.

Chehabi, Houchang E., "Staging the Emperor's New Clothes: Dress Codes and Nation-Building under Reza Shah," *Iranian Studies*, Vol. 26, No. 3–4 (Summer/Fall 1993), pp. 209–29.

Chubin, Shahram, "The Politics of Iran's Nuclear Program: Power, Politics, and US Policy," *The Iran Primer*, 2010, http://iranprimer.usip.org/resource/politics-irans-nuclear-program, retrieved: September 15, 2014.

Cohen, Ronen A., "The Hojjatiyeh—From Anti-Baha'i and Anti-Revolutionary Movement to the Real Creators of the Islamic Revolution in Iran," *The New East—Journal of the Middle East and Islamic Studies Association of Israel* (MEISAI), Vol. 51 (Summer 2012), pp. 69–92.

Cohen, Ronen A., *The Hojjatiyeh Society in Iran: Ideology and Practice from the 1950s to the Present* (New York: Macmillan Palgrave, 2013).

Dareini, Ali Akbar, "Iran Hits Milestone in Nuclear Technology," *Associated Press* (April 11, 2006).

De Bellaigue, Christopher, "Talk Like an Iranian: As the author learned in Tehran, yes sometimes means no," August 22, 2012, http://www.theatlantic.com/magazine/archive/2012/09/talk-like-an-iranian/309056/, retrieved: October 5, 2014.

Dehghan, Saeed Kamali, "Iranians hit back at Israeli PM by tweeting pictures of their jeans," October 7, 2013, http://www.theguardian.com/world/iran-blog/2013/oct/07/iranians-israeli-pm-tweeting-jeans, retrieved: September 3, 2014.

Dehghan, Saeed Kamali, "Noam Chomsky Calls on Iran to Release Imprisoned Journalist Marzieh Rasouli," *The Guardian* (July 12, 2014).

Dovey, Kim, "Silent Complicities: Bourdieu, Habitus, Field," in *Becoming Places: Urbanism/Architecture/Identity/Power* (New York: Routledge, 2010), pp. 31–42.

Drezner, Daniel W., "Five Myths about Sanctions," *The Washington Post*, retrieved: May 2, 2014.

Escribà-Folch, Abel, "Authoritarian Responses to Foreign Pressure Spending, Repression, and Sanctions," *Comparative Political Studies*, Vol. 45, No. 6 (2012), pp. 683–713.

Esfandiari, Golnaz, "The Twitter Devolution," *Foreign Policy*, June 7, 2010, http://www.foreignpolicy.com/articles/2010/06/07/the_twitter_revolution_that_wasnt, retrieved: August 26, 2014.

Fair, Christine, and Shellman, Stephen M., "Determinants of Popular Support for Iran's Nuclear Program: Insights from a Nationally Representative Survey," *Contemporary Security Policy*, Vol. 29, No. 3 (2008), pp. 538–58.

Farhi, Farideh, "The Antinomies of Iran's War Generation," in Lawrence G. Potterand Garry G. Sick (eds.), *Iran, Iraq and the Legacies of War* (New York: Palgrave Macmillan, 2004), pp. 101–20.

Farmanfarmaian, Fatema Soudavar, "Haft Qalam Arayish: Cosmetics in the Iranian World," *Iranian Studies*, Vol. 33, No. 3/4 (Summer-Autumn, 2000), pp. 285–326.

Farshian, Jafar, "The Double Lives of Tehran's Middle Class," March 20, 2010, http://iwpr.net/report-news/double-lives-tehrans-middle-class, retrieved: September 3, 2014.

Farshneshani, Beheshteh, "In Iran, the Wrong People Are Suffering," *New York Times* (January 22, 2014).

Fisher, Max, "9 Questions about Iran's Nuclear Program You Were Too Embarrassed to Ask," *The Washington Post* (November 25, 2013).

Gharaati, Mehran, "Who Knows? An Overview of Reconstruction after the Earthquake in Bam," *i-Rec* (2008), pp. 1–13.

Giacobino, L., Abadpour, A., Anderson, C., Petrossian F., and Nellemann, C., "Whither Blogestan: Evaluating Shifts in Persian Cyberspace," March 2014, http://www.iran> mediaresearch.org/en/research/download/1607, pp. 1–49.

The Global Jewish News Source, "Survey finds majority of Iranians would give up nuclear program," June 8, 2014, http://www.jta.org/2014/06/08/news-opinion/israel-middle-east/survey-finds-majority-of-iranians-would-give-up-nuclear-program, retrieved: July 19, 2014.

Gramaglia, Carla, and Marzola, Enrica, "Self-Esteem and Personality in Patients with Body Dysmorphic Disorder Undergoing Cosmetic Rhinoplasty," in Melvin A. Shiffman and Alberto Di Giuseppe (eds.), *Advanced Aesthetic Rhinoplasty—Art, Science, and New Clinical Techniques* (Springer: Verlag Berlin Heidelberg, 2013), pp. 77–92.

Grigor, Talinn, "Preserving the Antique Modern: Persepolis '71," *Conservation Information Network 2*, No. 1 (2005), pp. 22–29.

Haeri, Shahla, "Temporary Marriage: An Islamic Discourse on Female Sexuality in Iran," in Mahnaz Afkhami and Erika Friedl (eds.), *In the Eye of the Storm—Women in Post-Revolutionary Iran* (New York: Syracuse University Press, 1994), pp. 98–114.

Haffa Jr, Robert P., Hichkad, Ravi R., and Johnson, Dana J., "Deterrence and Defense in the Second Nuclear Age," *Northrop Grumman Analysis Center* (March, 2009).

Hendelman-Baavur, Liora, "'The Mirror Has Two Faces': The Islamic Republic's Dual Policy toward the Internet," *Orient*, 4 (2013), pp. 44–48.

Higgins, Patricia J., "Women in the Islamic Republic of Iran: Legal, Social, and Ideological Changes," *Signs*, Vol. 10, No. 3 (Spring 1985), pp. 477–94.

Hoodfar, Homa, "Devices and Desires: Population Policy and Gender Roles in the Islamic Republic," *Middle East Report*, No. 190, Gender, Population, Environment (Sep.–Oct. 1994), pp. 11–17.

HRW, "UN: Expose Iran's Appalling Rights Record," *Human Rights Watch*, September 21, 2011, http://www.hrw.org/news/2011/09/21/un-expose-iran-s-appalling-rights-record, retrieved: June 5, 2014.

Hunter, Shirin T., "Iran and the Arab World," in Miron Rezun (ed.), *Iran at the Crossroads: Global Relations in a Turbulent Decade* (Boulder, San Francisco, and Oxford, 1990), pp. 97–114.

ICHRI, "Hold Ahmadinejad Accountable for Iran's Human Rights Crisis During UN Visit," *International Campaign for Human Rights in Iran*, September 14, 2011, http://www.iranhumanrights.org/2011/09/ahmadinejad-accountable-for-human-rights-crisis/, retrieved: June 5, 2014

IIPJHR, "The Impact of Sanctions on the Iranian People's Healthcare System," *Global Research* (October 18, 2013).

ILNA, "Ayatollah Khomeini Confidential Letter, published by Hashemi Rafsanjani," *Iranian Labour News Agency*, Sep. 29, 2006.

Iran Media Program Center for Global Communication Studies & Annenberg School for Communication University of Pennsylvania, "Liking Facebook in Tehran: Social Networking in Iran," March 2014, http://www.iranmediaresearch.org/en/blog/227/14/03/14/1610, pp. 1–38.

"Iranian Cultural Heritage," *Bam and Its Cultural Landscape World Heritage: Property, Comprehensive Management Plan* (Tehran: Iranian Cultural Heritage, 2008), p. ii, http://whc.unesco.org/en/list/1208, retrieved: October 6, 2011.

"Iran's Twitter Revolution," *Washington Times*, June 16, 2009, http://www.washingtontimes.com/news/2009/jun/16/irans-twitter-revolution/, retrieved: September 2, 2014.

IRNA, "Ahmadinejad: Iran Will Continue Nuclear Program, Says Does Not Need US Help," *Islamic Republic News Agency*, June 26, 2005.

Kaempfer, William H., Lowenberg, Anton D., and Mertens, William, "International Economic Sanctions against a Dictator," *Economics & Politics*, Vol. 16, No. 1 (2004), pp. 29–51.

Kalantar-Hormozi, Abdoljalil, "A Brief History of Plastic Surgery in Iran," *Archives of Iranian Medicine*, Vol. 16, No. 3 (March, 2013), pp. 201–6.

Karagiannopoulos, Vasileios, "The Role of the Internet in Political Struggles: Some Conclusions from Iran and Egypt," *New Political Science*, Vol. 34, No. 2 (2012), pp. 151–71.

Kashani-Sabet, Firoozeh, "Cultures of Iranianness: The Evolving Polemic of Iranian Nationalism," in Nikkie R. Keddie and Rudi Matthee, *Iran and the Surrounding World: Interactions in Culture and Cultural Politics* (Seattle and London, 2002), pp. 162–81.

Kashani-Sabet, Firoozeh, "Who Is Fatima?—Gender, Culture, and Representation in Islam," *Journal of Middle East Women's Studies*, Vol. 1, No. 2 (Spring 2005), pp. 1–24.

Kaufman, Ned, "Heritage and the Cultural Politics of Preservation," *Places*, Vol. 11, No. 3 (1998), pp. 58–65.

Kershner, Isabel, "Openness on Israeli Issues Seen in Survey of Iranians," *New York Times*, June 6, 2014, http://www.nytimes.com/2014/06/06/world/middleeast/israeli-survey-iranians-found-support-giving-up-nuclear-arms-in-exchange-for-lifting-sanctions.html, retrieved: September 3, 2014.

Khiabani, Gholam, and Sreberny, Annabelle, "The Politics of/in Blogging in Iran," *Comparative Studies of South Asia, Africa & the Middle East*, Vol. 27, No. 3 (2007), pp. 563–79.

"Learn Persian (Farsi) with Chai and Conversation- —About Tarof (Taarof), an Iranian tradition," http://www.youtube.com/watch?v=u5oX2n1-diA, retrieved: October 5, 2014.

Loschky, Jay, and Pugliese, Anita, "Iranians Split, 40% to 35%, on Nuclear Military Power, Gallup," February 15, 2012, http://www.gallup.com/poll/152633/Iranians-Split-Nuclear-Military-Power.aspx, retrieved: July 9, 2014.

Lotfian, Saideh, "Nuclear Policy and International Relations," in Homa Katouzian and Mohamad Tavakoli (eds.), *Iran in the 21st Century: Politics, Economics, and Conflict* (London: Routledge, 2008), pp. 158–80.

Maghen, Ze'ev, "Occultation in Perpetuum: Shi'ite Messianism and the Policies of the Islamic Republic," *The Middle East Journal*, Vol. 62, No. 2 (Spring 2008), pp. 232–57.

Mahdavi, Shireen, "Shawhar Ahu Khanum: Passion, Polygamy and Tragedy," *Middle Eastern Studies*, Vol. 24, No. 1 (Jan. 1988), pp. 113–17.

Mamouri, Ali, "Facebook use among the seminary in Qom," *Almonitor*, January 3, 2014, http://www.al-monitor.com/pulse/iw/originals/2014/01/qom-seminary-facebook.html #ixzz361C9zo8l, retrieved: September 2, 2014.

Milani, Mohsen M. "Reform and Resistance in the Islamic Republic of Iran," in John L. Esposito and R.K. Ramazani (eds.), *Iran at the Crossroads* (New York: Palgrave, 2001), pp. 96–104.

Mohammadi, Majid, "Zealous Militants in Citizens' Bedrooms," Gozaar, Freedom House (July 2, 2010), http://www.gozaar.org/english/articles-en/Zealous-Militants-in-Citizens-Bedrooms.html, retrieved: June 5, 2014.

Mokhtari, Eskandar, "Lesson Learned From Recovery Project of Bam's Cultural Heritage (RPBCH)," pp. 1–8, http://www.iitk.ac.in/nicee/wcee/article/14_01-1021.PDF, retrieved: June 21, 2014.

Moshirzadeh, Homeira, "Discursive Foundations of Iran's Nuclear Policy," *Security Dialogue*, Vol. 38, No. 4 (2007), pp. 521–43.

Mousavian, Seyed Hossein, "Twelve Consequences of Sanctions on Iran," *Al-Monitor*, May 3, 2013, http://www.al-monitor.com/pulse/originals/2013/04/iran-sanctions-consequences-list.html#, retrieved: July 7, 2014.

Nader, Alireza, and Elson, Sara Beth, "What Do Iranians Think? A Survey of Attitudes on the United States, the Nuclear Program, and the Economy," 2011, http://www.rand.org/content/dam/rand/pubs/technical_reports/2011/RAND_TR910.pdf, retrieved: June, 11, 2014.

Najmabadi, Afsaneh, "Gendered Transformations: Beauty, Love, and Sexuality in Qajar Iran," *Iranian Studies*, Vol. 34, No. 1/4 (2001), pp. 89–102.

Najmabadi, Afsaneh, "Transing and Transpassing across Sex-Gender Walls in Iran," *Women's Studies Quarterly*, Vol. 36, No. 3/4, (Fall–Winter, 2008), pp. 23–42.

Namakydoust, Azadeh, "Covered in Messages: The Veil as a Political Tool," *The Iranian*, May 8, 2003, http://iranian.com/Women/2003/May/Veil/p.html, retrieved: June 5, 2014.

PBS, "Economic Sanctions Have Tangible Consequences for Average Iranians," *PBS Newshour*, February 10, 2014, http://www.pbs.org/newshour/bb/economic-sanctions-have-tangible-consequences-average-iranians/, retrieved: May 25, 2014.

"Persian Culture," Part One, http://www.youtube.com/watch?v=9ZTnBMQjr0A, retrieved: October 5, 2014.

Pesaran, Hashem, "Iran Sanctions: Now is the Time to Negotiate," *The Guardian*, September 17, 2013, http://www.theguardian.com/world/2013/sep/17/world-powers-negotiate-nucle ar-iran, retrieved: June 25, 2014.

Posch, Walter, "Prospects for Iran's 2009 Presidential Elections," *Middle East Institute Policy Brief*, No. 24 (June 2009), http://www.mei.edu/sites/default/files/publications/Posch2.pdf, retrieved: May 14, 2014.

Rahimi, Babak, "The Politics of the Internet in Iran," in M. Semati (ed.), *Media, Culture and Society in Iran: Living with Globalization* (New York, 2008), pp. 37–56.

Reuters, "Negroponte: Internet is way to world peace," November 25, 1997, http://edition.cnn.com/TECH/9711/25/internet.peace.reut/, retrieved: September 3, 2014.

Rhode, Harold, "Review on Laurence Louër's *Shiism and Politics in the Middle East*," (London: Hurst, 2012), http://www.israelcfr.com/documents/8-1/8-1-7-HaroldRhode.pdf.

Rhode, Harold, "The Sources of Iranian Negotiating Behavior," www.jcpa.org.

Rogers, Elizabeth S., "Using Economic Sanctions to Control Regional Conflicts," *Security Studies*, Vol. 5, No. 4 (1996), pp. 43–72

Rubino, Rich, "The Counterproductive Effects of Leveling Sanctions on Iran," *Huffington Post* (June 2, 2013).

Sagan, Scott D., "Realist Perspectives on Ethical Norms and Weapons of Mass Destruction," in Sohail H. Hashmi and Steven Lee (eds.), *Ethics and Weapons of Mass Destruction: Religious and Secular Perspectives* (Cambridge: Cambridge University Press, 2004), pp. 73–95.

Sagan, Scott D., "Why Do States Build Nuclear Weapons?: Three Models in Search of a Bomb," *International Security*, Vol. 21, No. 3 (1996), pp. 54–86.

Samii, A. William, "Candidates and Quitters," *Iran Report*, Vol. 3, No. 38 (October 9, 2000), http://www.globalsecurity.org/wmd/library/news/iran/2000/38-091000.html, retrieved: July 12, 2014.

Samii, Bill, "Iran: A Rising Star in Iran Politics," *Radio Free Europe/Radio Liberty* (November 7, 2005).

Seher, Jason, "Ex-national Security Adviser: 'Direct line' between Iran Sanctions and Rouhani's Election," *CNN* (December 1, 2013).

Seliktar, Ofira, "Reading Tehran in Washington: The Problem of Defining the Fundamentalist Regime in Iran and Assessing the Prospect for Political Change," in Joseph Morrison Skelly (ed.), *Political Islam from Muhammad to Ahmadinejad: Defenders, Detractors, and Definitions* (Santa Barbara, CA: Praeger, 2010), pp. 163–81.

Shahi, Afshin, "Iran's New Wave of Social Engineering," *Open Democracy*, September 29, 2010, http://www.opendemocracy.net/afshin-shahi/irans-new-wave-of-social-engineering, retrieved: June 5, 2014.

Shilandari, Farah, "Iranian Woman: Veil and Identity," *Gozaar.org*, September 7, 2010, http://www.gozaar.org/english/articles-en/Iranian-Woman-Veil-and-Identity.html, retrieved: June 5, 2014.

Sigurdsson, Harald, "Battle of Dara Byzantines Defeat Persians," http://burnpit.us/2012/06/battle-dara-byzantines-defeat-persians, June 6, 2012, retrieved: October 5, 2014.

Tabari, Azar, "The Enigma of Veiled Iranian Women," *Feminist Review*, No. 5 (1980), pp. 19–31.

Tabatabai, Ariane, "Iran's Evolving Nuclear Narrative," *Iran Matters*, Harvard's Belfer Center (February 7, 2014).

Tavakoli-Targhi, Mohammad, "From Patriotism to Matriotism: A Tropological Study of Iranian Nationalism, 1870–1909," *International Journal of Middle East Studies*, Vol. 34, No. 2 (May 2002), pp. 217–38.

Tehranian, Majid, "Communication and Revolution in Iran: The Passing of a Paradigm," *Iranian Studies*, Vol. 13, No. 1–4 (1980), pp. 5–30.

Terror Free Tomorrow, "Polling Iranian Public Opinion: An Unprecedented Nationwide Survey of Iran," Washington, DC, June 5–18, 2007, http://www.angusreidglobal.com/wp-content/uploads/archived-pdf/Iran_TFT.pdf, retrieved: June 11, 2014.

TheTower.org Staff, "CNN Host Describes Diplomatic 'Train Wreck' as Iran President Rules Out Dismantling Nuclear Centrifuges," *The Tower*, January 24, 2014, http://www.thetower.org/cnn-host-describes-diplomatic-train-wreck-iran-president-rules-dismantling-nuclear-centrifuges/&strip=1, retrieved: July 7, 2014.

Torbat, Akbar E., "Financial Corruption in Iran," *Information Clearinghouse*, March 2, 2013, http://web.calstatela.edu/faculty/atorbat/docs/Corruption%20in%20Iran.pdf, retrieved: May 14, 2014.

UNODC, "Islamic Criminal Code, Approved by Law Affairs Committee of the Islamic Consultative Assembly (Parliament)," *Tehran, 1363*, 1983, https://www.unodc.org/tldb/pdf/Islamic_Penal_Code_in_Farsi.pdf, retrieved: July 12, 2014.

Wojcieszak, Magdalena, and Smith, Briar, "Will politics be tweeted? New media use by Iranian youth in 2011," *New Media & Society*, 16 (2014), pp. 91–109.

Wright, Robin, "Islam and Liberal Democracy: Two Visions of Reformation," *Journal of Democracy*, Vol. 7, No. 2 (1996), pp. 64–75.

Yaron, Oded, "Iranians respond to Israeli Facebook initiative: Israel, we love you too," March 19, 2012, http://www.haaretz.com/news/national/iranians-respond-to-israeli-facebook-initiative-israel-we-love-you-too-1.419505, retrieved: September 3, 2014.

Zahed, Saeid, "Iranian National Identity in the Context of Globalization: Dialogue or Resistance?," *Center for the Study of Globalization and Regionalisation (CSGR)*, No. 162/05 (2004), pp. 1–27.

Zandiye, M., Mohammad-Poor, K. N., and Rezaee, H. R., "The Totemic Signs of Simorgh and Dragon in Shahnameh," *Journal of Basic and Applied Scientific Research 2*, No. 1 (2012), pp. 788–94.

Zimmt, Raz, "Conference in support of Khuzestani Arabs convenes in Cairo during Foreign Minister Salehi's visit to Egypt provoking anger from Iran," *Spotlight on Iran*, January 14, 2012, http://www.terrorism-info.org.il/Data/articles/Art_20462/E_009_13_503708825.pdf, retrieved: September 3, 2014.

SPEECH IN ENGLISH

Keddie, Nikki, "Iran: Understanding the Enigma: A Historian's View," Lecture presented at Teachers' seminar at UCLA, Los Angeles, California, 1998.

BOOKS AND ARTICLES IN PERSIAN

Ahmadinejad, Mahmoud, "Masaaley-e Hastehee Iran Sahneye Taghabole Zibaeeha va Zeshtiha Bode Hast," September 9, 2007, http://www.president.ir/fa/6569, retrieved: June 11, 2014.

Arg-e Bam." ichodoc.ir. http://www.ichodoc.ir/argebam/, retrieved: October 6, 2011.

Asr-e Iran, "Vazir-e Ershad: 4 Milion Irani a'dhu Facebook," January 23, 2014, http://bit.ly/1ohpb9u, retrieved: September 1, 2014.

BBC Persian, "Sokhtan-e bahth barangiz debirkol hezballah darbara-e tamadan-e irani," November 8, 2010, http://www.bbc.co.uk/persian/world/2010/11/101107_u03_nasrallah_iran.shtml, retrieved: September 2, 2014.

BBC Persian, Business Reporter, "Vazir-e eqtesad-e iran: Ahmadi-nezhad eshtebah-e shah ra tekrar kard," August 17, 2013, http://www.bbc.co.uk/persian/business/2013/08/130817

_l01_tayebnia_economy_iran.shtml, retrieved: September 1, 2014.

Botian News, "Facebook Zarif va jazire abu-musa," December 4, 2013, http://fa.botianews.com/2013/12/87677/, retrieved: August 23, 2014, https://www.facebook.com/mehdi.parpanchi/posts/452643708191276.

Edalat News, March 23, 2014, http://edaalatnews.blogspot.co.il/2014/03/blog-post_8549.html, retrieved: September 3, 2014.

Edalat News' Facebook page, https://www.facebook.com/pages/%D8%B9%D8%AF%D8%A77%D9%84%D8%AA-%D9%86%DB%8C%D9%88%D8%B2/224122577778684, retrieved: September 2, 2014.

Harf-ha-ye Nagofte, "Astan-ha-ye Jomhuri-ye Eslami-ye Iran," http://harfhaye-nagofte-elham.blogspot.co.il/2013/02/blog-post_14.html, retrieved: September 3, 2014.

Jaish al-Adl Twitter account, https://twitter.com/jaishaladl_, retrieved: September 3, 2014.

Javad Zarif's Facebook page, March 28, 2014, https://www.facebook.com/jzarif/posts/776295132381937.

Kalemeh, "Tae'b: Suriya astan si va panjam iran ast," February 14, 2013, http://www.kaleme.com/1391/11/26/klm-133479/, retrieved: September 3, 2014.

Khaleghi-Motlagh, Djalal, "Ferdowsi, Abu'l Qāsem-i.Life," *Encyclopædia Iranica* (January 26, 2012).

Khamenei, Seyyed Ali, "20 Year National Vision," website of the Ministry of Economy and Financial Affairs, December 4, 2003, http://asl44.mefa.gov.ir/Portal/Home/Default.aspx?CategoryID=c08d0272-f684-4d5b-9836-bc13a45d04bb, retrieved: June 11, 2014.

Khomeini, Rouhollah Mosavi, *Velayat-e Faqih (Government of Jurisprudence)*, (Tehran: Tanzim va Nashr-e Asar-e Imam Khomeini, 1993).

Leo Messi's Facebook page, December 4, 2013, https://www.facebook.com/LeoMessi/posts/713193608700236.

Mehr News Agency, "Fanavary taht-e taathir-e jam jahani / jaded-tarin Amar karbaran-e internet dar iran ee'lam shod," 26 June, 2014, http://www.mehrnews.com/detail/News/2319958, retrieved: September 1, 2014.

Mehr News Agency, "Zarif: Omadgi baray-e goftegu mowzue' hamishegi-ye iran dar khasus-e jazireh abu-musa ast," December 2, 2013, http://mehrnews.com/detail/news/2187411, retrieved: September 3, 2014.

Mehryar, Mohammad, "Arg-e Bam," *Iranian Cultural Heritage Organization*, http://www.ichodoc.ir/scripts/wxis.exe, retrieved: November 2011.

Molana, Hamid, *Syasat Khareji Jomhory-e Islami-e Iran Dar Dawlat-e Ahmadinejad (Iran's Foreign Policy during Ahmadinejad)* (Tehran: Dadgostar, 2009).

Rafsanjani, Akbar Hashemi, *Payan-e Defa, Aghaz-e Bazsazi; Khaterate Ayatollah Hashemi Rafsanjani Dar Sal-e 1367 (The End of Defense, Start of Reconstruction; Memoir of 1988)* (Tehran: Maaref-e Enghelab, 2011).

Rouhani, Hassan, *Amniat-e meli va-diplomaci-e haste-i* (Tehran: Majma-e tashkhis-e maslahat-e nezam, Markaz-e tahqiqat-e estratezhik, 2012), pp 594–96.

Said-e Najafi Moqadam, Mohammad, "Matn-e kamel-e sokhanan-e doktor rouhani dar shast-o-hashtomin majma-e omumi-e sazeman-e melal-e motahad," September 25, 2013, http://www.president.ir/fa/71572, retrieved: August 27, 2014.

Said-e Najafi Moqadam, Mohammad, "Matn-e kamel-e sokhanan-e doktor rouhani dar marasem-e tanfiz-e hokm-e riasat jomhouri az sui-e rahbar-e moazam-e enqelab," August 4, 2013, http://www.president.ir/fa/70471, retrieved: August 27, 2014.

Sight, "Hassan Nasrallah ba tamam bi shauriyesh fahmid ke iran be garugan gerefted shode ast," http://bit.ly/1pPXAk3, retrieved: September 3, 2014.

Tabnak, "Javab-e Messi be Irani-ha dar Facebook," December 7, 2013, http://www.tabnak.ir/fa/news/362982, retrieved: September 3, 2014.

Zahedi, Alborz, "Criticism of Iranian Middle [Class]," October 16, 2012, originally published in: http://bamdadkhabar.com, available in: https://plus.google.com/11528790926368 2590925/posts/GGjjCc5DaKg, retrieved; September 1, 2014. [in Persian].

Zimmt, Raz, "'Iran has to prefer Syria to the Khuzestan region': Ammar Headquarters chief's announcement draws angry reactions," *Spotlight on Iran*, February 17, 2013, http://

www.terrorism-info.org.il/Data/articles/Art_20477/E_031_13_734144126.pdf,   retrieved: August 16, 2014.

SPEECHES IN PERSIAN

Ahmadinejad, Mahmoud, "In meeting with IRGC commanders" (September 11, 2007).

Ahmadinejad, Mahmoud, "In meeting with supreme council of Islamic propagation organization at Qom Seminary" (August 29, 2008).

Ahmadi-nezhād, Mahmūd, "Bardashthai-e nadorost az sokhanaon-e rais jomhour darbare emdadhai-e emam-e asr (aj) nesbat be melat-e iran" ("The erroneous impressions from the speech of the president concerning the Mehdi's help to the Iranian people"), Iranian and foreign reporters (Iran: May 13, 2008) [interview], http://www.president.ir/fa/president/out looks, retrieved: September/October 2009.

Ahmadi-nezhād, Mahmūd, "Bazgasht be eslam, tanha rah-e hal-e moshkelat-e alam" ("The return to Islam is the only way to solving all the world's problems"), Friday prayer (Gambia: June 30, 2006) [speech], http://www.president.ir/fa/president/outlooks, retrieved: September/October 2009.

Ahmadi-nezhād, Mahmūd, "Bozorg kardan-e mas'ale-ye holocast az sui-e qodratha-ye solte dar moqayese ba setamhaye rafte bar sayer-e melatha" ("The inflating of the Holocaust question on the part of the Great Powers, compared with the great exploitation amongst the rest of the nations"), Convention of heads of African states (July 1, 2006) [speech], http://www.president.ir/fa/president/outlooks, retrieved: September/October 2009.

Ahmadi-nezhād, Mahmūd, "Chahar shoar-e doulat, bargerefte az farhang-e entezar" ("The four slogans of the government were taken from the culture of anticipating the Mehdi"), *Daftar-e Tablighat-e Eslami* (Qom: Islamic Propagation Office, September 28, 2005) [speech], http://www.president.ir/fa/president/outlooks, retrieved: September/October 2009.

Ahmadi-nezhād, Mahmūd, "Da'vat be emam-e asr, mohemtarin kar-e dar donia" ("The invitation of the Mehdi is the most important action in the world"), Exhibition "The Messianic Doctrine" (Iran: August 24, 2007) [speech], http://www.president.ir/fa/president/outlooks, retrieved: September/October 2009.

Ahmadi-nezhād, Mahmūd, "Doulat-e amrika, bozorg'tarin tahdid-e khavar-e miane va jahan" ("The American government, the greatest threat to the Middle East and the world"), At the D-8 summit (Kuala Lumpur, Malaysia: June 27, 2008) [interview], http://www.president.ir/ fa/president/outlooks, retrieved: September/October 2009.

Ahmadi-nezhād, Mahmūd, "Edeai-e vahi-e qodratha-ye solte mabna bar hemayat az hoquq-e bashar va demokrasi" ("The false claims of the Great Powers that they are based on the support in human rights and democracy"), Meeting with residents (Pakdasht: October 30, 2006) [speech], http://www.president.ir/fa/president/outlooks, retrieved: September/October 2009.

Ahmadi-nezhād, Mahmūd, "Elat-e asli-e mas'ale-ye felestin" ("The main reason for the Palestinian problem"), Meeting with spiritual leaders, (Iran: Convention on the subject of the Holocaust, December 12, 2006) [speech], http://www.president.ir/fa/president/outlooks, retrieved: September/October 2009.

Ahmadi-nezhād, Mahmūd, "Emam (aj), ramz-e vahdat-e bein-e hame adian" ("The Mehdi is a symbol of unity amongst the religions"), Visiting religious leaders and the "Friday Imams" (Bushehr province: January 31, 2008) [speech], http://www.president.ir/fa/president/out looks, retrieved: September/October 2009.

Ahmadi-nezhād, Mahmūd, "Emam-e zaman vasete feiz-e elahi braai-e hamegan" ("The Mehdi is the divine channel of abundance for all"), Members of "pezhoheshkade mahdaviat" (Iran: The Messianic Research Institute, August 26, 2006) [speech], http://www.president.ir/fa/ president/outlooks, retrieved: September/October 2009.

Ahmadi-nezhād, Mahmūd, "Enqelab-e eslami tablor-e khoast va-erade-e mardom-e iran" ("The Islamic Revolution is the consolidation of the wills and demands of the Iranian nation"), Visiting ambassadors from different countries who are present in Iran, in preparation for

Revolution Day (Iran: February 10, 2008) [speech], http://www.president.ir/fa/president/outlooks, retrieved: September/October 2009.

Ahmadi-nezhād, Mahmūd, "Enqelab-e eslami va daheh fajr, bozorgtarin havades ba'ad az sadr-e eslam" ("The Islamic revolution and the ten days of the Fajr are the greatest events following the establishment of Islam"), Members of the group organizing the "ten days of the Fajr" plan (Iran: January 29, 2008) [speech], http://www.president.ir/fa/president/out looks, retrieved: September/October 2009.

Ahmadi-nezhād, Mahmūd, "Eslam, bonyan-e farhang va tafakor-e melat-e iran va talash bra'ai-e por'rang kardan-e naqsh-e din dar zendegi-e fardi va jam'ei" ("Islam, the cornerstone of Iranian culture and thinking, and the effort to create a diversity in the individual and general spheres with the help of religion"), The ceremony of replacing the president of the state (Tehran: August 6, 2005) [speech], http://www.president.ir/fa/president/outlooks, retrieved: September/October 2009.

Ahmadi-nezhād, Mahmūd, "Eslam dini jahani va jahan shomul" ("Islam, a global and universal religion"), Visiting religious leaders (Qom: January 5, 2006) [speech], http://www.president.ir/fa/president/outlooks, retrieved: September/October 2009.

Ahmadi-nezhād, Mahmūd, "Eslam, din-e hame Payambaran-e elahi va noqte ta'ali-e adyian" ("Islam, the religion of the prophets, and the high point of all other religions"), Visiting religious leaders and Muslim religious leaders from across the United States (New York: September 24, 2007) [speech], http://www.president.ir/fa/president/outlooks, retrieved: September/October 2009.

Ahmadi-nezhād, Mahmūd, "Eslam, maktab-e rehai-e bakhsh-e donia-ye sarkhorde az maka'teb elhadi va liberal" ("Islam, the school freed from the frustration existing in the atheistic and liberal part of the world"), The convention of the heads of Islamic states (Saudi Arabia: December 7, 2005) [speech], http://www.president.ir/fa/president/outlooks, retrieved: September/October 2009.

Ahmadi-nezhād, Mahmūd, "Felestin sahne-ye azmayesh-e andishe liberalism va nezam-e sar-maie dari" ("Palestine is a trial arena for liberalism and the capitalistic regimes"), Cabinet meeting (Tehran: January 2, 2008) [interview], http://www.president.ir/fa/president/out looks, retrieved: September/October 2009.

Ahmadi-nezhād, Mahmūd, "Jaigah-e ensan dar didgah-e eslam" ("The place of man in the point of view of Islam"), Meeting with political researchers and media people (New York: September 25, 2007) [speech], http://www.president.ir/fa/president/outlooks, retrieved: September/October 2009.

Ahmadi-nezhād, Mahmūd, "Kemal-e jame'e bashari dar barpayi-e jame'e mahdavi" ("The place of all men in the bringing forth and the creation of the messianic community"), (Ardabil: November 21, 2007) [speech], http://www.president.ir/fa/president/outlooks, retrieved: September/October 2009.

Ahmadi-nezhād, Mahmūd, "Masa'le holocast va sahionism" ("The subject of the Holocaust and Zionism"), The sixth exhibition of the celebration of the world mosques day (July 28, 2008) [speech], http://www.president.ir/fa/president/outlooks, retrieved: September/October 2009.

Ahmadi-nezhād, Mahmūd, "Mavaze osuli-e jomouri-e eslami-e iran dar ersehai-e bein olmela-li" ("The Central Stances of the Islamic Republic of Iran in International Matters"), Meeting with ambassadors and delegates from the various embassies of the Islamic Republic of Iran (Iran: August 11, 2008) [speech], http://www.president.ir/fa/president/outlooks, retrieved: September/October 2009.

Ahmadi-nezhād, Mahmūd, "Mouj-e dovom-e enqelab" ("The second wave of the revolution"), The senior circle of the members of Jihad and Shahada (Iran: September 27, 2006) [speech], http://www.president.ir/fa/president/outlooks, retrieved: September/October 2009.

Ahmadi-nezhād, Mahmūd, "Mouj-e dovom-e enqelab, gostarde'tar va amiq'tar az mouj-e aval" ("The second wave of the revolution is wider and deeper than the first one"), (Iran: October 14, 2006) [speech], http://www.president.ir/fa/president/outlooks, retrieved: September/October 2009.

Ahmadi-nezhād, Mahmūd, "Mouzo-e haste'i va muz'e iran" ("The nuclear matter and the stances of Iran"), (Tajikistan: Iranian residence, April 20, 2008) [speech], http://www.president.ir/fa/president/outlooks, retrieved: September/October 2009.

Ahmadi-nezhād, Mahmūd, "Omid'ha va forsat'ha-ye omat-e eslam dar doniaye konuni" ("The hopes and opportunities of the nation of Islam in today's world"), A convention of heads of Islamic states (Saudi Arabia: December 7, 2005) [speech], http://www.president.ir/fa/president/outlooks, retrieved: September/October 2009.

Ahmadi-nezhād, Mahmūd, "Qur'an, ketab-e rahnamai-e zendegi-e ensan" ("The Qur'an, a guidebook for life"), Awards-giving ceremony to those diligent in the study of the Qur'an (Iran: October 9, 2006) [speech], http://www.president.ir/fa/president/outlooks, retrieved: September/October 2009.

Ahmadi-nezhād, Mahmūd, "Rah'kar-e asli-e ensejam-e eslami" ("The main road to Islamic solidarity"), The experts' council of the leadership (Iran: February 24, 2008) [speech], http://www.president.ir/fa/president/outlooks, retrieved: September/October 2009.

Ahmadi-nezhād, Mahmūd, "Rishe-haye moshkelat-e bashar-e emruz" ("The roots of the problems of humanity today"), Meeting with representatives of states that are members of UNESCO (November 15, 2007) [speech], http://www.president.ir/fa/president/outlooks, retrieved: September/October 2009.

Ahmadi-nezhād, Mahmūd, "Sahionistha a'omel-e ijad-e tefreqe bein-e shi'e va-soni" ("The activity of the Zionists to drive a wedge between the Shi'ites and the Sunnis"), Foreign correspondents (Senegal: February 12, 2008) [interview], http://www.president.ir/fa/president/outlooks, retrieved: September/October 2009.

Ahmadi-nezhād, Mahmūd, "Sharayet-e ijad-e solh-e paidar dar jahan" ("The conditions for the creation of sustainable peace in the world"), (New York: The 61st General Assembly of the United Nations, September 20, 2006) [speech], http://www.president.ir/fa/president/out looks, retrieved: September/October 2009.

Ahmadi-nezhād, Mahmūd, "Tabdil-e holocast be boti brai-e qodrathai-e solte" ("The turning of the Holocaust into a statue to which all Great Powers bow"), (Qa'em Shahr: December 7, 2006) [speech], http://www.president.ir/fa/president/outlooks, retrieved: September/October 2009.

Ahmadi-nezhād, Mahmūd, "Talash-e estekbar-e jahani barai-e takhrib-e bonianhaye akhlaqi dar iran"—("The arrogant global effortsfor the destruction of the foundation of morals in Iran"), Visiting religious leaders (Ilam: December 6, 2007) [speech], http://www.president.ir/fa/president/outlooks, retrieved: September/October 2009.

Ahmadi-nezhād, Mahmūd, "Zorurat-e nazrie pardazi-e masa'el bar asas-e farhang-e entezar" ("The importance of expressing an opinion regarding questions relating to the culture of anticipation"), Visiting religious leaders and their pupils (Qom: January 5, 2006) [speech], http://www.president.ir/fa/president/outlooks, retrieved: September/October 2009.

Ahmadi-nezhād, Mahmūd, "Zorurat-e nazrie pardazi-e mojadad-e vazaef-e montazer dar doran-e gheibat" ("The important need for a reassessment of the mission of the man expecting the Mehdi during the time of occultation"), *Daftar-e Tablighat-e Eslami* (Qom: Islamic Propagation Office, September 28, 2005) [speech], http://www.president.ir/fa/president/out looks, retrieved: September/October 2009.

BOOKS AND ARTICLES IN HEBREW

Gil, Moshe, "Ha-Mifgash Ha-Bavli" (The Babylonian Encounter), *Tarbitz*, Vol. 48.

Hendelman-Baavur, Liora, "Live Protest: the Islamic Republic and the Green Revolution on the Internet," *Zman Iran*, No. 10 (July 2009), http://humanities.tau.ac.il/iranian/he/pre/9-iran-pulse-he/67-10, retrieved: September 3, 2014. [In Hebrew.]

Litvak, Meir, "Iran and Israel: The Ideological Enmity and its Roots," *Iyunim be-Tkumat Yisrael*, Vol. 14 (2004), pp. 367–92. [In Hebrew.]

Mishna, *Shabbat*, chapter 6, article 6.

Zimmt, Raz, "Nationalism, Shi'ite Islam & National Interests in Iran's Foreign Policy," in Daniel Zissenwine (ed.), *Nationalism, Secularism, and Religion in the Middle East* (Tel Aviv, 2012), pp. 87–95. [In Hebrew.]

Index

About the Contributors

Ronen A. Cohen is an assistant professor and the chair of the Department of Middle Eastern Studies and Political Science at Ariel University, Israel. He has published several books including *The Rise and Fall of the Mojahedin Khalq, 1987–1997: Their Survival after the Islamic Revolution and Resistance to the Islamic Republic of Iran* (UK: Sussex Academic Press, 2009); *Modern Persian, A Textbook* (Ariel: Ariel University Center, 2009); *The Hojjatiyeh Society in Iran: Ideology and Practice from the 1950s to the Present* (USA: Macmillan Palgrave, 2013); and *The Upheavals in the Middle East: The Theory and Practice of a Revolution* (Lanham, MD: Lexington Books, 2014); *Revolution Under Attack: The Forqan Group of Iran* (USA: Macmillan Palgrave, forthcoming). He has also published numerous academic and commentary articles and has occasionally been interviewed on radio shows and in newspapers.

Ofira Seliktar is professor of political science (emerita) at Gratz College and Temple University. Previously, she was a scholar-in-residence at the Middle East Center at the University of Pennsylvania and a visiting professor at the Security Studies Program at Tel Aviv University. She is the author of seven books, scores of articles in referred journals, and chapters in books. She specializes in predictive failures in intelligence with a special emphasis on the Middle East. Her latest book is *Navigating Iran: From Carter to Obama* (Palgrave Macmillan, 2012) and she is now working on a new book: *American Intelligence and Jihadism: From Al Qaeda to ISIS*.

Harold Rhode is a distinguished senior fellow at Gatestone Institute (formerly Hudson Institute, New York). He was a former advisor on Middle

Eastern and Islamic Affairs in the Office of the Secretary of the US Department of Defense.

Farhad Rezaei is a PhD candidate in international relations at the Department of International and Strategic Studies, at the University of Malaysia, Kuala Lumpur. He has a BA in political science and an MA in international relations from Azad University in Iran. He has published several articles including "Iran's Nuclear Program and the Israeli-Iranian Hostility at the Post-Revolutionary Era," in the *British Journal of Middle Eastern Studies*, and "Iran's Nuclear Project under Hassan Rouhani: Proliferation under New Management?" in the *Middle East Quarterly*. His book, entitled *Iran's Nuclear Weapons Project, 1979–2014: Proliferation and Rollback?*, has been submitted to the Oxford University Press. His areas of expertise are nuclear weapons proliferation, Iran's nuclear weapons program, Sanctions theory, International Sanctions Regimes (with special application to nuclear proliferation), and rational choice theory.

Ladan Zarabadi is a PhD student in the School of Architecture and Interior Design at the University of Cincinnati, United States. She is the author of "From Imam Hussein to Azadi Square: Politicized Venues" published in *epolis journal*. She received her MA in architecture from Iran's Qazvin Azad University in 2001. Her dissertation was written on politicized public spaces in the Middle East focusing on Iran, under the supervision of Prof. Adrian Parr. She is also interested in discourses of feminist movements and women's studies and the social and political roles women play in place-making in the public sphere.

Raz Zimmt is a research fellow at the Alliance Center for Iranian Studies at Tel Aviv University. He completed his PhD at Tel Aviv University in 2011 under the supervision of Prof. David Menashri and Prof. Eyal Zisser. His dissertation focused on *Iranian Policy towards Nasserism and Arab Radicalism: 1954 –1967*. He is a graduate of the Hebrew University of Jerusalem and has a MA and doctorate from Tel Aviv University. His main academic interests are politics, society, and social networks in the Islamic Republic of Iran. His fields of specialization include the modern political history of Iran, contemporary Iranian politics, and society and social networks in Iran.

Moshe-hay S. Hagigat is a researcher into modern Iranian society, politics, and the military during the last ten years. He received his PhD in Middle Eastern studies from Bar-Ilan University, Israel. His dissertation (2013), written under the supervision of Prof. Ze'ev Maghen, focuses on the theological, political, and socioeconomic doctrines of Iran's sixth president, Mahmud Ahmadi-nezhād. Dr. Hagigat has been a researcher in the Israeli Prime

Minister's office and is currently a commentator on Iranian issues and pundit at the Israeli "Walla! News" website.

Lightning Source UK Ltd.
Milton Keynes UK
UKOW04n1410170216

268561UK00001B/11/P